Innocents in the Dry Valleys

Innocents in the Dry Valleys

AN ACCOUNT OF THE VICTORIA UNIVERSITY OF WELLINGTON
ANTARCTIC EXPEDITION, 1958–59

BY COLIN BULL

With massive contributions by Dick Barwick, Barrie McKelvey and
Peter Webb, my uncomplaining, contubernial accomplices in this
wonderful adventure

Graphics by Richard Barwick – that's Dick

UNIVERSITY OF ALASKA PRESS
Fairbanks, Alaska

UNIVERSITY OF ALASKA PRESS
PO Box 756240 Fairbanks
Alaska 99775-6240

www.uaf.edu/uapress

First published by Victoria University Press
and University of Alaska Press 2009

Printed in Singapore

Contents

Maps   6

Foreword, by Dr Eddie Robertson   9

Introduction, by Dr Peter Barrett   11

Author's note   15

Dramatis Personae   19

Chapter 1. An idea   21

Chapter 2. Loife in Noo Zillun   31

Chapter 3. Dear Sir, I write on behalf . . .   40

Chapter 4. Go. No, stop! No, go! Scott Base   52

Chapter 5. Landed gentry   79

Chapter 6. An enigmatic lake and a remarkable saga   120

Chapter 7. A trip to the seaside   133

Chapter 8. And the walk back 'home' again   154

Chapter 9. Alone for a short while, maybe   163

Chapter 10. The End. Wait for the applause!   177

Chapter 11. Aftermath   196

Publications   243

Glossary   245

Place-Names   251

Conversion table   256

Index   257

Maps

Map 1. (p. 20) Dry Valley area, in relation to the Antarctic continent and part of the Southern Hemisphere.

Map 2. (p. 20) Outline map, showing Dry Valley Map area (Map 4) in relation to Ross Island and McMurdo Sound.

Map 3. (p. 54) Copy of Griffith Taylor's 1916 map of the Dry Valleys, showing how little was known of the area until 1957.

Map 4. (fold-out) Wright and Victoria Valleys, showing routes of VUWAE 1958–59. (Based on US Geological Survey map, Satellite Image Map, McMurdo Dry Valleys.)

Map 5. (fold-out) Copy of original map of Dry Valley area drawn by Guyon Warren in 1958.

Dedicated to the memory of
Professor Robin (Bob) H. Clark
(1921–1987)

Without his relentless zeal for smashing through administrative obstacles,
and encouraging us to do the same, our task in organizing this summer
'vacation' would have been so much more difficult.

'One of the advantages of being disorderly is that one is constantly making exciting discoveries.'

A.A. Milne (1882–1956)

Research progress 'results from the free play of intellects, working on subjects of their own choice in the manner dictated by their curiosity for explanation of the unknown.'

Vannevar Bush (1890–1974)
'a master craftsman at steering around obstacles' (New York Times obituary)

'contubernial' (adj.) sharing the same tent. *(Oxford English Dictionary)*

Foreword

Way back when the world was a little less complicated than now, in the 1950s, we in New Zealand realized that, instead of merely helping other nations with their studies in Antarctica, we could make great contributions of our own to the knowledge of our continental neighbour. One of my particular pleasures and duties at that time was in being Chairman of the Ross Dependency Research Committee, the body charged with the responsibility for New Zealand's work in the Antarctic. It was exciting and immensely difficult, for we had too little money and logistics with which to undertake all the work we wanted to do, with New Zealand's contribution to the work of the International Geophysical Year (1957–58) and its successor programs, with the aftermath of our part in that great enterprise, the Commonwealth Trans-Antarctic Expedition, the first crossing of the continent, and with all the new projects, both for field and laboratory studies.

At one of our Committee meetings in July 1958 an incredibly enthusiastic young man from the Victoria University of Wellington, 'that place up the hill', came along with a different idea. Together with three other equally enthusiastic people, who had all been summer assistants to the Trans-Antarctic Expedition the previous summer, he had put together plans for a little scientific venture into Wright Valley, an area of south Victoria Land, not far from Scott Base, the main New Zealand base. He didn't want money, merely approval of his plans, so that he could approach our US colleagues for a ride on one of their helicopters, from neighbouring McMurdo Station into his selected area – and presumably a ride back to Scott Base at the end of the season. Colin Bull was articulate and forceful, and was strongly supported by Professor Bob Clark, Professor of Geology at the University and also a member of our Committee.

I chided Colin for making our Committee's task even more difficult, but we approved the plans – and the four of them made a great success of that first University expedition, the forerunner of more than 50 from the Victoria University of Wellington.

I am delighted that, at long last, he has taken the time to write this lively account of the expedition that followed.

Eddie Robertson,
lately Chairman,
Ross Dependency Research Committee.

Introduction

Since the earliest days of man's inquiry into the nature of the Antarctic continent, New Zealand has played a most important role. Indeed when Abel Tasman, the European discoverer of New Zealand, first sighted that 'land uplifted high' in 1641, he was seeking Terra Australis Incognita, the unknown south land, and thought that he had found it. Captain James Cook, who in 1773, with his two ships, *Resolution* and *Adventure*, became the first man to sail south of the Antarctic Circle, had also been, in 1769, the first European to circumnavigate and map New Zealand. Thaddeus von Bellingshausen, one of the contenders for being the first to sight the Antarctic continent, in 1820 visited the part of New Zealand later called Wellington.

The rest of the first half of the 19th century saw many other ships' captains, bound for or returning from the far southern seas, spending time in New Zealand waters; William Stewart, the Enderby brothers, John Biscoe, John Balleny, Dumont d'Urville, Charles Wilkes, and most importantly from our point of view, Captain James Clark Ross, with his two ships, *Erebus* and *Terror*. Ross's discoveries in the south, in 1840 and 1841, include the Ross Sea, Victoria Land and its magnificent mountains, Franklin Island, McMurdo Sound, Ross Island and the Barrier, later called the Ross Ice Shelf. Nearly all of these places feature in the current story by Colin Bull.

The *Challenger*, the first steamship to circumnavigate the Antarctic continent, visited New Zealand in 1874 and the first proposal for a New Zealand expedition to the Antarctic seems to have been in 1878, when C.W. Purnell from Otago suggested sending two steamers south to make a thorough exploration of the southern seas and perhaps to winter on the continent. Unfortunately nothing came of the proposal, and it was not until 1895, after visiting Port Chalmers, that men from H.J. Bull's Antarctic fursealing expedition first landed on the main part of the Antarctic continent, at Cape Adare, at the northern tip of Victoria Land. One of those men was Carsten Borchgrevink, who returned to Cape Adare in 1899 with the *Southern Cross*, built two huts there, and wintered over with ten men, one of whom died during the winter.

New Zealand played a major role as the base for four of the largest expeditions during the Heroic Age of Antarctic exploration; they were Scott's *Discovery* expedition of 1901–04, Shackleton's *Nimrod* expedition of 1907–09, Scott's last expedition, the *Terra Nova* expedition of 1910–13, and the New Zealand part of Shackleton's Trans-Antarctic Expedition of 1914–17. Even Roald Amundsen, who reached the South Pole first, in December 1911, visited New Zealand after his return and gave a few lectures.

On the *Discovery* expedition Scott and two of his men found and briefly examined an ice-free valley that extended many miles between the glacier at its head and McMurdo Sound. This was later named Taylor Valley. Among many interesting features they found a mummified Weddell seal. Hartley Ferrar, the expedition's geologist, was the first to map the geology of the area, and was especially impressed with the thick brown horizontal sheets of columnar-jointed rock, now termed Ferrar Dolerite, which can be traced throughout the region and indeed the length of the Transantarctic Mountains

On Scott's second expedition the first Western Party, Griffith Taylor, Charles Wright, Frank Debenham and Taffy Evans, spent several days in Taylor Valley. They named many features, conducted a limited amount of surveying, and found cavernously eroded boulders, more mummified seals and eight mummified Adélie penguins; the same sort of things that the present expedition found in the valley to the north of Taylor Valley that they named for Charles Wright.

New Zealand was also a staging post for the next phase of Antarctic exploration. Beginning in 1928, and continuing until 1955, Admiral Richard E. Byrd led a series of expeditions to the Antarctic sector south and east of New Zealand and now called Marie Byrd Land. These paved the way, with vastly improved logistics, especially in the use of aircraft and radio, for the modern era of Antarctic science, initiated by the 'Maudheim' expedition of 1949–52 and the International Geophysical Year (IGY) in 1957–58.

New Zealand's position changed from being an interested bystander to being an active participant in Antarctic affairs in the period preceding the International Geophysical Year, the collaborative effort of many nations to gain scientific information about the earth and its environs in space.

Initially 11 scientific research stations were planned on the Antarctic continent. Scott Base, on Ross Island near the old Scott and Shackleton bases, would be solely a New Zealand responsibility and Cape Hallett, at 72°S on the shore of Victoria Land, would be operated jointly by New

Zealand and the United States. The New Zealand National Committee for the IGY included Dr Eddie Robertson, Chairman, and Geoffrey Markham, Secretary, both of whom are involved in this story. So is Dr Trevor Hatherton, who was appointed leader of the five-man IGY team who wintered over at Scott Base.

At about the same time Dr Vivian (Bunny) Fuchs, then Director of the Falkland Islands Dependencies Survey, was planning his Commonwealth Trans-Antarctic Expedition (TAE), in which a New Zealand team, also working from Scott Base, was expected to establish a series of fuel and food depots between there and close to the South Pole. The leader of this group was Sir Edmund Hillary, and members included Ron Balham, Bernie Gunn, Guyon Warren and Dickie Brooke, and others the reader will meet again.

The summer support team of the TAE in 1956–57 included Dick Barwick, a junior faculty member from the Victoria University College of Wellington. His talks at the University after his return inspired Professor Bob Clark, newly appointed to the Chairmanship of the Geology Department, and two of his undergraduate students, Barrie McKelvey and Peter Webb. In a remarkable example of student persistence, ability and fortitude, Barrie and Peter persuaded Bob Clark to support their successful efforts to gain places on the New Zealand ship supplying Scott Base in the 1957–58 season. Among many other activities, one of them joined with Ron Balham and Dick Barwick in the team that first looked at Victoria Valley, which Peter named for our University. The events that followed are perhaps best given in the words of L.B. (Les) Quartermain, doyen of New Zealand's Antarctic historians, in his book *New Zealand and the Antarctic*.

Les wrote

> The following summer, 1958–59, the same enterprising pair (McKelvey and Webb) formed with physicist Colin Bull (leader) and biologist Barwick (both lecturers on the staff) a Victoria University College [sic] team whose objective was to survey and to make a thorough biological, geological and geophysical examination of the Wright Valley, between the Taylor and Victoria Valleys. Bull had taken a prominent part in the British North Greenland Expedition a few years earlier . . . It was approved by the Ross Dependency Research Committee in August 1958, and later became known as VUWAE 2 (Victoria University of Wellington Antarctic Expedition No. 2), VUWAE 1 being the term applied to the extraordinary intrusion into Antarctic history of Peter Webb and Barry [sic] McKelvey the year before. Admittedly, to use Dr Bull's term in his report, it was a 'try-out', the first independently sponsored expedition of New Zealand's Antarctic programme: the first of many.

Since that first unofficial student visit by Webb and McKelvey and the first University-sponsored expedition that followed it, described by Colin

Bull, its leader, in the pages that follow, there has been a further expedition each year, for a total so far of 50, a most remarkable accomplishment.

In those 50 years more than 300 staff members and students have participated in the VUW Antarctic expeditions and over 400 scientific publications have resulted. The geological emphasis of the original effort has continued, with the theme in recent years being the history and behaviour of past climate and ice sheets. This has entailed the development of offshore drilling systems and more recently an ice-coring system, and collaboration with other institutions and countries. The expeditions have changed greatly in character as science and society have changed, but they are still fulfilling that original purpose – to educate the best of our young people and to expand our knowledge of the Antarctic continent. They are therefore necessarily rather different in style and scale: Colin's little enterprise in 1958–59 cost less than $1000, whereas the current annual budget for our eight staff in the Antarctic Research Centre of the Victoria University of Wellington is close to $1 million. But the spirit continues.

I have been very happy, as Director of the University's Antarctic program from 1970 to 2007, to pen these words of introduction to Colin's lively tale of its origins, and especially so, as Colin was also one of my PhD supervisors at The Ohio State University. I have also had the good fortune to sail with Peter Webb on the deep-sea drilling ship *Glomar Challenger*, to drill the Antarctic continental shelf in the Ross Sea in 1972–73, and Peter and I have continued promoting this fascinating and productive enterprise ever since. Barrie McKelvey and Dick Barwick have visited a number of times, often in the company of Colin or Peter, sometimes to entertain us with the story of that expedition. I am delighted that it is finally appearing in print, and I sincerely hope it will spur others to follow this lead with their own stories.

Peter J. Barrett,
Antarctic Research Centre,
Victoria University of Wellington
January 2008

Author's Note

A few years ago, in 2001, I was one of the members of a reunion – the 50th anniversary of the Birmingham University Spitsbergen Expedition, 1951, my first polar adventure. As usual at reunions every conversation started with either 'Do you remember when . . .?' Or 'What do you think would have happened if . . .?' Then Dave suggested that one of us collect all these remembrances, and try to make a book from them. Of the ten members of the expedition, seven were at that reunion. All the others had kept diaries or extensive field notes. I hadn't, so obviously I was the one called upon to do the compilation and book preparation. It was all much more fun than I could ever have expected or imagined and took far too long, but, with great help from all the others, we made it – and the book, *Innocents in the Arctic*, was published in 2005.

Following that effort I was greatly concerned that I would be obliged to revert to digging ditches, or some other form of honest employment, Most fortunately, exactly at the right moment, somebody else decided to hold a reunion, 'The First And Last Reunion of the Vandals', the name given to the former inhabitants of a little remote New Zealand station on the shores of Lake Vanda, in Wright Valley, Antarctica. Well, I had never been an inhabitant of that station but I had had the great good fortune to be able to take there a party of four like-minded souls (Dick Barwick, Peter Webb, Barrie McKelvey and myself – you'll grow heartily sick of those names quite soon!) on the first University expedition to the Antarctic. We had been the first people to visit Wright Valley; we had named Lake Vanda and had done lots of other exciting things. The Vandal reunion organizers invited us to their reunion, 'to provide historical perspective', as one of them said, and all four of us turned up. The presentations that we made at the banquet about our 1958–59 adventure were immensely well received, and that was not entirely due to the questionable sobriety of the audience – and I decided that writing up an account of the expedition could be more fun than weeding rows of carrots.

A few months later Gillian, my wife – you'll meet her again later – was helping with a painting workshop in the Chianti valley of Tuscany, and while she worked her fingers to the skin, painting those gorgeous scenes,

I sat in the sun, drinking Chianti (what else?), and trying hard to translate the immensely detailed diary I had kept all those years before. It was in the form of a huge letter to Gillian and few-months-old son Nicky. In parts it was more difficult to decipher, I'm sure, than understanding Etruscan, but I persisted. In any case there is much merit in having more than one interpretation to choose from.

Well, wouldn't you know it, around Christmas 2006, Peter Barrett – the chap who wrote the Introduction (isn't it useful to have former students in important positions?) – decided we needed a reunion, to be held in late June 2007, to celebrate 50 years of work in the Antarctic by the University. Not only were the four of us invited but also all the members of the 50 expeditions that had followed ours, from that little University. To force a deadline on myself I promised Peter that I would bring him a first draft, and I managed it, with copies for the other three members of the 1958–59 party. I asked them for their corrections, contributions and additions – and those have been plentiful and are still (June 2008) arriving.

In the field we worked as two pairs. I worked with Dick and spent 52 consecutive nights (except one) in the same tent with him. We ate the same meals, climbed the same ridiculously exhausting mountains, pulled the same over-loaded sledge, and laughed at the same inane jokes. You have the picture. Shortly after the reunion, Dick unearthed his diary from 50 years of accumulated junk – I mean 50 years of carefully collected and meticulously catalogued treasures. Dick's diary is not quite as detailed as mine, but nearly so. Well, it is obvious that the pair of us were on the same expedition, but we saw many things with quite interestingly different eyes. Dick was amazingly reticent in his comments on my stupid actions (as I hope I was with his), but his diary made me see all of our expedition from another point of view, and there isn't much similarity between the first and second drafts.

Peter added some great descriptions of events that occurred when I wasn't around and Barrie showed that he had a better-developed soul than any of the rest of us, by scolding me for failing to describe properly the breathtaking views that very frequently stunned our senses. My original description of our first view of that superlative panorama at the head of Wright Valley he dismissed as a 'leaden underkill'. I hope I've done better in rewriting that – and in many other places.

And Isobel Gabites, daughter of an old friend of 50 years ago, has done us all a huge favour in reading carefully through the manuscript, translating some of my English into good Kiwi, and pointing out innumerable unjustified assumptions I had made. We all owe her a very big 'thank you'. Thank you so much Isobel!

Of course there are dozens of other people to whom we are indebted for help of many kinds in generating the expedition and launching it, at least moderately successfully. First off, naturally, there's good friend Gillian, my incredibly tolerant wife, who wouldn't let me not go. 'You must go! You may never have another chance!' Darcy Walker, Chairman of the Physics Department, and my boss, allowed me to go, and invited Gillian and baby Nicky for Christmas dinner – and two other notable New Zealand scientists helped immeasurably, Eddie Robertson and Bob Clark. Eddie, back then, was the Superintendent of the Geophysical Division of the Department of Scientific and Industrial Research, perhaps the person in New Zealand whose scientific interests most closely mirrored my own. He was also Chairman of the Ross Dependency Research Committee, the body from which we had to gain approval of our plans. I'm delighted that he was able to write that very generous Foreword. And Bob Clark! He had been appointed Chairman of the Geology Department in 1954, when he was 32 years old, and was busy building up an outstanding department. He was the fellow who had eased the way for Barrie and Peter to reach Antarctica in 1957. With that and the administrative help that he gave us, he was well entitled to the honour that he claimed: 'Founder of the Antarctic efforts of the University'. Bob was definitely an iconoclast, although he enjoyed good relationships with the powers in the University, the government and the Antarctic. A great guy!

Then there are the many people who allowed us to borrow instruments and equipment, and the manufacturers who supplied us with much of the food we delighted in consuming, and some of our field clothing. We would have liked to place their individual or company names on many of the features of that beautiful, stark and wind-swept land, but the New Zealand Geographic Board didn't like that idea, so instead we eventually named one notable mountain 'Sponsors' Peak'.

When we went to Wright Valley none of us was very adept with a camera but by virtue of statistics and taking enough exposures some of them are fairly presentable. All of those reproduced, except the cover photo of Bull Pass, are by one of the four of us, but we've swapped them around so much that the original photographer is often 'shrouded in the mists of time'. The cover photo is by Josh Landis, one of the contributors to the Antarctic Photograph Archive organized by the National Science Foundation. In the last 50 years Dick Barwick has blossomed as a photographic artist, to add to his other considerable artistic talents, which is why I'm so pleased he volunteered to look after the illustrations. Dick is also a highly competent cartographer, and has produced four of the maps for the book. Dick, in turn, is grateful to Paul Sjoberg, Facilities and Services, Australian National University, for his help in converting the US Geological Survey map of the McMurdo Dry Valleys into the one we have included in the book. Just for interest, we've also included an illustration based on Guyon Warren's 1958 map, the best one we had to take into the field. For the last 50 years Barrie has been standing coffee cups on it.

Lots of other people have helped by reading bits of the manuscript and suggesting improvements. In the same way that we named Sponsors' Peak to represent all the generous folk who helped with supplies and so on, I'm going to name my great friend Henry Brecher to represent all the readers who helped in this way.

Finally I am also very grateful to Eileen, my 11-year-old granddaughter, who pointed out that I had written 'Chapter One', but 'Chapter 2', that you shouldn't put a period after the chapter title, and lots more similar boo-boos. Perhaps when she grows up she will attain the stature of Kyleigh Hodgson, Editor, who with her gentle and considerate touch has done much to convert my crude blabberings into readable English. Would you like to come on our next Expedition, Kyleigh, and write it up on the spot?

Dramatis Personae

Richard Barwick, BSc (New Zealand) Biology, 1956; MSc (New Zealand) Biology, 1957. Member, NZ TAE, Summers 1956–57 and 1957–58. Junior Lecturer, Zoology, Victoria University of Wellington. 29 years old.

Colin Bull, BSc (Birmingham) Physics, 1948; PhD (Birmingham) Physics, 1951. Member, Birmingham University Spitsbergen Expedition, 1951. Geophysicist and later Chief Scientist, British North Greenland Expedition, 1952–54. Senior Lecturer, Physics, Victoria University of Wellington. 30 years old.

Barrie McKelvey, BSc (VUW) Geology, December 1958. Member VUWAE 1. 21 years old.

Peter Webb, BSc (VUW) Geology, December, 1958. Member VUWAE 1. 22 years old.

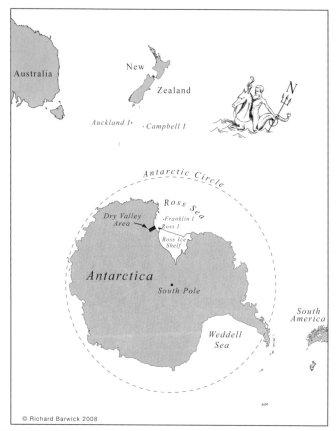

Map 1. Dry Valley area, in relation to the Antarctic continent and part of the Southern Hemisphere.

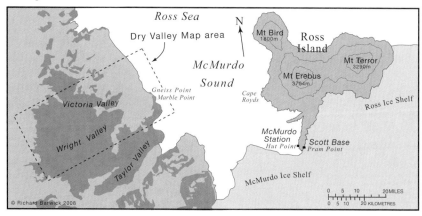

Map 2. Outline map, showing Dry Valley Map area (Map 4) in relation to Ross Island and McMurdo Sound.

CHAPTER 1

An idea

'Oh damn the calorie count! What we're going to need is food.' This was the rangy, ever-hungry Peter Webb talking. His audience comprised co-third year geology undergraduate Barrie McKelvey, Dick Barwick, a junior lecturer in the Zoology Department and me, Colin Bull, a senior lecturer in physics. Together we made up the Victoria University of Wellington, New Zealand, Antarctic Expedition, 1958–59, the first expedition organized and planned from a university, that we know of, ever to visit 'the white continent'. The other three had all been to the Antarctic in the previous year, as summer members of the New Zealand part of the Commonwealth Antarctic Research Programme, and Dick had also been there in 1956–57.

I'd not been to the Antarctic but did have some Arctic experience. I had been an organizer and member of a university expedition to Spitsbergen in the summer of 1951, and then a member of the large national (Queen Elizabeth was our patron and Winston Churchill our vice-patron) British North Greenland Expedition, 1952–54.

Our challenge was to work out the food rations that the four of us would need for three months of fieldwork. That wouldn't have been difficult usually but we had another condition to satisfy: we were paying for most of it ourselves and we had rather little money, in fact very little.

Peter and Barrie were keen as mustard, and always game for any unusual activity. In July 1957 they urged their professor, Bob Clark, to write to the Ross Sea Committee, who then looked after the Antarctic efforts of the New Zealand government, asking for assistance in sending these two immensely enthusiastic young men to the Antarctic to undertake unspecified geological work. Bob was a persuasive and enthusiastic advocate and the Committee promised the students transport to Scott Base, nominally in return for their help with unloading the ship. At the last minute they were nearly dumped, in favour of two carpenters, but they prevailed and eventually found themselves bound for McMurdo Sound on

HMNZS *Endeavour*. After helping with the unloading, they'd be free to fend for themselves.

The wee wooden warship of the New Zealand Navy, *Endeavour*, had had several lives. Her previous service had been with the British Government's Falkland Islands Dependencies Survey, in the Antarctic Peninsula area, as HMS *John Biscoe*, and in that role she had become very well known. Before that, she was HMS *Pretext*, and she had been born, in 1944, as USCGC *Satinwood*, in the service of the United States Coastguard as a harbour-boom maintenance vessel. After WWII the Americans transferred the vessel to the British and they in turn sold her to New Zealand. (Her cost to the New Zealanders, Dick Barwick believes, was less than £60,000.)

Peter and Barrie, just by being themselves, made an excellent impression on Captain Kirkwood, Captain of the *Endeavour*, who, with Dick Barwick as the joint author, sent a signal commending them to Mr Bowden, Chairman of the Ross Sea Committee. The members of the Committee, quite properly, had been just a bit dubious about having two unsupervised students gadding about on the continent.

In McMurdo Sound they helped unload the *Endeavour*, Peter driving a farm tractor between the ship and the New Zealand base, similar to the ones that Edmund Hillary and his team were driving to the South Pole to meet Bunny Fuchs and the crossing party. Peter learned his tractor-driving skills in his childhood, spent partly on a farm near beautiful Mount Taranaki. (Barrie avers that at this stage of his life he could barely drive a nail.) They had planned to conduct a small gravity-coring program around McMurdo Sound, from the *Endeavour*, but that had to be cancelled, probably because there was insufficient fuel available. When they were not away on field trips Barrie and Peter lived on the *Endeavour* but they took every opportunity to see as much of the country as they could.

Dick Barwick, the short and wiry biologist, was a remarkably tough outdoorsman, and an excellent black and white artist (one of his designs, a leaping rainbow trout, had been selected for the one shilling and three pence postage stamp in the New Zealand 1955 nature series). He'd completed his Master's degree with a thesis on the life history of a New Zealand scincid lizard, carrying out the field work in a local cemetery. He then spent quite long periods living alone on the isolated Brothers Island in Cook Strait, studying the giant gecko and doing some research on the tuatara, in which he was occasionally aided by Peter Webb, who worked briefly as a lighthouse keeper there. For the summers of 1956–57 and of 1957–58 Dick had been a biologist seconded by Victoria University to the official New Zealand summer support party of the Trans-Antarctic Expedition.

Fig. 2. Wharfies. Barrie and Peter sailing from Wellington on HMNZS *Endeavour*, 1957.

Fig. 3. Dick, looking coy, Wright Valley, 1958.

He had spent most of the first season helping to build Scott Base and driving a tractor for six weeks, seemingly around the clock. Biology was occasionally sandwiched between other activities. In the second year things improved and he had been able to travel around quite a lot. On 11th February 1957 he and three others had made a landing from HMNZS *Endeavour* onto Franklin Island, in the Ross Sea. It was the first such landing since Borchgrevink had visited the island in 1900. They landed on the same beach where James Ross had landed when discovering the island in 1841. They only had a couple of hours ashore but Dick climbed the steep 150-metre cliffs to take a photographic panorama, in order to estimate the size of the large Adélie penguin colony. The following year, while the two of us were tent-bound by snow in the Antarctic, Dick told me more than I had ever expected to know about Franklin Island, but obviously Dick's biggest problem had been in deciding what to do on shore, to make best use of his limited time in such a fascinating place. Nothing seemed to have escaped the young biologist's attention. He even reported that the volcanic rock he found on the way up the cliff showed some spectacular phenocrysts.

Three days later, on 14th February, Dick went ashore again at Botany Bay in Granite Harbour. Captain Kirkwood described it: 'Sandstone and granite cliffs topped by a sheer ice cliff rose above the beach and it looked a most uninviting place.' When the party was collected from the beach three hours later, 'Barwick was loaded with geological and botanical specimens.' Dick found and collected some luxuriant mosses in a steep coastal gully, which he was able to send back by air to the DSIR a few days later – absolutely fresh.

All three of them, Dick, Barrie and Peter, had leapt at opportunities to see a number of fascinating places on the west side of McMurdo Sound. Their new friend, Phil Smith, the chief representative in McMurdo of the US IGY organization, arranged their helicopter rides with the US Navy VX-6 Squadron, part of the US Operation Deep Freeze.

The young geologists had visited the previously unnamed Beacon Valley, one of the side valleys of the Taylor Valley. Once upon a time Beacon Valley had been filled with a glacier which flowed into the Taylor Glacier. An undersized Taylor Glacier still exists but it no longer flows all the way to McMurdo Sound. Nowadays it stops perhaps 50 kilometres short of the coast and the ice-free lower valley forms one of the most fascinating areas in the Antarctic. The valley had been investigated by parties from both of the Scott expeditions, in 1901 and in 1911, and Scott's parties had also named Beacon Heights, overlooking Beacon Valley, but had not named the valley itself.

Peter and Barrie, in the company of Gordon Turnbull, a young English geologist from Cambridge, flew to Beacon Valley in a big lumbering piston-engine Sikorsky helicopter, called *King Pin*, which was painted in a faded and oil-streaked Day-Glo orange. They camped on the west side of the valley and worked on the geology of the sandstone and dolerite rocks. Gordon was collecting oriented samples, in order to make a study of their paleomagnetism. He collected many sandstone specimens and a few dolerites, but later when he worked them up in Newcastle, England, was disappointed to find that the sandstones had all been heated when the dolerite was intruded, and they didn't produce anything useful.

Peter and Barrie also enjoyed two other novel experiences. The first was to give names to features that they had mapped. Mount Weller, which they named after Isaac Weller, one of the Royal Navy men who worked in that area during the *Discovery* expedition, and Aztec and Maya Mountains, were all subsequently approved by the New Zealand Geographic Board.

The second experience was with their tent companion, not the most adroit camper. Peter described it later:

> We were sitting in our tent on our air mattresses after dinner and just relaxing. Our friend was sitting there smiling and all seemed to be fine and tranquil with him. He had a large and very sharp pointed skinning knife and was idly plunging it between his legs and awfully close to his manhood. Suddenly there was a whistling noise of escaping air, accompanied by Gordon screaming 'Oh dear!' (Barrie explained that Gordon did not swear at all. He just said 'Oh dear', on a variable scale of passion.) 'I've done it! I've done it! What am I going to do?'
>
> Barrie looked as if he was going to lose his dinner all over us. First I assumed that Gordon had severed his intestines or bladder with his idle knife thrusting. But then it came to me that something truly awful had occurred and he had lopped off a testicle or his penis and someone was going to have to look for them inside his pants (remember that Barrie and I were very young and innocent at the time). Poor Gordon was moaning about not being able to sleep that night and I assumed that shock had set in. Amidst the excitement it became apparent that he had missed his vitals by millimetres but had cut through both sides of the air mattress and hit rock under the tent.

On other occasions *King Pin* took them to the Inland Forts, high on the north side of the upper Taylor Glacier, and to the area of Mount Handsley (again named by Peter and Barrie, after another of Scott's Royal Navy men who had sledged in the area) and Knobhead, near the confluence of the Taylor and Ferrar Glaciers. After being deposited by *King Pin* directly below Beehive, they scrambled up West Groin, the first visitors to the area since Hartley Ferrar had been there as the geologist on the *Discovery* expedition. Although members of Scott's expeditions had seen all these areas, Barrie and Peter were the first to map their geology.

Fig. 4. Peter and Barrie on the flanks of Mount Knobhead, Quartermain Range, above the junction of the Ferrar and Taylor Glaciers, January 1958.

Dick and Peter were two members of a four-man party who were the first ever to set foot in another ice-free valley, 80 kilometres or so to the north, at that time unnamed. One of the New Zealand pilots, Squadron Leader John Claydon, was flying near Gneiss Point when he saw what he thought was an ice-free lake further inland in a glacier-free valley. The people at Scott Base were excited and persuaded Phil Smith, over at McMurdo, to arrange a helicopter flight over there. The party formed to investigate the lake and valley included Dick and Peter, Andrew Packard, a biologist from Auckland, and Ron Balham, another biologist and a member of the wintering-over party of the Trans-Antarctic Expedition.

At the time that Ron was asked to take charge of the party he was driving a tractor towards the South Pole, in Hillary's Trans-Antarctic party. Ron later joined the faculty of Victoria University and he became the leader of the University Expedition the year following our venture.

The New Zealand party was fortunate to have the support once again of Phil Smith who organized a US helicopter to take four people to a spot near the lake (Peter and Barrie tossed a coin for the fourth place: Peter said that he had won; Barrie is still disputing the validity of the toss). Over the following ten days they had a most interesting time in the valley, which they named Victoria Valley, for our University. Peter made a first reconnaissance geology map of the topographically complicated area, investigated some of the weird land forms, including the desert sand dunes, and named the two largest lakes, Lake Vashka and Lake Vida, after two dogs from Scott's parties.

The biologists found very little life in the area: some red and blue-green algae in the streams, a few bits of lichen high up in the surrounding peaks, and a few mummified crabeater seals, similar to those found 50 years earlier in Taylor Valley but even further from the coast. They brought one of these seals back to New Zealand, where radiocarbon dating showed it to be 300 years old.

They'd all had an absolutely wonderful and productive time and were all desperately keen to go again. The two geological publications that Peter and Barrie produced from their visits were the first on this part of Antarctica to appear since the reports of the Scott and Shackleton expeditions.

And Peter and Barrie had other treats. Several times they went on *Endeavour* to the sites of Scott's second hut, at Cape Evans, and to Shackleton's hut at Cape Royds, usually going ashore in a lifeboat, but once they went to Cape Royds by trekking over the sea ice. They were able to cover quite a lot of territory on foot. They sampled material from the perched strandlines, gained data from the erratics, found one of the sledges abandoned by either Scott's or Shackleton's parties, and made a nearly calamitous attempt to reach Tent Island.

No wonder they were keen to return! Together with Bob Clark they had started a tradition of work and adventure in Antarctica by members of the University and particularly by members of the Geology Department that has continued to this day.

My approach to the idea of going to the Antarctic was quite different. At the University of Birmingham, England, I had completed a PhD degree in solid-state physics. This work was deemed to be 'Scientific Work of National Importance' and was considered by the powers-that-be to be an acceptable alternative to military service. In the last year of that time, in 1951, I had helped organize and had been a member of my first polar expedition, to Spitsbergen. This had helped me to achieve an ambition that had been generated by reading a book about Scott's Last Expedition, when I was a ten-year old, 'to become a polar explorer' (according to my father's accounts), and had also gained me a position on the British North Greenland Expedition of 1952–54. That was perhaps the last of the large British Navy-based Arctic expeditions, in which everybody wintered over, whether or not they could do anything useful during the winter.

I'd enjoyed myself greatly for most of those two years. We'd done some good science. For the second winter I had been the weather observer, and leader of three people living at 2345 metres elevation for eight months. My companions, Hal Lister (a glaciologist) and Dixie (the radio operator), and I spent the winter of 1953–54 completely isolated, 500 kilometres from our nearest neighbour, in a four-metre-square hut we called 'Northice'. During that time the air temperature dropped on two occasions below −65°C and once below −68°C. It was all highly enjoyable, especially in retrospect.

Except for the first winter, when I was the self-appointed chief pastry cook for the 20-odd members wintering at the Main Base in Dronning Louise Land in northeast Greenland, and the second winter at Northice, most of the rest of my time was spent in making a levelling and gravity traverse from coast to coast, finishing near the US Air Force Base at Thule. The four-man 'gravity team' thereby established 'The World Record for the Slowest Crossing of Greenland', two years and a month, a record that no one has yet tried to beat. In addition we showed that the ice sheet was as much as 2800 metres thick!

Back at Cambridge University I spent the rest of 1954 and most of 1955 working up the results of our work in Greenland. One of our visitors during that time was Bunny Fuchs, who had come to Cambridge to try to entice Hal Lister and me to become members of his Commonwealth Trans-Antarctic Expedition. Hal succumbed and became the expedition's glaciologist, initially with the wintering party at the Advanced Base, which he called 'South Ice', and then with the crossing party. But I recalled two of the sayings we had generated in Greenland: 'Everyone should winter over on a two-year expedition once but no one should do it more than once,' and 'If you've seen one square metre of an ice sheet, you've seen it all.' Obviously Hal had forgotten these bon mots. Furthermore I had just become engaged to Gillian, the sister of one of my Spitsbergen colleagues. So I declined Bunny's offer.

Hal Lister re-enters the story a little later, although he probably doesn't realize it. When he and the rest of Bunny's crossing party reached Scott Base, Hal discarded the anorak that he had been using for the last two years. Dick Barwick retrieved it from the rubbish dump and gave it to me. (We didn't have money enough to buy new ones.) At Scott Base I repaired it, and wore it during our time in the Antarctic in 1958–59, before returning it to the 'used but usable again' store.

While Bunny Fuchs and I were talking, however, he showed me some aerial photographs, taken by a fairly recent US expedition, of the ice-free areas in southern Victoria Land. From the southern part of this area there was a magnificent photograph looking westwards up the entire Taylor

Valley. There were also some photographs of parts of the complicated valley system in the north, which Dick, Barrie and Peter had since named Victoria Valley. Between these two places was a breathtaking, high-walled ice-free valley, largely east-west, perhaps 70 kilometres long, with a large ice-covered lake towards the western end.

Fig. 5. Colin, looking detached.

In the far west (the inland end) two thin icefalls spilled from the inland ice beyond, over huge walls of rock, to form a flat-lying apron of ice extending a few miles down the valley. At the other end of the valley (the eastern end) the low-lying Wilson Piedmont Glacier – also named by Scott's Last Expedition – blocked access from McMurdo Sound to the unnamed valley. Members of Scott's and Shackleton's parties, including Griffith Taylor, for whom Taylor Glacier and Valley were named, had walked along the coastal end of the area but no one had seen into the valley, except, nearly 50 years later, from the air. It looked a most intriguing place! Although I'd disappointed Bunny I remembered his great photographs.

Gillian and I were married in June 1956 and we sailed almost immediately for New Zealand. After we had become engaged, a year earlier, Gillian casually remarked that it might be a good idea if one of us got a job that might last more than a few months. As she had yet to finish her degree at

Art School, I supposed that that should be me. There was a junior faculty position available in my Cambridge department, and Ben Browne, the Chairman, said he would support my application for it. I duly applied – and didn't get it! At the last minute there was another applicant, Sir Edward Bullard, KBE, FRS. He got the job, and quit his current one as Director of the National Physical Laboratories, so that he could give up administration, and indulge in science. I couldn't understand why Cambridge preferred Teddy to me, but at least Teddy did apologize for stealing the junior job.

I was offered two other employment possibilities: one was a somewhat staid-sounding (although academically far, far superior) lectureship in geophysics at Imperial College, London; the other was a lectureship in physics at Victoria University of Wellington, New Zealand, for which we applied simply for the sheer adventure of it. I was very surprised when Victoria University offered me a senior lectureship instead, which we accepted.

CHAPTER 2

Loife in Noo Zillun

New Zealand turned out to be a wonderful place to live and certainly the best place to raise a family in the whole world. Our voyage from Britain had been exciting; a month on SS *Strathmore*, so long indeed that we felt we had become part of the superstructure. We were one of the last ships through the Suez Canal before the 1956 imbroglio. We gloried in the fascination of Bombay and Colombo; and the tedium of writing geophysics lectures all morning, while Gillian learned to type, and deck quoits and other competitions in the afternoon. The Australian ports were young, clean and refreshing, although we didn't like the rough seas in the Australian Bight. I'd hoped to sail on the famous MV *Rangitiki* from Sydney to Wellington but that would have meant a month's delay in Sydney, which we couldn't afford, so instead we travelled on MV *Rangitane*, newer and perhaps more comfortable. Wellington Harbour was beautiful and the compact and clean city appeared most welcoming.

Darcy Walker, the Chairman of the Physics Department, and June, his wife, both of whom I knew from my graduate student days in Birmingham, met us at the dock in Wellington and within minutes, prevented me from generating my first industrial dispute. Our small pile of luggage was on the dock; all the dock workers had gone to lunch; Darcy's car was a couple of hundred metres away; dozens of luggage carts were stacked against a neighbouring wall. I walked over to bring one to our luggage. Darcy ran after me, and warned me not to touch the cart. 'Certain labour strike,' he said.

Initially we had borrowed a house belonging to a lecturer in Greek who was away on leave, only a very short walk from the rather pretty collection of red brick buildings that was, and is, the University. At the University I had to share a room with Noel Ryder, the other senior lecturer in the Department. When Darcy took me round to meet the staff and the rest of the faculty, every conversation started the same way. 'Weel! Wilcum to Noo Zillun! D'you see the goime?' The previous Saturday the

combined Universities rugby football team had most unexpectedly beaten
the touring national team from South Africa. That was the 'goime'. No one
mentioned physics.

After those few months Gillian and I moved our trivial possessions to
Paremata, on the west coast of the North Island, 'over the hill' and about
20 kilometres north of Wellington, and out of the wind. Home there was
a diminutive rustic cottage, about the same size as the garage of our next
house. It was midway between our landlord's house (he was a Professor in
the Chemistry Department, Bobby Munro) at the top of the slope and the
shore of Paremata Harbour at the bottom. The view from our dining/living
room, across the mouth of the bay to the proper coast, was just exquisite,
and more than compensated for the absence of indoor plumbing. And if
we needed a change of scenery we could go and sleep in the bunkhouse at
the water's edge, and wake to hear the waves lapping around the footings,
and the seagulls sliding down the corrugated iron roof, just for fun. Did I
say it was the best place to live in the whole world?

Gillian had a position that she much enjoyed, as the junior Art Teacher
at Wellington East Girls' School, although she didn't like the chore of
measuring the height of the girls' socks. However, she would be giving
up that job at the end of Winter Term, late in June 1958, because we were
expecting our first child in July. I felt a complete heel for even thinking
of planning to be away for nearly three months while our baby was
still so young. Gillian, however, said, 'Go! You may never have another
opportunity!'

Victoria University was a delightful, impoverished place. It was a
small 'liberal arts' school, without medical, dental, engineering, or even
agricultural departments. Even in those days it was a crowded little campus,
three hectares or so of steep hillside overlooking downtown Wellington,
the beautiful harbour and the Hutt Valley. We had a few more than 100
faculty members and 2000 or so students, perhaps two-thirds of them part-
time, and very nearly all undergraduates. Everyone on the faculty knew
everyone else's business and interests. Money was always tight, spare cash
did not exist, and consequently it was far from being the best place in the
world to attempt cutting-edge research in geophysics or solid-state physics.
We had no equipment, no money to buy it, no facilities to make it, and no
one with whom to discuss it.

In New Zealand, at that time, if one studied any subject for two whole
weeks, even something as prosaic as the best shape for table legs, one
became the national expert. Some people like to work in a vacuum like
that but I really wanted someone to rub ideas with; someone, if you please,

to ride pillion passenger on my hobbyhorse. In November 1957, while I was working on some ideas to explain the strange geophysical results we had obtained on the Greenland Ice Sheet, I travelled down to Christchurch in the South Island (at my own expense), merely to talk for a few hours to Charlie Bentley and Ned Ostenso, two glaciologists from the USA, on their way to Antarctica to take part in the work of the International Geophysical Year. Charlie had also carried out geophysical work on the Greenland Ice Sheet, and knew what I was talking about! I was so grateful to him for giving up an afternoon when he could have been exploring Christchurch. I had the best conversation and scientific discussion I had had in the 16 months since leaving Britain.

On another occasion I needed a few inches of quartz fibre of a particular thickness, to make an astatic magnetometer with which we were intending to measure the magnetic properties of rock samples. There didn't seem to be anything suitable anywhere in the length and breadth of New Zealand. If I could acquire the money – we wouldn't need much – and the required import license I could buy suitable material from Britain. However that would take six months! Or I could try to make it myself. How? Dr Eddie Robertson, head of the Geophysics Division of the government's Department of Scientific and Industrial Research, didn't have any quartz fibre but told me that, years ago, one of his colleagues in London had made some, though he didn't know how successful the experiment had been. All one had to do was to take a bow and arrow, the arrow being a solid rod of quartz, heat up part of the rod until it was molten and then shoot the arrow across the room, holding on to the back end.

Well, parts of the experiment worked. Jim Gellen, my graduate student, and I spent many hours trying to find the fibre, which was very uneven, either too thick or too thin. Rather quickly I despaired of the possibilities of being a laboratory research scientist in New Zealand.

Apart from my research training in solid-state physics, which had produced my dissertation (and lots of offers of jobs in industrial laboratories, all of which were easy to reject) but which didn't seem to fit readily into the Physics Department of the Victoria University of Wellington, the only other work at which I'd shown any prowess, if that's what it was, was my cooking and the geophysics and glaciology that I had picked up in Spitsbergen and Greenland. Research in some branches of those sciences could be carried out with relatively unsophisticated equipment, or even just a good pair of eyes and a lively imagination. I wondered if I could organize a little expedition down south to the Antarctic and do some work of one kind or another to justify myself.

Three of my good friends from the Greenland expedition, Hal Lister, Dickie Brooke, surveyor, and Roy Homard, vehicle mechanic, were already in Antarctica. Hal and Roy were with the crossing party of Bunny Fuchs's expedition and Dickie Brooke was one of the surveyors with the New Zealand end of that expedition. I was still pleased that I hadn't accepted Bunny's invitation to go with him for maybe two complete years, but perhaps it would be possible to organize matters so that I could go down there just for the summer. I started playing with a few ideas of how to make this possible.

And then, one day in March 1958 I went to hear a talk in the Geology Department, given by Peter and Barrie, on their work and adventures in Antarctica in the preceding months. I knew about New Zealand's part in the International Geophysical Year, 1957–58, and in the Commonwealth Trans-Antarctic Expedition, of course, but both of those were parts of large organizations. From Peter and Barrie's talk, for the first time I realized that university people, acting for themselves, had already been involved in New Zealand's Antarctic science, even if only as student assistants – so far! It looked as though the pair, Barrie and Peter, had had a thoroughly stimulating, satisfying, and rewarding time.

I thought to myself that at least two of the other members of my hypothetical expedition were already lined up, even if they didn't know it yet. And the place to aim at was clear – that was the unnamed and unvisited valley between the Taylor and Victoria Valleys. Peter and Barrie could very readily and profitably continue their geological mapping work into the western part of the Victoria Valley complex, as well as into the unnamed valley and the upland areas north and south of it.

I chewed over the idea for a day or two with Gillian, who, as ever was highly supportive ('You should go. You may never have another chance.') and then went along to see Bob Clark, the recently appointed Professor of Geology, and the inspiration and driving force behind Barrie and Peter's adventures of the previous year. Bob was a jovial and dynamic geologist, part of whose training had been in gaining a PhD, with the redoubtable Arthur Holmes as supervisor, at Edinburgh University. There he had become friends with Lionel Weiss, my friend and the instigator of our Spitsbergen expedition of 1951. Lionel, from California, told me lots of good things about Bob and urged me to meet him.

Bob had seen the immense potential of the Antarctic as a training and research area, and was incredibly keen to establish some sort of continuing work there from his Department. A couple of years later he even entitled the serendipitous work by Peter and Barrie as 'Victoria University of Wellington

Antarctic Expedition #1'. In me, Bob quickly saw the possibilities of generating further expeditions. In Bob, because he was a senior member of the University, who knew his way around the tricky paths of academia, I saw the means of gathering backing, of an academic if not financial nature, for a first 'proper' university expedition to the continent. We clicked.

Soon after that I first met Dick Barwick, who, as I've said, had already had a first glimpse of the Antarctic biology in the ice-free areas of south Victoria Land, and wanted to see more of it. Most particularly he wanted to have a close look at the mummified seals that they had found in Victoria Valley, and which the men of one of the 'Western Parties' of Scott's Last Expedition had seen in Taylor Valley. There were sure to be more of them in that unnamed valley, weren't there? Dick had lots of other ideas. What sort of life was there in the 'soil' on the surface of the valley? What was in the lake?

Four people would be enough for a first attempt at a quasi-independent expedition. We were complete, without even trying!

Members of Scott's polar party, on their fatal return journey, had found fossils of *Glossopteris*, a temperate or perhaps tropical plant, in the moraines of the Beardmore Glacier, far to the south. They represented a huge difference in the climate from the present conditions. Was that because the climate had changed all over the world, or was that change caused because the latitude of the *Glossopteris* site had changed?

My friend Ted Irving, who had been a graduate student in geophysics at Cambridge while I was a post-doctoral fellow, had demonstrated, using the paleomagnetic properties of ancient rocks from Scotland, that polar wandering (movement of the site of the rocks relative to the North Magnetic Pole) and continental drift (of Europe relative to North America) had both occurred, and on a very large scale. Now he was at the Australian National University in Canberra, where he had built a magnetometer to measure the same properties of Australian rocks. Using the direction of the remnant magnetization of rocks, inherited from the Earth's magnetic field when the rocks were first formed, and trapped in them from that time, was a new way of determining the latitude at which the rocks were formed.

By comparing the fossil magnetization directions of the Antarctic rocks with those from rocks of the same age from the other southern continents, it should be possible to make a solid test of the idea, first formulated by Alfred Wegener in 1911, that all the southern continents were once joined together to form a supercontinent, Gondwana. The magnetization of rocks of Jurassic age from South America, South Africa, Tasmania and India had been measured and I knew the dolerite rocks in the Taylor Valley were about the same age. Gordon Turnbull had collected a few specimens from there, with Barrie and Peter (although I didn't know that at the time), but no one had yet made a good set of measurements of Antarctic rocks in that way. I hadn't managed to build the necessary magnetometer in Wellington but perhaps I could collect suitable rocks and measure them on Ted's machine.

As if that wasn't tantalizing enough, the whole valley looked as though a glacier had carved it out. When was that? Where was that glacier now? And why did the glaciers flowing from the inland ice sheet into that valley and into the Taylor and Victoria Valleys now stop 70 kilometres before they reached the coast, while all the rest of the glaciers flowing through the Transantarctic Mountains ploughed on straight down to the sea? The photographs that Bunny had showed me of that inland ice-covered lake appeared to show benches cut into the scree slopes above the edge of the lake. Former higher lake levels?

The first possible diversion came and went very quickly. George Woollard, University of Wisconsin, was trying hard to fill in some of the most significant blank spots in the International Gravity Network, of which in some fashion he seemed to be in charge. He knew of my gravity work in Greenland. Would I like to spend the summer making gravity ties between Wellington and Auckland in New Zealand, Sydney, Melbourne and Canberra in Australia, and as many islands in the south Pacific as we could fit into the schedule? It sounded fascinating, utterly! But I don't like hot weather! I'd been miserable in the Red Sea on our voyage from England.

With many misgivings I turned it down, but asked if I could borrow Dr Woollard's Worden gravity meter to make a traverse along 'our' Antarctic valley. We might gain some useful information about whether the mountain range was really a horst (a block of elevated land forced up between two north-south, near-vertical faults), as some of the geologists from Scott's and Shackleton's expeditions had suggested. Unfortunately the idea of borrowing that gravity meter didn't work out, but a couple of months later I arranged to borrow another Worden meter, the only one in New Zealand, which belonged to the Geophysics Division of the Department of Scientific and Industrial Research. That came to me through the good offices of Eddie Robertson, the Director. By that time Eddie was becoming more and more a friend to the expedition. So I did the traverse. Years later I met the fellow who had done that initial gravity work in the South Pacific. Indeed it was fascinating but he said he'd suffered from yaws, beriberi, malaria and a dozen other tropical diseases. 'You were lucky not to go,' he said. I never did discover whether he was pulling my leg.

What did we need to launch our expedition, to go to that unnamed valley, do some worthwhile scientific work – and come back safely? Money would help but we had very little and the University wasn't likely to give us much, if any. Still, it was clear that we would be better off with the University's official blessing, even if we couldn't spend it. Bob Clark would obviously put our case to the University Council, of which all department heads were members.

I went to see our Physics Department Chairman, Darcy Walker, to tell him of my embryonic ideas and of the support offered to them by Bob Clark. Perhaps the difference between Bob and Darcy in the response to the idea of outdoor work in a remote area just reflects the difference between a volcanic petrologist and a nuclear physicist. Darcy could see very little purpose in trying to do science in uncomfortable places, but of course he agreed to support Bob's request to the Council for approval for the expedition.

I also visited Dr Williams, the University's Vice-Chancellor, and I was most pleased to find that he was thoroughly enthusiastic. Bob Clark had obviously talked to him earlier, for he seemed to know more about me and the whole idea of our trip than I had expected. Furthermore he suggested that I apply for a New Zealand University Research Grant, and after spending far too much time writing my proposal to that body I was gratified to receive, in September 1958, a grant of £300, which was soon supplemented with £410 from the Council at Vic. Very good! I hadn't expected that! Most of the £410 was spent on insurance for ourselves and the scientific and survey equipment we borrowed. We didn't need the £300 and most of it was spent in the following year by the successor expedition.

The other body from which I knew we must gain approval was the Ross Dependency Research Committee (RDRC), successor to the Ross Sea Committee, which was charged with overseeing all of New Zealand's activities in the Antarctic. Several members of the Committee had been with the earlier New Zealand effort in the south, the British, Australian and New Zealand Antarctic Research Expedition (BANZARE) of 1931–33, led by the Australian, Sir Douglas Mawson. Now, in 1958, several of that expedition's scientific members had risen to become the leaders of New Zealand's science community. Bob Clark was also a member of the Committee, one of the youngest, and he told the Committee something about me. What he said I don't know, but shortly after Bob had made his presentation I was called in. The Chairman, Eddie Robertson, whom I had met several times when he was wearing his other hat as head of the Geophysics Division, admonished me for making the work of the Committee even more difficult, but we left the meeting with their approval for our expedition and, much more important to me, with that approval being given to an only slightly official university expedition, not to an authorized government effort. The four of us would be able to decide what scientific work we would do, where we would go and so on and so on.

Fig. 6. Vice-Chancellor J. Williams, discussing Expedition plans with Colin, Barrie and Peter (*Evening Post*, Wellington, September 1958).

For that meeting I had rewritten the proposal I had sent to the University Grants Committee, with a bit more science and a bit less food in it and sent it to Geoffrey Markham, Secretary of the RDRC. Just before we left for Antarctica Eddie Robertson sent me the same material back, but this time as a set of instructions regarding the work we must do in our selected area. Apparently the RDRC didn't like the idea of having people working independently of the government. Ah, well!

Obviously we would have to cooperate with many others, in order to gain the logistic support we needed, to borrow some of the field equipment and a host of other matters. Being even just a little bit independent seemed to carry lots of responsibilities with it.

CHAPTER 3

Dear Sir, I write on behalf . . .

At the end of July 1958 Gillian woke me one Sunday night and said that there was an urgent need to go to the hospital in Wellington. Fortunately the car started quite easily. It did that sometimes. (Two years later, for the birth of our second child, it didn't start and the family joke is that Gillian had to push it!) Shortly afterwards son Nicholas appeared. By the rules of the times Gillian was constrained to the hospital for 12 days, during which she fretted to come home. She had already built the baby's cot (while I bought the electric fire for night-time feedings – the windows of the cottage weren't very tight) but there were lots of other preparations to do. I felt even more of a heel, but Gillian refused to give me permission to withdraw from the expedition.

Well it wasn't quite true that I could only cook, do scientific work in geophysics, bits of glaciology and solid-state physics. I also had a demonstrated ability for organizing shoestring expeditions – just one, to be honest. Back in 1951 I had been a member of and had helped to organize the Birmingham University Spitsbergen Expedition. The only money that the ten of us had then, for getting ourselves to Spitsbergen, spending two or three months attempting to solve a most intriguing geological problem, and returning to Britain in at least moderate order, were our own miserable contributions from our stipends as students and impoverished junior faculty.

We had supplemented that with contributions from the Lord Mayor's fund – that amounted to £10, of which exactly half came from the Lord Mayor himself – and from our winnings from investing a little bit of our 'cash in hand' (probably from the Lord Mayor's largesse) on the horse that became the winner of the Derby. Arctic Prince won the race, at odds of 40 to 1, and we had bet £1 on it, 'each way', whatever that means. When the Birmingham University bursar went through our fiscal records after the expedition was all over and done with, he was very cross, in fact quite apoplectic, that we had been so improper as to bet public money on a horse race!

We had been so impoverished that, when we read somewhere that it never rains inland in Spitsbergen, we saved money by not buying flysheets for the tents of the people who would be working inland. For further economy we had decided to stuff three people into each two-man tent. As one of us said shortly afterwards, 'If you've never spent the first hours of each day for a month or more, wringing cold rain water from the sleeping bag in which you are going to spend the next night, you just don't know how character-forming it is.' But it wouldn't rain inland in Antarctica, would it? And anyway the official New Zealanders at Scott Base had said we could borrow tents from them.

In our naïveté, back in 1951, we had chartered a wooden-hulled motor launch, the *Miss Mabel*, but fortunately the Ships Controller in Tromsø had prevented us from committing suicide in the ice-infested seas of the high Arctic. We hated him at the time, when he wisely condemned the vessel, with a note pinned to the mast which read 'This vessel is unfit to proceed in any direction'. But some of our planning did go well. Gordon Brace and I wrote 400 or so letters, all following the simple format:

> Dear Sir,
>
> I write on behalf of the Birmingham University Spitsbergen Expedition. . . . will conduct geological investigations in the St. John's Fiord region of Spitsbergen . . . as outlined . . . accompanying brochure. This Expedition, like many scientific efforts of these days . . . needs support.
>
> Of your products we need . . .
>
> If you are able . . . free or at a much reduced price, we can assure you . . .
>
> Yours sincerely,

Everyone was most generous and we collected boots, sweaters, toilet paper, vitamin tablets, splints for broken legs, whistles and food galore. Smedleys, the people who take practically every type of food and put it into cans, told us we could have as much as we liked – free. The only drawback was that the cans were all completely unlabelled, and identical, except for the amount of 'slosh' when shaken, but David Gossage and I, the two cooks on *Miss Mabel*, regarded that as just one more challenge. Our rule became: you may open any six cans for the next meal but you must use them up before opening any more. Have you ever eaten salmon with strawberry jam?

For our Antarctic venture we wouldn't have to charter our own vessel. The RDRC had promised to include our travel to Scott Base (and presumably back to Wellington) with the plans for the official New Zealand parties, so that we would travel there and back by ship, New Zealand or US, or perhaps even by air with the US Navy VX-6 Squadron, and all without charge. The RDRC, and particularly its Chairman, Eddie Robertson, were marvellously supportive.

However, no one in the official world had offered us food for the time we would be in the field. The mukluks that we could borrow from Scott Base weren't the least bit suitable for walking on the bare snow-free surfaces we should have in most places in that deep valley and in the Victoria Valley area. There were stacks of things we needed; I'd try the Spitsbergen approach. The four of us sat down one afternoon in my room in the Physics Department and we thought hard of all the items to put on our 'want list'. We even toyed with making ration lists, with balanced meals containing the approved amounts of carbohydrates, fats, proteins, and calories, which provoked Peter's remark about wanting food.

Dick became the self-appointed 'King of the Lists' and gloried in producing lists of first-aid items we would need, (complete with a note of what was in the standard TAE medical field kit – in the end we borrowed one of those from Scott Base, and used very little of it, not even the 12 ounces of medicinal brandy), clothing needs, hardware items, and likely sources, free from financial encumbrances, for many of them:

hammer, heavy . . . Department;
hammer, light . . . home;
tea chests, six . . . Barrie's parents

and a little note of despair at the end of that very long list:

To be purchased:
    one tin red paint,
    one tin white paint
    one pair crampons.

Another little note reads: 'Pemmican, Egg Powder – NZ Poultry Board, A.M.P. Chambers, Mr Cowdrey.' Soon afterwards Mr Cowdrey produced for us considerable quantities of egg powder, which, after we had all learned to cook it properly, was delicious.

Our field and cooking equipment list is still highly instructional for it has attached to it the cost of all the items we were forced to buy. 'Climbing ropes, two . . . one from Colin, one from Tisdall's, £5..5..0.' My climbing rope, new in Spitsbergen seven years earlier, was being used as a clothes line to hang out Nicky's nappies and other clothes, but Gillian found a length of cord to replace it. The total of the main 'need to buy' list, largely items too small and too diverse to cadge, came to £48..1..2, something less than $100. When Dick found the lists in his tons of clutter in 2007, he sent them to me with the comment 'My God! A quid went a long way in those days'.

TISDALS LTD

	Unit price	TOTAL
2 Lilos	£ 3 - 5 - 6	£ 6 - 11 - 0
2 Climbing ropes	£ 5 - 5- 6	£ 10 - 11 - 0
2 Ice axes		£ 4 - 17 - 6
		£ 5 - 5 - 0
Meta fuel . . x 10 pkts	£ - 6 - 9	£ 3 - 7 - 6
3 Pairs Plastic-leather faced mitts	£ - 17 - 6	£ 2 - 12 - 6
2 string singlets	£ 1- 3 - 6	£ 2 - 7 - 0
2 Tea Infusers	£ - 2 - 3	£ - 4 - 6
4 Mugs small plastic	£ - 1 - 6	£ - 6 - 0
2 Frying pans	£ - 11 - 9	£ 1 - 3 - 6
4 plates	£ - 5 - 9	£ 1 - 3 - 6
5 pr goggles	£ - 11 - 9	£ 2 - 18 - 9
2 pr goggles	£ - 4 - 9	£ - 9 - 0
		£ 41 - 16 - 3
[Possible extras]		
2 pr Green Snow [goggles]	£ - 3 - 6	
Shirts - Blue	£ 2 - 18 - 9	
Diving Jersey	£ 3 - 17 - 6	£ 6 - 4 - 11
		£ 48 - 1 - 2

The sum of NZ£ 50 is approximately equal to US$ 150.00
at the September 10 2008 exchange rate

Fig. 7. One of Dick's supplies lists, 'Gear purchases'.

Peter and Barrie came out to Paremata one bright spring Sunday to continue the discussion and list-making. After a few hours at that task and lunch they both squeezed themselves into our Klepper canoe and set off onto Paremata Harbour, not noticing that the tide was going out very quickly. Equally quickly the boys found themselves swept out of the harbour, under the railway bridge and into the open Tasman Sea. Naturally they assumed that all of this was deliberate on my part. Peter thought I was trying to murder them both; Barrie felt that I was just trying to avoid giving them tea and dinner. They struggled hard, managed to reach shore and carried the canoe back to the cottage, perhaps a bit silent and thoughtful. However, they had no difficulty in managing the next meal.

Armed with our lists I went along to see the venerable Harold Miller, the University Librarian for countless years. Mr Miller had been very enthusiastic about our little expedition ever since I'd mentioned it a month before. Now he could help us. Very soon one of the metal tables in the main reading room was covered with reference books on New Zealand's industry and commerce. As usual Harold was apologetic: 'You're not supposed to have metal tables in a library. But there wasn't enough money for both wooden tables and books!'

Contents of the Pots and Pans Box (for 2 men)

1. Primus box contains
   1 Primus
   3 Primus Legs
   1 Kerosene Filter Funnel
   1 Kerosene Filter spout
   1 Adjustable Spanner
   1 Pump Nipple Key
   3 Burner Prickers
2. Primus Spares Tin containing:
   1 burner complete
   1   "   ring
   4 pump washers
   4 burner   "
   6 filter cap   "
   2 burner cap "
   1 filter cap
   1 burner cap
   5 burner nipples
   1 pump complete (handle, piston, valve, cap)
   1 spare leg
   18 burner prickers
   1 burner nipple key
3. Solid fuel (for lighting Primus) (- for at least 20 days)
4. Matches in Tin (sufficient for 30 days)
5. Candles (sufficient for 20 days)
6. Candle holders 2
7. Alarm Clock 1
8. Two plates
9.   "   enamel mugs
10.   "   pots with lids
11.   "   pot holder
12.   "   Knives. Forks, spoons
12. Tin Openers – 4 'butterfly' openers
13. Dish Cloth – 4 Wettex
14. Torch, spare bulb and batteries - 2 cycle lamps & spare batteries
15. Bag of clothes pegs and pins
16. Tea infuser
17. Compound Vitamin tablets
18. Milk Shaker
19. Toilet Rolls
20. 4 stainless steel pot Scourers

Fig. 8a. Another of Dick's lists, 'Contents of the Pots and Pans Box', Spring 1958.

Sledging Medical Kit

Right Pocket – Dressing materials

   (A)   One plastic bag containing:-

Compressed absorbent gauze	4 pkts
" " cotton wool	4 pkts

   (B)   One plastic bag containing:-

Bandages 3"	4
2"	4
1"	4
crepe	2
triangular pictorial	4

   (C)   Two tins of 3" elastic adhesive bandage
          One tin of 1"   "   "   "

Left Pocket – drugs: instruments

   (A)   Drugs

Boric acid powder	1 dredger
Acriflex Cream	2 tubes
Chloroform ampoules	6
Iodine pencil	1
Triple Dye Jelly	1 tube
Aqueous zinc oxide ointment	1 tin
Brulidene cream	2 tubes
Aspirin tablets	50
Cantrisin tablets	25
Gelusil tablets	50
Trafuril cream	1 tube
Golden Eye ointment	1 tube
One tin containing:-	
Lamellae Adrenalin (0.0006 gr.)	1 tube
Lamellae cocaine (1/20 gr.)	2 tubes
Morphine Tartrate (1/4 gr.)	12 tablets
Procaine HCl with Adrenaline 2%	6 2cc ampoules
Omnopon syrettes (1/4 gr.)	2

   (B)   Instruments

One case containing syringe and needles	
Eyeshade	
Safety pins	
Dressing scissors	
Canvas Roll containing;-	
Artery Forceps	2
Scissors	
Forceps	2
Scalpel and packet of Blades	
Emergency suture with needles	4 tubes
Clinical thermometer	
Dental forceps - upper and lower	

In Lid

First Aid Field Dressings	2
Penicillin distaquaine	15 vials

Fig. 8b. Sledging medical kit list (an ex-NZ TAE kit).

In very little time I had discovered the name of the current Managing Director of Cadbury, Fry, Hudson (New Zealand). I knew who made Anson boots, and who was the headman there. Socks were more difficult; it seemed that there were at least three largish manufacturers of high quality durable socks. In the end Wellington Woollen Manufacturing Company turned out to be our saviour. After a couple of hours of this sort of work, we stopped and walked down the hall to the Common Room, for afternoon tea. In those days the University faculty was a delightfully small group of convivial people, and perhaps half of the 120 or so faculty would come along for tea each afternoon. In this way we all knew a little of what the rest of the University was doing. My particular friends, other than my Departmental colleagues, included Bobby Munro, Chemistry, who was also our landlord, and charged us £2 a month rent for the cottage until we objected and made him put it up to £10 a month, John Beaglehole, History, who was deep into his magnum opus *The Life of James Cook*, Douglas Lilburn, Music, whose compositions we still hear on the radio from time to time, and Mr Miller, the librarian.

Back in the Physics Department I asked Darcy if I might have the services of the Department secretary to type out some of my begging letters. He agreed. For the first letter I hand-wrote the draft in full:

Mr John Oliver, Managing Director,
Cadbury, Fry, Hudson Ltd. (New Zealand),

Dear Sir,

I write on behalf of the Victoria University of Wellington Antarctic Expedition, 1958–59. This Expedition will be leaving this country in early December and expects to spend the following three months working in the unexplored area of south Victoria Land, north of Taylor Valley, as described in the accompanying brochure.

We have received abundant encouragement and help from the University, and from the Ross Dependency Research Committee, but this has all been of the academic and advisory type, so that the expedition, like many scientific ventures of these years, finds itself still greatly in need of financial support.

In planning for our 12 weeks of fieldwork we find ourselves in need of the following of your products:

168 bars of Cadbury's Dairy Milk Chocolate, each 4 ounces;
12 jars of Cadbury's Drinking Chocolate, each 8.8 ounces.

If you find yourselves able to donate these items to the Expedition, or to supply them at a reduced price, we can assure you that you will be supporting a most worthwhile scientific endeavour.

If I can provide any more information about the Expedition and its proposed work, please ask us. I look forward to your response.

Yours sincerely,

Colin Bull

In reply, the kind folk at Cadbury's pointed out that they packed their four-ounce bars of Cadbury's Dairy Milk in boxes of 144 bars. Perhaps we would like to take two such boxes, one of Dairy Milk, and one of Fruit and Nut bars. Were we sure that 12 jars of Drinking Chocolate was sufficient? That was only one each week, and Mr Oliver was sure that those young students – what were their names? – Webb and Mcwhat? – would manage twice as much! Did I think we could take an intrepid photograph or two, showing somebody hanging by one hand from a rock knob on a vertical rock face, and eating a bar of chocolate held in the other hand, while smiling contentedly at the camera? We promised to oblige and were greatly encouraged.

For the second trial letter, to Mr Foot, the Managing Director of Messrs Bing Harris, the makers of Anson boots, I drafted the following, with the segments here in parentheses being written in red ink, so that it was obvious, I thought, that they were different from the part to be typed:

> Dear Mr Foot,
>
> (Same as last letter down to end of second paragraph, and then as follows:)
> 8 pairs of standard Anson boots, with Vibram soles, in the following sizes: . . .
> (Then the concluding paragraph from last letter)

And that's exactly how the secretary typed it:

> Dear Mr Foot,
>
> (Same as last letter down to end of second paragraph, and then as follows:)
> 8 pairs of standard Anson boots . . .

I took the draft and the typed letter to Darcy and asked if we could find another secretary. Darcy explained that the lady was Dutch, was a very recent immigrant and had had a rough time during the war. I took many of the rest of the letters home for Gillian to type and managed the rest of them myself. The secretary in Dick's department, Dorothy Freed, was very helpful with Dick's part of our chores – but we really expected that. Her father was Gerald Doorly, who had been second officer on HMS *Morning*, one of the relief ships on Scott's *Discovery* expedition, and the author of one of the greatest books from that period, *The Voyages of the 'Morning'*. Another of Doorly's books, his autobiography, *In the Wake*, is dedicated to Dorothy and her sister.

Nearly all our 'soliciting' letters generated very generous responses. Twenty-four or more companies gave us contributions that I considered were worth a name on a map. In the end the New Zealand Geographic Board didn't approve the names we put on 30-odd peaks so we had to clear our collective conscience by naming one handsome peak 'Sponsors' Peak'.

No one in New Zealand made the kind of beef pemmican that we had eaten, and usually enjoyed, in Spitsbergen and Greenland, but a kind friend at Cadbury's offered to try making some if I could produce the recipe. I think he tried but in the end we were supplied with 'meat-bars' made from mutton, nicely spiced and perhaps even tastier than pemmican. We were given dozens of pairs of woollen socks by some kind soul at Wellington Woollen Manufacturing; soft, warm and incredibly hardwearing. More than 40 years later I gave my last remaining pair, very well worn, but with no holes and fairly recently washed, to the Antarctic Museum in Christchurch. What an odd way to become famous!

Somebody gave us nearly all the string vests we needed, but we had to buy two more. I'd worn British Army versions of them in Greenland for two years (not completely without washing, but nearly so). There they had come in two sizes, 'bra length' and 'evening dress length' and seemed to be made from softened barbed wire. These New Zealand ones were approximately the right length and were much softer. I divided the dozen vests among the four of us.

Dick Barwick and Dorothy Freed typed letters galore and he also visited many commercial people in Wellington. One of the most enjoyable of these visits was to Roy Parsons, probably Wellington's most discriminating bookshop owner. Roy had heard about the expedition and phoned to say that he had a swag of publishers' proofs, sent to Roy pre-publishing for early orderings. Would we like some? We jumped at the chance, and one Friday evening Dick, Barrie and Peter went down (I was attending a faculty meeting) and spent happy hours selecting from the shelves in Roy's back rooms. They came away with a barrow-load of books, nearly all of them new books, and nearly all non-fiction. Many of them were without covers, some without page numbers, or otherwise deficient – but all readable. Dick promised Roy that we would all write reviews of the ones we read. One of the books, I remember, was John Kenneth Galbraith's *The Affluent Society*, recently published in the USA. I looked forward to reading it, but there wasn't time to do that now. Eventually we made some rules for the books. We would divide the books among the food chests. No one was to open a food chest merely to get the books. No one must discuss a book (except to say, 'Don't bother to read this') until all had had a chance to read it. This rule was often broken when one had to explain why one was laughing.

On another day Dick visited a little electronics firm, Collier and Beale, who had just started producing small ship-to-shore radios, modified from taxi radios, which looked as though they might be very valuable to us in the field. We borrowed two and promised to report on their use when we returned.

By now the Spring Term, August to November, was well under way. My teaching responsibilities that session were a course in geophysics to a small class of final-year undergraduates and a couple of graduate students, part of the introductory physics course to a large class of medical, veterinary and dental students, and also the supervision of their laboratory work. I liked the lecturing very much but was much less keen on looking after the laboratory classes, because many of the embryonic medical people were strangely incompetent with simple bits of equipment. It worried me to think that perhaps one day I would be operated on by a surgeon to whom I had given a grade of C, or lower, because he or she couldn't wire up a Wheatstone Bridge.

Bob Clark had taken academic leave that Spring Term to go up to White Island, in the Bay of Plenty, eastern North Island, to conduct some studies on the island's volcanism. He had been good enough to ask me to be his deputy on the Ross Dependency Research Committee, so I was able to attend a couple of meetings and to give some account of the progress we were making with our preparations. Dick and I also visited the offices of the Antarctic Division of DSIR, the people who did all the administrative, planning and financial work for the fast-growing New Zealand Antarctic effort. Mr Geoffrey Markham, the Superintendent, was very helpful and assured us that there would be space for us at Scott Base in the days before and after our fieldwork, but warned us that we would have to do our share of the chores while we were there. He hadn't managed to make any definite arrangements for us to fly by helicopter from Scott Base to our field area: we would have to talk with VX-6 Squadron when we reached there, but they did know that we wanted to go and had the RDRC's approval. He still had no definite dates for our leaving New Zealand, but it looked as though it would be around 25 November, a few days before the end of the term. We assured him that we'd be ready.

In the early days of November I went along to Darcy's office to tell him that we were nearly ready with the expedition plans, to say that my classes were going well and to give him the drafts of the examination papers I had proposed for my two lecture classes. In those days all examinations had to be approved by the Department, though I could never understand why. 'Oh, and by the way, it looks as though we shall be able to fly to McMurdo Sound, but the plane will probably be flying out about 25th November, and that's a couple of days before the end of term. I suppose that's alright.' Darcy's reply amazed me: 'No, Colin! I can't let you go then! If I let you go early all the rest (of the faculty) will want to get away early.'

I wasn't sure I could trust myself with a response but after taking several deep breaths I said, 'Darcy, that's unfair and it's rubbish. I am proposing to do scientific work through the long vacation, mainly at my own expense, while all the rest of you will spend the time gardening, camping, and fishing. I will have given my exams, marked them, and had my marks "authenticated" all by the previous weekend. I have no departmental duties at all during that last week of term and I haven't been invited to the University Convocation (the event that marked the official end of the University year, when degree certificates were presented to the graduates) in December. Do you mind if I take the matter to the Vice-Chancellor?' Darcy backtracked and said he would think about it overnight.

I didn't have a very good night, but the following morning Darcy acknowledged that he'd made a mistake. I could go early. We shook hands and remained friends. I went to see Dr Williams anyway, but my message was now quite different. Dick had no problem with leaving in time for that plane, while Peter and Barrie could leave immediately after taking their exams, a week or more before Dick and me.

Fig. 9. Colin (right) loading stores onto DSIR truck from the Easterfield Building, Victoria University, to accompany Peter and Barrie on their flight to McMurdo.

Our final weeks were hectic. We boxed up the loot we had already acquired, so that Barrie and Peter could take it with them. Their flight from Christchurch to McMurdo was on 15th November. Dick still had to find a little rubber boat for his sampling work on the ice-free ponds and lakes. I had to make sure that all was going well with the construction, in the Physics Department workshop, of the Stephenson screen for housing the meteorological instruments. It looked fine, except that they had put the louvered sides in upside down.

I went over to the Meteorological Office on Salamanca Road to collect the charts for the met instruments I had already borrowed, and which we proposed to put in the Stephenson screen. We were going to make a simple meteorological station at our main base, which we had decided should be close to the big lake. Richie Simmers, the Director, suggested we take a couple of spare thermometers, 'just in case'.

What had we forgotten? Oh yes! The aerial photographs! Geoffrey Markham at the Antarctic Division offices had promised to find us a bunch of Trimetrogon photos of the unnamed valley, taken a few weeks before by VX-6. They should be very valuable to Dick and me, as we decided where to put our survey stations. The photos were waiting for us and we were told that there were some maps in the parcel as well. There was a second parcel to be taken for Larry Harrington's party. Would I take them down to Christchurch? Larry, a geologist with the New Zealand Geological Survey, was leading an exceedingly well-equipped group of government geologists working along the coast of south Victoria Land. Someone rumoured to us that they all had been issued with red silk pyjamas. I've no idea whether that was true but rather soon they became known to us as 'the pyjama gang'.

My students had taken their exams; I marked them and took them down to Darcy. He asked someone, probably George Peddie, the associate professor, to check my marking standards – another of the rules at the time that didn't make sense.

I checked Gillian's ticket to Melbourne, where she was to spend the summer with Ann, an old friend, confirmed that Bobby and Elsie Munro, our landlords and surrogate parents, would look after her and Nicky and take them to the airport in early January, and I was ready to go.

CHAPTER 4

Go. No, stop! No, go!
Scott Base

Well, half of us, Peter and Barrie, were already in the Antarctic and, Dick and I hoped, were looking after our interests and not eating all our food. After long farewells on 24th November Gillian drove me and a load of boxes and assorted rubbish down to the ferry terminal in Wellington, to catch the night ferry to Lyttelton, the port of Christchurch. Elsie Munro looked after Nicky, now a chunky, placid four-month-old. As usual I tied the back doors of our shaky van closed with a piece of rope, for they had a propensity to fly open on the most trivial excuse. Dick was waiting for me and in due time we, and our baggage, boarded the *Maori*, the new 'Inter-island Steamer Express', about which songwriter Barry Humphries made so much fun. Our cabin was down in the bowels of the ship (we were paying our own expenses) a long way from the bathroom, and there wasn't room for the intended third passenger. He never turned up, anyway, which was just as well!

At 9.40 p.m. we went along to the dining room, only to be turned away because they stopped serving at 9.45 p.m. We wondered if this was a harbinger of the months ahead but didn't argue. Back in the cabin we ate a packet of dried apple – a bit heavy on the sulphur dioxide preservative, I thought. Dick climbed into his bunk and soon cried out a complaint about the string singlet: 'They don't protect you when you drop hot ash on your chest!' I suggested that he not smoke in bed and continued to look through the bundle of maps and photographs from Mr Markham.

Most of the maps were enlargements of US Air Force Aeronautical Charts, made when very little of the land, apart from the coast, had been seen, so they wouldn't be much use. One set of maps, however, was much more recent and showed the places in south Victoria Land where the Americans needed ground control points in order to make proper maps from the aerial photographs. In my diary I noted 'two of these ground control points are in the mountains north and south of Wright Valley'. This was the first time I had written the name I had proposed (only to our quartet so far) for our target unnamed valley.

Charles Wright was the young Canadian physicist who joined the scientific staff of Scott's Last Expedition as the glaciologist. He was one of the Western Party who explored Taylor Valley – named for Griffith Taylor, leader of that party. During the expedition, the piedmont glacier blocking access inland from McMurdo Sound, just north of the mouth of Taylor Valley, had been named 'Wilson Piedmont Glacier', for Edward Wilson, Scott's second-in-command and chief scientist, and the part of the piedmont that seemed to be flowing inland was called 'Wright Glacier'. However, no one had set foot on Wright Glacier and no one realized that the glacier only extended westwards for a mile or two, before ending in our ice-free valley. Charles Wright, nicknamed Silas, kept a diary during his two years in the Antarctic and nearly 40 years later I converted the diary into a book, duly entitled *Silas*.

It really was very exciting. Here we were, bound for the Antarctic, and intending to follow on the work of those men, who, just over 40 years earlier, had become the heroes for every British and British Commonwealth lad. I recognized that I was luckier than most; when I returned to Cambridge University from the British North Greenland Expedition I resumed my position as a post-doc student at Gonville and Caius College, the same College where Edward Wilson and, later, Charles Wright had been students. The room in the Department of Geodesy and Geophysics to which Stan Paterson (the surveyor on the crossing party) and I were assigned had previously been occupied by Frank Debenham, whom we met quite often when we walked round to the Scott Polar Research Institute, where he had been the first Director, and still continued as an emeritus staff member and friend to all. Wright and Debenham had been members of Griff Taylor's Western Party, who had worked in Taylor Valley, but Taylor's map of his journeys showed a complete blank inland of the Wilson Piedmont Glacier in the areas of Wright and Victoria Valleys, where we were hoping to go.

When he visited Victoria Valley the year before Peter had drawn a rough map of the area, a copy of which he subsequently sent to Griffith Taylor. Taylor's acknowledgment reads, in part:

> I am greatly pleased to have an advance copy of the N.Z. Antarctic Expedition's map of Victoria Land. It is amazing that the hinterland of Wright Valley should be a series of low, dry valleys. I should think something like Taylor Dry Valley but on a larger scale.

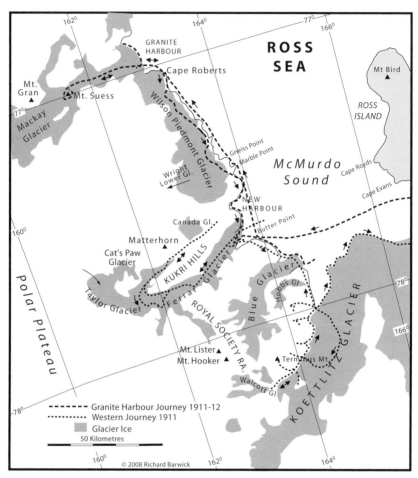

Map 3. Copy of Griffith Taylor's 1916 map of the Dry Valleys, showing how little was known of the area until 1957.

I woke at 4.30 a.m. with sun shining through the porthole. I decided to shave – the last time for three months, perhaps – and then went on deck to watch our very impressive entry into Lyttelton Heads. We passed a couple of tankers and made our way into the crowded but peaceful inner harbour, with a scatter of neat, clean houses up the sides of the Port Hills, making it all very beautiful. As we were rushing to get all our boxes and bags on the seven a.m. train for the 20-kilometre trip through the tunnels to Christchurch I remembered that I had left my exposure meter on the cupboard in the living room. Dick had one. We'd get by!

At the railway station in Christchurch I found that an ice axe and a vital kitbag had been left behind in Lyttelton. Back there to retrieve them.

Back to Christchurch and a miserably hectic day, overdressed (those string singlets!) and stewing under a sun blazing from an azure sky flecked with cirrus clouds. Hire a van to take the luggage to Harewood Airport. Fail to find anyone who knows anything about where to stow it. We made a pile of the luggage under the wing of a Super Constellation C-121 named *Pegasus*, one of four unattended aeroplanes with American markings, covered the pile with a tarpaulin and hoped it would be safe. Then back into town to the US Deep Freeze Headquarters, where we learned that our plane was due to depart at eight p.m. and we should be at the airport at seven p.m.

At the New Zealand Geological Survey office we met Bernie Gunn and Guyon Warren, the two people, completely different from each other in character, who were working up the survey data collected by the NZ IGY and TAE parties during the previous two years. Guyon drew for us a little 'geographic map' of the area in which we hoped to be working, and as I write this, in January 2008, I'm delighted to report that Barrie still has it, although somewhat aged and stained – the map, that is, not Barrie. Several members of Larry Harrington's Geological Survey party were there; all dressed identically, very expensively and very spiffily in their field jackets and tailored ski pants. Dick and I looked out of place with our surplus army trousers, bought second-hand from the Army and Navy Stores.

As I knew already, my Greenland friend Dickie Brooke had established a survey station on Mount Newall, just inland from the Wilson Piedmont Glacier, on the south side of Wright Valley. From there he had a good view of the eastern half of Wright Valley itself. We spent several hours with Guyon trying to decide where we should make our survey stations, to be of maximum use to both the US and the NZ mapmakers. We came away with lots of ideas, copies of the photographs from Dickie's survey station and some disdain (or perhaps it was just envy) for Harrington's party. Tailored ski pants indeed! And I'd paid for them with my income tax!

We thumbed a lift back to the airport, had a whitebait fritter dinner, unearthed our baggage, and made sure it was all going to be loaded on the same four-engined Super Constellation C-121 aircraft in which we had been assigned seats. Just after seven p.m. I climbed aboard, found my very uncomfortable canvas seat, facing backwards, and went to sleep. An hour later the flight commander, a certified stand-up comedian, came back to shout to us all the safety instructions. 'The exposure suits,' he said, holding up an example, in fetching pink, 'are behind the seats. They aren't much good, and it'll take you ten minutes to get into them. But they're all we've got, and if you can get in them quickly enough, if we have to ditch, put 'em on and you might last five minutes longer.' He explained that there were two US Navy air-sea rescue vessels in the ocean below, one of them a third of the way from New Zealand to McMurdo Sound, the other two thirds of the distance. Their real function was to report the weather. The flight from Christchurch took ten hours and there was a 'point of no return' because the plane couldn't carry enough fuel to allow a return trip to Christchurch from positions south of that. Then, after the commander had told us where the escape hatches and the life rafts were, he found a rubber mattress and went to sleep on the floor by the coffee pot.

The engines were particularly thunderous, but I didn't notice them until I woke up again at 2.45 a.m. My left leg was dead, my right one was dying and I wished I were elsewhere. There were 60 seats, all filled and all uncomfortable. Apart from Dick I knew only two passengers, a physics department lecturer from the University of Canterbury, Christchurch, named John Gregory and his student assistant Mike Randall. Both of them were bound for Scott Base, but they were the only Kiwis on board except us. The back half of the plane was completely filled with kitbags and boxes, variously labeled 'South Pole', 'Wilkes Station', 'Crary's Traverse' and here and there one labeled 'V.U.W. Ant. Exp.'.

There was no point in looking through the window. We could see only one engine, and that continually emitted flames from the exhaust, which was disconcerting to me, although no one else seemed the least bit concerned. Beyond the wing was a continuous sheet of cloud.

An hour later it was quite light. They switched the lights on in the cabin and treated us all to a quite incomprehensible event.

Here we were, enjoying a free flight, which must have cost the US taxpayers some thousands of dollars for each of us, and then they charged us five shillings each for a box breakfast. Good value, though: four ham sandwiches, a hard-boiled egg, a banana, chocolate bar, a lemon-cheese tart and endless coffee. The cloud cover continued so we saw only an occasional peak down the length of Victoria Land, and one or two glimpses of the sea ice below. This was all very disappointing for we were flying along some of the most spectacular scenery on the continent, the northern section of the Transantarctic Mountains, which extend from Cape Adare at about 70°S to the Rawson Mountains, near 87°S – a span of more than 2000 kilometres.

Eventually the plane descended below the clouds and, bang on six a.m. as promised, we landed on the runway cut on the fixed sea ice attached to the McMurdo Ice Shelf. A bearded local came aboard and said, 'Welcome to McMurdo. The temperature is +17°F and there's no wind!' Stiffly we emerged, and took a breath of the frigid air. Dick said he could hear his

Fig. 10. Super Constellation *Pegasus* at Christchurch Airport, with our baggage dumped under the wing. Lockhead Globemaster (C–124) at right.

Fig. 11. And Super Constellation *Pegasus* on sea-ice runway at McMurdo, Antarctica.

lungs give a quiet scream. Then we put on our sun-specs and gloried in the sights of Mounts Erebus, Terror, Discovery and all the places I had read about for nearly 20 years. Peter Webb was there to meet us with a Ferguson tractor and a big sled.

Peter explained that all the decorated American vehicles around about were not to welcome us but were part of the farewell ceremony for Admiral Dufek, the Commander of Deep Freeze, who at ten a.m. would be leaving his command by helicopter for the flagship, USS *Glacier*, at the fast ice edge, 20 kilometres away. We decided not to wait. It was cold, even in our army windproof pants and anoraks.

We collected our luggage. The ominous trickle from one of the boxes turned out to be the 'medicinal' brandy. Dick said he was going to cry. Our trip back to Scott Base was very, very cold, sitting on the loaded sledge, though it was only a few kilometres. Scott Base in those days was a compact group of yellow-painted flat-roofed buildings, some of them modified from 'reefers' of a meat-packing plant, spread out on the scree slope below a low hill, and facing south. Sometimes the place was known locally as the Banana Belt, although that term was usually reserved for Cape Hallett, the joint New Zealand-United States station 800 kilometres to the north. The views all around (except due north) were quite superb: the volcanic mountains Erebus and Terror (named after Ross's two ships in 1841, and known to us usually as Error and Terebus) to the northeast, and the gorgeous white peaks of the Royal Society Range over to the west, across McMurdo Sound.

Everyone from Scott Base was at the farewell for Dufek, except Grahame, the seismic station technician, who was the watchman, and charged with visiting every hut every half hour, in case of fire. In the communal bathroom he had just put up the sophomoric placard 'Please do not throw cigarette butts in the urinal. It makes them soggy and difficult to light'. That was the first time I had seen the slogan, and I laughed loudly.

Breakfast was bacon, beans and pineapple and then I sat in the only armchair, playing with the kitten, named Tucker (Grahame explained that the kitten was not a cat, 'S'no-cat', and all the local Sno-Cats were made by Tucker), while Peter and Barrie brought us up-to-date on their activities. Their most significant events had been meetings with Phil Smith, the head US official at McMurdo (who had been so helpful to them the previous year), his new assistant Ken Moulton, and the two US Geological Survey geologists, the small, inconsiderate and quite experienced Warren Hamilton and his young assistant Phil Hayes. Peter had flown with Hayes and Hamilton on a recce flight by Otter aeroplane around the Taylor and Wright Valleys.

Somehow in subsequent conversations he and Barrie had managed to persuade the Americans out of their idea of working in the Wright Valley and to confine their geological efforts to the south side of the Taylor Glacier.

Nearly all the people at Scott Base were filled with derision to learn of their subsequent minor disasters. Despite Warren's experience they were novices in the field and had taken kerosene for their white gas (unleaded petroleum) stoves. Consequently they nearly killed themselves from malnutrition ('The poor buggers ate cold food the whole time') as well as from carbon monoxide poisoning. Apparently they didn't know about the standard 'sand desert cooker' used by all the troops, including Americans, in North Africa, but still they did invent a brand-new cooking device – flaming kerosene-soaked socks – and Warren distinguished himself by recognizing that the pink granite on the south side of Taylor Glacier (and also in the Wright and Victoria Valleys) was analogous to rocks found near Adelaide in South Australia. This eventually led him to conclude that Australia and East Antarctica had once been joined – another early example from Antarctica of the break-up of the super-continent Gondwana.

An even more nagging worry came from Larry Harrington and his quite large party from the New Zealand Geological Survey. They were all nice chaps but their presence did concern us just a bit. Their main purpose in life was to 'do the geology' and the surveying ground control of the coastal part of Victoria Land, north of the area already studied by the 'northern party' of the New Zealand Trans-Antarctic Expedition, and especially around Wood Bay, 74°S, a safe distance away from us. So far the party had not had much luck with their intended landings. We felt sorry for them about that but our main concern was that they might decide to invade the Wright-Victoria Valley area – and overwhelm us, with disastrous effects on the MSc theses of Peter and Barrie. This worry continued throughout our time in the field, so that we were always pleased when we heard that Larry's party had visited some other site. In the end Larry's surveyors came into Wright Valley and surveyed from one peak only. Because our survey work was entirely a 'service' activity, solely for the sake of the NZ and US mapmakers, we didn't mind at all! Well, not much!

There were big delays because one of the two helicopters was awaiting parts from Honolulu. VX-6 wouldn't fly without a rescue helicopter available, but they were keen to help and had flown Peter for two hours in the single-engine Otter looking for possible landing places. They'd found two, one on the Wilson Piedmont Glacier and the other high on the shoulder of the north wall of the valley, at its inland end – although, from the sober depths of the Scott Base armchair, that sounded horribly hair-raising. Even without the helicopter we should manage to reach our valley and, we all hoped, do something useful.

Then Barrie showed us around the base. All of the 'living huts', the three sleeping huts, the ablution and scientific laboratory huts, and the generator room were connected by a covered way, perhaps 40 metres long. Only the garage and the aircraft hangar were separate. There was a double door from the covered way for each hut, each being a small metal door set in a larger door. Each sleeping hut had eight bunks in single cabins; about two and a half metres by two, and very cleverly designed so that the bunks took up minimal room. All were heated by hot-air ducts and were at shirtsleeve temperature. The living/dining room had a diesel fuel drip stove, a piano, a good record player and a fairly good library. Leading off the main room were the well-equipped kitchen, the station leader's room and the radio room.

It all looked greatly superior to our Greenland main base, and designed to last for 50 years, or more. And then there was the kitten, obviously in charge of everything. An American had smuggled it into the US base, but had not been allowed to keep it. So it was put on the Scott Base pay roll, and obviously earned its keep in entertainment value. It was also useful in helping each successive 'house mouse' (as they called the duty cleaners) to sweep the linoleum-covered floor.

The summer crew at Scott Base numbered twelve, all 'nice chaps, selected for their equanimity as well as their competence', as it said in the newspaper article pinned on the notice board. We soon met nearly all of them as they returned from the Dufek farewell party at McMurdo, the US base. Dick and I showed the new aerial photographs we had brought down to Barrie, Peter and a few others and then I went to bed and soundly to sleep till suppertime: bangers (sausages) and diced potatoes, followed by tinned fruit salad. Maurice Speary was a pretty good cook.

After supper Dick and I walked over to McMurdo, a two-kilometre walk on hard snow, with a flag every few metres, through 'The Gap' between Observation Hill and the unnamed hill to the east. Compared with the pristine cleanliness of Scott Base, McMurdo was a shambles. At the edge of the sea ice two Dakotas (DC-3 aeroplanes) and three Otters, including Bunny Fuchs's one, which had recently flown across the continent, were parked, all facing in different directions. On land at the shoreline was the rubbish dump, huge and full of good stuff: timber, slightly damaged chairs, as well as vehicle engines and the like. A mass of Quonset and Jamesway huts, big and small, and interspersed with ablution and bucket toilet buildings (serviced by a quaint little cut-down Weasel, with the front and rear floatation tanks removed), were spread over a kilometre square, and housed about 400 people, including about 12 scientists, at that moment. Only the chapel, a Quonset hut with a wooden steeple built on one end, and surrounded by a neat little white picket fence, looked the least bit interesting as a building. I thought it all looked rather grotty, but when I said that to Barrie he pointed out that the Americans, with the airfield, 'Willy Field', and the maritime freight facility, were stretched beyond their limit in coping with all the demands of the IGY and related programmes, spread across much of the continent. There simply was no time for cleanliness and town planning.

Dick had wanted to go over there to talk with the four biologists who had been hurriedly added to the research program when it was discovered that the Soviets had a big biology effort at their main base. When the American biologists arrived in McMurdo there was no accommodation for them so they spent their first two weeks sleeping in the chapel. They hadn't been able to find a proper table to work on and eventually they built their own, with salvaged timber from the rubbish dump. One of the four was a 'lichens and moss' man, very interesting and keen to come over to visit us in Wright Valley, if we ever got there. Another two were 'seal' men, who were somewhat despondent. They had just asked for volunteers to help catch seals for tagging, and one man only, out of 400, had volunteered. (The 'moss' man complained that he was having no luck at all finding moss but shortly after escaping from their overheated hut Dick spotted some mosses in a frost-heaved crevice in the local rocks. Nothing would avail but collecting a sample, which he took back to the poor chap!)

As background to our chat we listened to the radio operator of Dufek's ice-breaker, trying to make contact with the driver of one of the Weasels, the small tracked vehicles used for running around the place and for light towing jobs. For half an hour the operator kept repeating 'Glacier to Weasel 35', 'Glacier to Weasel 35', 'Glacier to Weasel 35'. Eventually the McMurdo radio operator came on and said 'For Pete's sake! There is no radio in Weasel 35!'

Phil Smith, the head US IGY man, and the chap through whom we would have to work with the helicopter people, was very cooperative and an easy man to work with, as Peter had told us earlier. He had suggested to Peter and Barrie that he'd like to try parachuting our food supplies and kerosene to us, but Barrie pointed out that we didn't have any spare food with which to make such experiments. Anyway, Phil was at Little America for a few days, so that all we could do was to busy ourselves acclimatizing.

Fig. 12. Main Street, McMurdo, December 1958.

Fig. 13. First Street, McMurdo. 'Our Lady of the Snows', with Observation Hill in the background.

We stayed much too late and it was two a.m. before we started back to Scott Base. The sun was shining brightly.

The station leader, Lynden (Lyn) Martin, was the watchman when we reached the mess hall. He made us a cup of cocoa and we stopped and talked for another hour. Chiefly, he urged us to be patient with US logistics. They meant well, he said, but hadn't really got themselves properly organized yet.

We thought of Lyn's advice many times in the following days for there were so many changes in the plans that I began to despair. We tried hard to fill our days with useful occupations. One day Barrie and I spent the morning checking out the tents that we were borrowing from Scott Base. The two big pyramid tents, 'Scott tents', had belonged to the New Zealand part of the TAE. They had inner walls and were in excellent condition. They would be our Main Base, somewhere near the lake. The two small tents, one green and one yellow, our travelling tents, were in a fairly good state but had a few holes, which we mended. I commented that the tents were going to be a bit cold at the beginning of our stay in the ice-free area.

Then I spent a few hours showing the other three how to take 'star' shots with a theodolite to determine position. The only visible star was the sun but, knowing where we were I 'worked backwards' and set the theodolite to where a star should be. It was! I made them all look through the theodolite and see the star in broad daylight. They were very impressed, so I didn't tell them how much luck there had been in the operation.

And then we all spent time weighing out rations and making up boxes, actually tea chests, for the three depots we had decided on. As usual it proved impossible not to read the slogans and instructions on each food container, generally out loud. Dick liked, best of all, the Cadbury's slogan 'It's good and its good to eat often!' and he could be heard repeating this for several hours afterwards, in fact throughout the expedition, varying the cadence and intonation from time to time. I could understand that slogan. The one that bothered me – and still does – was the packet of dates, special for Christmas, that proclaimed itself 'Loose packed for thrift!' And Barrie, after reading that another Christmas delicacy was 'The finest product of sun and air', wondered why it was so heavy.

To the Main Base, most of the material would go: 240 kilograms of food, 45 kilograms of kerosene, the Scott tents (73 kilograms), radios (45 kilograms), one two-metre fibreglass sledge for working on the lake ice (15 kilograms), survey and scientific gear (90 kilograms) – total 500 kilograms.

One fibreglass sledge for use on the Wilson Piedmont Glacier, along with three weeks of food (130 kilograms), and a jerry can of kerosene would be depoted at the east end of the valley, as close to the Lower Wright Glacier as we could manage.

We had lots of fun in this collecting, scavenging and packing work, occasionally joined by proper Scott Base inhabitants. We had an addict in our foursome, although we didn't know it at the time – Barrie was addicted to mushroom soup, and during our packing lots of containers of other kinds of soup (ham and pea soup, vegetable soup, chicken noodle soup) would disappear, to be replaced by mushroom soup. Fifty years later Barrie confessed that one of his proudest moments was when he realized that 71% of our total soup supply was mushroom soup.

Another three weeks' supply of food, or perhaps just a bit more (Barrie and Peter would be depending on this depot more than the others), were to be placed high on the north shoulder of the valley, close to the inland ice. With all the food boxes, but especially those in the two smaller food depots, we put a few of Roy Parsons's books. Into the little depots we added a spare pair of socks, and we placed, close at hand, but not too close, a can of kerosene. Dick, who had been sorting out his biology gear, wandered over, looked at the piles of food, sucked on his pipe and said, to no one in particular, 'Far too much'. Barrie disagreed, vehemently!

A steady stream of visitors entertained us at Scott Base, especially people who had wintered over at Pole and Byrd Stations. Most of the scientists were very well versed in their subjects but a few of them were very young and did not seem to have much of a background. A few years later I spent much time analyzing their glaciology reports and these initial feelings were all too often confirmed. The work lacked depth and sophistication – but then, there were no university courses in glaciology in the USA.

One of the men who had wintered at the South Pole told us of his problem there. He was ill; they thought he had appendicitis. One of the technicians offered to carry out an appendectomy, but they decided against it, and stuffed the patient with Aureomycin instead. He said he was fine now but attributed this to his being scared stiff of the technician, rather than to the antibiotic. Another fellow, an Italian naval officer named Franco, quite openly said that he had not enjoyed his winter at Scott Base because he found he was expected to do a share of the menial chores.

Several times in the next week I walked, or begged a lift over to McMudhole, as the locals called it. Phil Smith was still at Little America and his assistant, Ken Moulton, was very new in the job and knew rather little.

Fig. 14. Moving stores at Scott Base on a banana-boat sledge, Dick pulling and Peter pushing.

Fig. 15. Quartet at Scott Base, sorting rations. (Peter entitled this 'Contemplating future feasts'. Barrie's preferred caption was 'Sorting stores, at Scott Base. "Just where the hell do you find the marked prices on these darned packages?"')

Over two metres tall, taciturn and cautious, Ken was completely different from his assistant, Bill Smith – short, a psychiatrist by training, and an enthusiastic but not very realistic chap. Over the following 20 years I grew to know and like Ken very much, but at the first meetings he made me cross. 'Tomorrow,' he said at our first meeting, 'we are going to talk to the parachute guys. The following day we are going to land you by Otter at the head of the Taylor Glacier, and parachute 30 days of food onto the ice on the lake.'

Well, that might be better than nothing, but certainly wasn't at all suitable. It would take us most of the season to carry ourselves and all the fragile equipment – the met and survey equipment, the radios and so on – from any possible landing place, across the glacier, up the side of the steep mountain range (later called Asgard Range), across the unknown top and down into Wright Valley.

I think Ken, and his assistant Smith the psychiatrist, felt they had satisfied our needs but as our conversation ended who should walk in but Palle Mogensen, summer chief at Pole Station, and at that moment in charge of the big convoy of tractors and sledges making its way up to Byrd Station. I'd last seen him at Sierra Camp on the Greenland Ice Sheet in 1954. We compared ice sheets for a while and we told him our current tale of woe. What he said to Ken I don't know, but Ken then told us that he might be able to do something better for us.

The next time we went over to the US station Peter had 'house-mouse' duties. It was windy so the other three of us were happy for a lift in a Weasel with Peter Yeates, the Scott Base radio operator. Ken told us that Phil Smith would be staying at Little America and that Ken would be in charge of us. We groaned, but silently, and followed Ken and Bill to the headquarters office of VX-6 Squadron.

The Squadron Commanding Officer was away so we talked to the Executive Officer, a Commander Barlow, to the Otter pilot who had flown Peter round last week, Lieutenant Commander Ellison, and to the helicopter pilot. They were all friendly people, but then the bomb dropped. They had never received any authorization to help us, and without that authorization they couldn't do a thing! I, for one, didn't understand. What were those plans, last time, for the Otter landing on Taylor Glacier? 'Not to worry,' said Barlow. 'We'll work it out! Assume we've got authorization. What comes next?'

The airmen had trouble with our next remarks. We said that once they had dropped our depots and us in the valley, we didn't need to see them for eight weeks or more. They seemed to think that once they had undertaken the job of landing us somewhere, we were completely their responsibility, with scheduled daily radio contacts and so on. Furthermore, they wouldn't land us anywhere unless they could with certainty extract us again from there. In other words they couldn't land us anywhere in the Otter unless the big helicopter was functioning. If that were the case, we pointed out, we didn't need to land in the Otter.

The vital part for the helicopter was said to be coming on the Constellation tomorrow, Sunday, 30th November, and we should be ready to fly in either the Otter or the big helicopter about three days later, say 3rd December. Tomorrow, we were told, Peter and I would fly in the Otter for a reconnaissance up the valley and we would also try to see if we could land the Otter on the lake ice. Bill Smith took us back to Scott Base, because he wanted to talk to Lyn Martin, and on his radio we heard that the next Connie (Constellation) flight was now scheduled for 2nd December. This was the slowest moving, fastest changing environment I'd ever lived in.

From that point my world went mad for a few hours. For the first time I learned, from Lyn, that an official request for full support had been sent by NZ IGY to Admiral Dufek's office back in October and had been refused. Yet I'd been told in Wellington that the helicopter trips and the depot laying had been promised. 'No,' said Lyn. 'All they promised was to take you to Marble Point airstrip.' It was all very confusing. I'd never heard that! Well, we had left Ken writing a cable to Commander Naval Support Force, asking for full support for us, and Lyn was worried that this might appear to come from the New Zealanders. I really didn't understand what was wrong with that, but Lyn seemed concerned.

So Bill and I dashed back to the McMurdo radio room and grabbed the cable before it was sent. It looked fine to me. It was obviously a request from the US IGY, emphasizing that our geology programme would supplement the studies being made in Taylor Valley by the two US geologists, Hayes and Hamilton. I'm amused to note that in my diary I wrote, 'They are somewhat old (probably about 40) and are obviously not interested in walking very far from the spot where they were landed.'

All appearing to be well, Bill took me to eat in the communal mess hall. The place held about 90 people and was grossly overheated, as was every other building that we went in, except the biologists' room, where they had eventually decided to close most of the hot-air ducts. The food was plentiful indeed but, apart from the peach ice cream, not as good as the fare at Scott Base. Perhaps that was due to the large number of mouths that they had to feed, but they could not have been kinder.

Fig. 16. The Joy of Food. Peter and Colin sorting food at Scott Base.

And, back at Scott Base I remembered the Memorandum that Eddie Robertson, Chairman of the RDRC, had given me just before we left Wellington. Copies had been sent to Martin, US IGY and to Admiral Dufek. It read, in part, 'Discussions have been held in New Zealand and in McMurdo regarding your air support in the field. Final arrangements should be made when you arrive.'

We still had time to kill. The next Connie flight would be the last mail flight. After that, mail would go by sea to New Zealand. I wrote Christmas cards to everyone – a rather poor photograph of South Pole Station – but I might have no other chance of sending cards from the Antarctic, ever.

With our close living conditions and frustrating delays, my three companions were revealing their characters to me, as I must have done to them, too. All three were incredibly fast of thought. Peter was the most serious and perhaps quickest to analyse a situation, and come forward with the solution. Dick seldom missed an opportunity to talk, but what he said was almost always germane and interesting. In group discussions he was often the taciturn one, until there was a need for someone to summarize, and he did that. Barrie, known to the other people at Scott Base as 'Gannet McKelvey' because of his prodigious appetite, had the sharpest wit and usually could turn any situation into a witticism.

One day we were carrying an RAF airdrop canister – cylindrical, a metre and a half long, perhaps 60 centimetres in diameter, and weighing 55 kilograms – between huts. Peter, Dick and two Americans, two on either side, were carrying the heavy cylinder by straps. Blowing snow flew all round. They looked intrepid! Barrie and I were trudging in the snow behind. He giggled, wiped the blowing snow from his face and said to me 'I suppose we must be the mourners.'

None of them treated me with the respect that I might have thought I deserved as leader, although Peter, passing me a cup of tea, added 'And would Sir wish to have sugar with his beverage?' I reckoned we would all get on just fine!

The recce flight for Peter and me was postponed from Sunday to Monday, and hence I volunteered to cook dinner on Sunday, Maurice's day off. Dinner was based on braised steak, and Maurice said it was OK. High praise! The cook's other duties were to pump water from the snow melter into the 'ready use' tank, pump up diesel fuel for the various diesel heaters, clean the living room, lay the tables, usually for 12 or 14 people, and clean up afterwards. Dick, who had made lunch, helped me. Altogether it wasn't very arduous. After dinner and the chores, on an exquisite calm, sunny evening, Barrie took me down to see the seals in the contorted ice in front of Scott Base. The McMurdo Ice Shelf, only 15 metres or so thick at its forward edge, moves forward against the land of Ross Island at a rate of about 20 or 30 centimetres a day, causing fantastic waves and buckles in the ice, most of them broken but a few intact. In some of the troughs were holes cut by seals, crabeaters Barrie told me, and around the holes were a couple of dozen mother seals and their pups, three or four weeks old, and all looking very sweet and cuddly. We petted one, but with a booted foot, just in case, admiring the fascinating 'oink, oink' sounds.

I wondered if we could work out some of the elastic properties of the ice from the shape of the waves, as I had tried to do in Greenland, where the local glacier, moving forward, made waves in the lake ice during the winter. The pleasant and gentle walk back to the dining room brought us to the surprising sight of a soot-faced Dick, standing with hands on hips, and obviously pouring abuse at the diesel-fuelled cooking stove that, equally obviously, had had a blowback. The kitchen, as well as Dick, was soot covered, but, with a lot of help, the clean-up job was quickly done.

In the morning Barrie remarked 'You can rely on everything being unreliable,' and, sure enough, our recce flight was cancelled. There was a bit of low cloud but not enough, I thought, to deter one of 'the brightest and the best', as it said on the placard in the VX-6 operations room we had visited. I helped John Humphries, the ionospheric physicist, with his ionosonde apparatus for an hour or two and was impressed with him and with his laboratory, where the library and the collection of small tools was far better than we had in the Physics Department at Victoria University.

Lyn Martin came in to find volunteers to help unload eight tons of scientific gear from a sledge hauled over from McMurdo behind a D-8 tractor. It seems that a bright young glaciologist had measured the rate of movement of the ice shelf on which Little America was built (although I didn't know how!) and reckoned that it would fall into the Ross Sea before the next year was over. The station was abandoned, the good stuff being brought back by sea on the *Glacier*, and then with the tractor from the sea ice edge in McMurdo, over to Scott Base. The aurora observer tower was built almost straight away and was in operation by the following winter. Much of the other science equipment was later installed at a new sub-station at Arrival Heights. The less fragile material from Little America was being transported to McMurdo by a 'tractor train' of huge D-8 tractors and sledges. While we were at Scott Base we learned that one of the D-8s had fallen 36 metres into a crevasse, with two people in it, both of whom, luckily, had survived. It reminded us that this beautiful land was also a hideously dangerous place.

Scott Base was an interesting place, full of interesting events and interesting people. But we were rapidly becoming disenchanted with being there. We searched for diversions – so that when the four men who had spent a month on a dog-sledge trip to inspect the emperor penguin colony at Cape Crozier returned (with their dog teams) after a strenuous and absorbing time, the only people who went to help them stake out the dog teams were the members of VUWAE.

The four men from Cape Crozier, Graeme Caughley, biologist, Bob Thomson, engineer, Don Thompson, chief scientist for the summer, and Murray Robb, strong man, had travelled 300 kilometres or more to the eastern end of Ross Island, and had followed the route taken by members of Scott's Last Expedition, in 1912, 'The Worst Journey in the World'. Graeme reckoned they had counted 450 emperor penguins and 260,000 Adélie penguins – although I was somewhat doubtful about their counting methods.

Another frustrating week followed. The spare parts for the helicopter duly arrived and presumably were duly installed, but we heard no more. The weather was nice, most of the time, but our reconnaissance flight did not materialize. We walked and scrambled to the top of Observation Hill and up to Castle Rock, from both of which we had wonderful views of McMurdo Sound, the US base and, across the sound, the place where we were supposed to be, with its backdrop of the imposing peaks of the Royal Society Range. We devoted two very energetic days to clearing the metre or so of snow and the half metre of ice from the area where the aurora tower from Little America was to be erected. We worked hard but there seemed to be much horseplay, too. Maurice, the cook, on a windy day, allowed me to make big batches of Anzac biscuits, and ginger-iced Heavenly Squares, dubbed 'Angel Pavement' by Dick.

And, twice a week, we watched the movie. The least unbearable of these was called *Blood and Sand*, introduced by the projectionist, John Humphries, with 'Come along and watch 10,000 feet of excruciating nausea!' After about five minutes Murray Robb suggested re-titling it *Lust in the Dust*, and John ran the last reel backwards. Still it was free and someone had liberated a huge can of popcorn from McMurdo. And, when there was nothing else to do, Barrie kept us entertained with his 'impressions'. The two I liked best were 'a spider doing press-ups on a mirror' and 'milking a mouse'. It was obvious that Barrie had a great future and would go far. We spent a lot of time trying to decide what and where it was most likely to be.

We did try one recce flight in the single-engined Otter. The pilot's first job was to drop mail to Messrs Hayes and Hamilton, who indeed were still where they had been landed on the Taylor Glacier, but there was a small patch of cloud and the pilot wouldn't fly through it. We retreated. There was also a line of cloud over the Wilson Piedmont Glacier. So, although we could see that it was cloudless over 'our' valley, we didn't get that far. Instead, to clock up his flying hours, the pilot spent a couple of hours buzzing lots of groups of penguins and seals. If the window had been anything like clean I could have taken lots of good photographs.

Another time we watched the Otter pilot carry out a clever experiment. The challenge was to develop a method of delivering a fragile package to an isolated field party, something like a radio or a theodolite, which could not be dropped and probably couldn't easily be parachuted. Someone told us that Phil Smith devised the solution. Anyway, from the Otter, in flight, the item is lowered on the end of a light cable 30–60 metres or more in length. The Otter then flies in tight circles over the intended recipient. Obviously the greater the diameter of the circle that the pilot must fly, the longer the cable must be. Over a small group of people on the sea ice just off McMurdo, the experiment worked and the bundle, whatever it was, landed safely in the arms of one of the men on the ground.

We hated all these delays but were having a most interesting time, too. On another Saturday we walked over to McMurdo, and while the others visited Club Erebus I walked, in infuriating sloppy mukluks, to Hut Point itself, to see the hut built there in 1901 by Scott's *Discovery* expedition. The hut was in quite good condition but, annoyingly, was stuffed full with snow, so that I couldn't see any of the inside. Outside there were no souvenirs (many such souvenirs had been liberated two years before), only a homemade pair of trousers made from sailcloth and a few Spratt's biscuits, presumably dog food. I visited the two crosses on the Hut Point peninsula; George Vince's from 1901, when he slid over the cliff and drowned in the sea below, and Richard Williams's cross (for whom Willy Field was named) from early 1956, when his 35-ton D-8 tractor broke through the ice in McMurdo Sound. Vince's was a fairly simple cross with a circle around it and Williams's had a small white statue of Mary, 'Our Lady of the Snows'. Salutary! Be careful!

Then we went up Castle Rock, all four of us, a short distance along the peninsula that ends in Scott Base. It was a tiring four-hour trudge in soft snow (still in sloppy mukluks) and then, when we were half a kilometre from the quite imposing summit the clouds came down, the wind came up and five Americans suddenly appeared. As we turned to walk back down, Bill Smith pointed out, over on the ice shelf beyond Cape MacKay, Major Dawson's heavy tractor train, bringing the stuff from Little America. I'd met Dawson in Greenland, and we had got on well together at their Camp Sierra, but the train was still 30 kilometres away, and they were making only two or three kilometres' progress a day, so I hoped I would not be around to welcome him when he reached McMurdo. With their huge tractors and sledges they were having all sorts of problems with crevasses. Their standard procedure, on meeting one, was to blow the top open with explosives, and then fill the crevasse with snow. They had been using 450 kilograms of explosive a day, and it wasn't surprising that they travelled only a few kilometres each day.

On 8th December our immediate frustration was blown away; we had our long-delayed recce flight. Peter Yeates drove the four of us out to the airfield where the pilot of the Otter, Chic Creech by name, and his very young co-pilot were ready for us. It was windy and growing windier, so Chic urged us to hurry in case Control decided to scrub the flight. The map that he had was, apart from the coastline, a blank piece of paper. Initially he was quite suspicious of the copy of Guyon Warren's map that we gave him but after a few minutes he accepted it as being at least comparatively accurate and he became more and more interested in our venture.

Once we were settled Chic took off, and flew westwards and quite low across the sea-ice covered McMurdo Sound. We crossed the coastline of Victoria Land somewhere between Marble Point and Gneiss Point, but I didn't see any of the buildings of the little US station, called Marble Point airstrip, where the Americans were trying to build their all-weather, all-year airstrip. Neither did Dick, which was a pity, because when later we walked to Marble Point airstrip we found it to be at Gneiss Point, several kilometres away.

Our first job was to find an easy (we hoped) route off the Wilson Piedmont Glacier. We found two; one by the side of Hogback Hill, near Marble Point at the south end of the Piedmont, and the other at the north end, north of Gneiss Point. Anyway, after flying along the edge of the glacier until we were satisfied with what we had seen, we buzzed a little outhouse perched over one of the little melt streams, without realizing where it was in relation to the coast or the camp. All of us thought it funny to see a man emerge, very hurriedly, with a toilet roll in one hand and his trousers round his knees.

We crossed the stretch of moraine-covered land and climbed a bit to cross the Wilson Piedmont Glacier. There seemed to be a lot of quite rough ice around the solitary nunatak, which we later called King Pin Nunatak, where a glacier flowed down from the mountains south of the valley ahead, but we could see no large crevasses. I reckoned that Dick and I should be able to walk across to the coast safely enough. We then looked hard at the end of the Wright Glacier, to find an easy way on from the valley. There were two main roads and we felt we'd have no great difficulty.

Now flying at 2100 metres and at a gentle 120 knots we all had absolutely terrific views of Wright Valley and the mountain ranges on either side. In the wonderfully clear and pristine air you could, quite literally, see for spectacular mile after spectacular mile. It truly was one of the most magnificent panoramas I've ever had the good fortune to see and the photographs, while they save me from excessive hyperbole, don't really do justice to the remarkable scene. The only aspect of the whole flight – and the photographs too – that deceived us was that we couldn't see the sand-laden wind. Over the next two months it wasn't perpetual, but nearly so, and was certainly the bane of our lives.

Fig. 17. Mouth of Wright Valley from Theseus Ridge, showing Lower Wright Glacier, backed by and merging with the Wilson Piedmont Glacier. Beyond, across McMurdo Sound, is Ross Island with Mount Erebus (right distance) and Cape Bird (centre distance). River Onyx flows westwards from Lower Wright Glacier into Wright Valley.

One of the most intriguing sights was of a tiny river meandering along the bottom of the valley, all the way between the small lake near the Wright Glacier and the big ice-covered lake towards the western end of the valley. We couldn't see which way the river flowed, or in fact whether it was flowing at all, but surely it must flow towards the coast. Wrong again! But whichever way it flowed we could see that on both sides of the river were some large areas of alluvium, as yet untrodden, along with great piles of material at the eastern end of the valley that looked as though they might be moraines, dumped by glaciers long ago.

The valley had a distinct curve to it. At the western end it ran west-east, but halfway along it turned quite a bit, 20 degrees or more, towards the northeast. The glacier that carved the valley didn't make a very symmetrical job of it. The northern side, especially towards the west, was steeper than the south, and down the southern wall there were many small cliff-sided glaciers, none of which reached the valley floor.

Chic did a complete circle over the ice-covered lake, so that we could perhaps pick out a site for our base. The lake was several kilometres long, and one or two broad – and even from that height we could see several beaches or benches cut into the steep scree slopes on the northern side. The ice looked rather dirty from up there, but we couldn't see how smooth or otherwise it was.

Right at the western end of the valley we looked hard at the two great icefalls, separated by an impressive hill, toppling over the dolerite-capped sandstone cliffs, and at the short flat-lying glacier that formed below. It really was a most exciting view in all directions, the huge sandstone cliffs, the monstrous icefalls, everything! How can I tell you easily how excited we all were?

At this point the engine gave several perturbing coughs and the co-pilot shouted back at us, 'Fasten your seat belts'. Then we heard the pilot say, 'I don't see any possible landing spot,' which disconcerted us rather more than somewhat, until we heard the co-pilot say, 'Chic, that really scared the Kiwis!' They'd throttled the engine back a notch too far, to reduce speed, so we'd have the best possible view!

Just after we had turned at the head of the valley, Control called us back to McMurdo because the weather was deteriorating quickly. That was a real pity because we were looking forward to an equally good look at the Victoria Valley system next door. However, back to McMurdo we went, and landed into such a stiff wind that Chic couldn't turn the plane when it was on the ground. He asked us all to get out and haul on ropes attached to the tail of the aircraft, to pull the tail round so we could taxi back to the fuel dumps. Apart from the fearsome wind it was a great, brilliantly sunny day. We all pulled mightily and were having some success in dragging the plane's nose into the wind, when Chic suddenly gunned the engine, and, laughing quite uncontrollably, towed the four of us for some distance through the snow before he cut the engine. Eventually we had to be towed home ignominiously behind a Weasel. What an absolutely wonderful day!

Fig. 18. Middle part of Wright Valley, showing Lake Vanda, and eastwards to hanging glaciers. Olympus Range and Asgard Range are on the left and right respectively.

Fig. 19. Western end of Wright Valley. Dais (left foreground) separates the North and South Forks. Asgard Range is on the left, Olympus Range on the right. Upper Wright Glacier is in the middle distance.

Someone in Washington DC had invented another rule to test our ingenuity. It was ordained that the helicopters could not be flown more than 30 minutes from base. We never discovered who generated the rule, or why, but Ken Moulton solved our problem, by declaring that the base for the helicopter was Marble Point Airstrip, about 30 minutes airtime from both McMurdo and from our lake in the valley. And the second helicopter was nearly ready, so there really was a chance that our agonizing delay was over. In a very optimistic mood we endured the chilly walk back to Scott Base.

Lyn and his Otter were marooned at Byrd Station, so strong man Murray Robb was in charge. Murray was a most interesting man, an engineer with a remarkable vocabulary and knowledge of Antarctic literature. He said that his 'standard' word was 'marmalade'. If the word that you had just spoken to him was longer than 'marmalade' he would make no attempt to understand it. He was a good listener and an excellent storyteller. One story that he told with great panache concerned Ted Gawn, the radio operator at Scott Base during the previous winter. One day, after a long windy spell that had irritated everyone, Ted said, 'Let's have a "be nice to the cook" day.' So they all did, and considered it a success. Next Ted suggested that they have a 'Let's be nice to everybody day,' and they did, even to the extent of passing the salt before being asked. Then, when Murray asked 'Well, Ted, what's next?' Ted replied 'Ah, Hell! Let's have a "bugger 'em all" week.'

At dinner Murray reported on his experiments with Tucker, the kitten. Last week it had dined exclusively on tinned salmon and had gained 60 grams in weight, as measured on the post office scales. This week he had been eating only fresh meat and had gained an improbable 450 grams, and now weighed 1450 grams. Altogether Murray and Maurice were most considerate and thoughtful men and almost entirely as a result of their efforts we found that we now had 14 weeks' supply of food, ten of our own, brought from New Zealand, and four weeks from other sources, and those extra four contained some of our best delicacies: canned chicken and fruit, as well as some pemmican left over from the crossing party of the TAE.

And at long last, on 9th December, we had a phone call from VX-6 saying that, weather permitting, we would be flown, in two flights, to Wright Valley. What's more, the helicopter would come over to Scott Base to collect us, so we wouldn't have to struggle with our luggage over to the heliport in McMurdo. We closed down the last three food boxes, each containing 40 man-days of food, and tossed coins to decide who went on the first flight. Dick and Barrie would go first, make the depot at the east end of the valley and take half of the stuff for the Main Base. Peter and I would fly to the western depot and then land at the Main Base with the remainder of the supplies. That being the case I could hope to have dinner cooked for me, at least for that first meal!

I phoned Gillian in Paremata and, because 'the band was in' we had a good conversation. We tidied our rooms and collected into boxes the few things we were leaving behind. I washed a few pairs of socks and had a necessary and delicious hot bath, although that meant losing the vital insulating surface layer of oil and grime. We were ready for action.

CHAPTER 5

Landed gentry

At half past one the next afternoon, 10th December, Lieutenant Potter, the pilot, brought the helicopter, *King Pin*, to the Scott Base helicopter landing site near the edge of the sea ice. He had brought a couple of his friends and the AD2. I didn't know what those letters stood for, and still don't, but he was the man in charge of loading the helicopter. The plans had changed: the first flight would put in the high-level, western depot, but the only difference between east and west depots was the banana-boat sledge for crossing the Piedmont Glacier.

Loading was done quite quickly, although our weights had increased remarkably overnight, by the addition to our pile of supplies of such things as 72 big cans of fruit, 16 kilograms of tinned bully beef, and sundry other items, like a big jar of curry powder, and more than a dozen frozen chicken stews, wrapped very carefully in plastic bags and aluminium foil, all courtesy of Maurice, the cook. A good man!

The pilot told us that he could only fly five hours that day, which meant that only one flight into the valley could be made. After that they had to 'torque the head', whatever that means. When the first flight had taken off with Barrie and Dick, I went back up to the mess hall for a cup of tea, to scribble a report to Bob Clark, and to wash up a pile of pots and pans. Maurice, the cook, often played the part of a great stuttering bully, awfully possessive of his kitchen, but he really was a kind-hearted and highly competent cook. 'Th- th- thank you Co- Co- Colin,' he said 'Th- th- thank God we've got a Po- Po- Pom- Pommie who isn't as mu- much of a bas- bas- bastard as they usually are.' And after that I typed a long letter to Gillian on the laboratory typewriter.

On the evening radio schedule we heard of all the mishaps to the Harrington party, the 'pyjama gang' from the New Zealand Geological Survey. They hadn't been able to land on Coulman Island, hadn't been able to organize themselves into Wood Bay, and were gently suggesting (or so I thought in my possessive paranoia) that they would come over and invade 'our' territory in Wright Valley. Well, I'd welcome help with the survey work. In fact I'd happily give them all of it, but I was really concerned that their geologists would come in and spoil the proposed work of Peter and Barrie for their MSc theses, as I've said before.

The helicopter had returned to McMurdo to take on 700 kilograms of gasoline and to 'torque the head'. Murray had told us, when I asked, that by that time the helicopter would have flown about seven hours since it had been reassembled; time to tighten up all the nuts and bolts. Maurice made us all an excellent dinner, with a large pork roast, applesauce, roast potatoes, peas and corn. Very good!

Dick and Barrie had taken two radios with them: the big TAE sledge radio which, we were assured, could receive anything, everywhere, but on which one could only transmit in Morse code, and one of the little ship-to-shore radios from Collier and Beale. At eight a.m. they failed to make themselves heard. Peter, the radio man, was concerned that the radios weren't working. I thought it much more likely that they had overslept. Shortly afterwards we heard the whap, whap, whap of the helicopter rotor. Murray announced, 'Taxi here.' Peter and I said hasty goodbyes, grabbed our packs and ran down to the helicopter landing spot.

It turned out they hadn't put in the Upper Depot – just left everything at the Main Base. Peter and I piled in, along with the rest of our stuff. The pilot, accompanied by his helicopter, very laboriously took off, loaded to the maximum, only to land again ten metres away. The second time it did take off, although with difficulty, I thought, and I was having kittens until I saw the AD2 yawning. The pilot flew with the door open (they always flew with the cabin door open, 'for escape purposes'!) and as we were sitting on canvas seats our nether parts froze. We flew slowly and at only 30 metres' altitude or less across the Sound and the Piedmont Glacier and could see very little of the ground because the opened door covered the window. The AD2 had a disconcerting habit of walking across the open doorway, without holding on to anything and with only 20 centimetres of space to put his feet, to ask us questions.

'Where exactly do you want the depot?'

'North side of the valley. As close to the glacier as possible.'

The pilot landed on a flat stretch, covered with frost polygons ten metres across, a kilometre from the glacier, just west of a prominent moraine loop, and close to the edge of the ice-covered lake formed by the summer melt of the glacier. The flat stretch I thought was possibly a beach from a higher lake level, so the four of us (the pilot's friends had evaporated) carried the depot to an elevated mound of moraine. Somehow the 40 man-days of

Fig. 20. *King Pin* at Main Base about to start up. Colin, Dick and Barrie look on as the crewman at the front of the machine monitors the start-up.

Fig. 21. *King Pin* unloading at Main Base, near Lake Vanda, Wright Valley.

food had grown to 80 man-days, along with 25 litres of kerosene, the banana-boat sledge, and 24 of Maurice's last-minute tins of fruit, as well as a few of his frozen chicken stews. It looked as though there was no way we could eat our way through all that! Peter called the depot 'Ostheim', but the other three of us, linguistically challenged, just stuck with 'Lower Depot', and pretty soon, lower depot.

In very pleasant conditions, cold but windless, we spent half an hour looking round for interesting bits of rock and patches of moss or lichen. The airmen were very, very interested indeed in everything around us, as were Peter and I. When we took off the altimeter read 300 metres and we vibrated along the huge valley for 15 minutes, something between 40 to 50 kilometres, to the main camp.

Dick and Barrie had selected and marked with a ring of boulders a flat pebbly spot near the west end of the lake, a hundred metres or so from the tents, for a landing spot for us. There the conditions were quite different. It was warm (about freezing point) and quite windy, the wind blowing towards the coast from the west. The altimeter read something like 180 metres, so the river was flowing inland. Strange!

On the previous day Dick, Barrie, the pilot and the AD2 had quickly unloaded and the chopper had taken off for McMurdo, using Erebus (as soon as they had gained enough height to see it) as their aiming point, without putting in the Upper Depot, but leaving Barrie and Dick as lords of all they surveyed. In the gusty wind they raked clear two sandy spots in the eroded granite, and then pitched the two Scott tents, the first one taking over an hour to erect in the 30-knot wind. By the time Peter and I arrived both tents were quite shipshape, with their valances (skirts) weighted down with large boulders, in a partially sheltered hollow between two dykes of the swarm that ran across the valley floor. Over the eons the hard rock of the dykes had resisted wind erosion much better than the granite of their surrounds, so they formed barricades to the wind of a metre or more in height. Barrie told me that the dykes were lamprophyre dykes – and who am I to argue?

To start with Barrie and Dick couldn't find a Primus, the screws to assemble the screen for the meteorological instruments, nor the alarm clock, but when a diligent search revealed the Primus, cleverly hiding in a box marked 'Primuses', they stopped for a meal before carrying the rest of the gear from the heliport to the tent site and erecting the radio aerials and the New Zealand flag. This was all completed by 2.30 a.m. They hadn't found the alarm clock and discussed having a 'watch' system so that they would be able to meet the scheduled eight a.m. radio contact. Barrie was sure he'd wake up in time, so they abandoned the watch plan, overslept and missed the schedule, as Peter and I at Scott Base had guessed they had.

By the time Peter and I arrived at the base, called (again by Peter) 'Mittelheim', Dick and Barrie had raked the heliport again and had erected a flag with a bright Day-Glo marker. Furthermore, by extracting screws from the packing boxes they had been able to assemble the Stephenson screen, and to erect it on a fine, firm platform of granite slabs. It all looked very professional and scientific.

We reloaded into the helicopter the stuff for the Upper Depot and in very turbulent conditions Dick and Peter – one from each two-man party – the pilot, the AD2 and two US passengers clambered into the helicopter. With great difficulty they climbed spirally to 1500 metres at the head of the valley, in magnificent scenery. The door was open as usual, and Dick had steeled himself to take photographs all the way. For the depot they chose a spot on rusty golden sandstone rock, in a prominent cirque basin surrounded by great sandstone towers up to 300 metres high, on the shoulder of the north side of the valley at 1600 metres' altitude. Dick and Peter unloaded the depot, fully 80 man-days (40 Barrie-Peter-days?) of food, with unnecessary haste because the pilot and his friends spent a leisurely 25 minutes or so taking photographs and collecting rocks. Dick, remarkably (in view of his subsequent cairn-building proclivities) didn't build a cairn and just put up a vivid pink Day-Glo flag to mark the depot, 'Hocheim', no less. The scenery was absolutely magnificent. The landscapes across what we later called Dais, Labyrinth and the Wright Upper Glacier, and across Wright Valley to the castellated dolerite and sandstone peaks of the Asgard Range, were truly outstanding, and by themselves, Dick said, 'were well worth the price of admission'. However, Dick also said he felt terribly exposed to westerly winds howling from the inland ice, 600 metres higher.

The return flight to the valley floor was quite tricky, with standing waves, strong updrafts, and much buffeting. We offered the AD2, the pilot and the others cups of instant coffee and our profuse thanks for all their great help. But they refused to stay any longer, and clattered off to the coast and to Williams Air Facility (named for the unfortunate tractor driver who had drowned two years earlier) and we were left alone, in 'our' valley, at last.

And what a stupendous valley it was, and is. We should have pitched our tents looking westward up valley towards the inland ice, for the best possible view, but for some reason the two tent openings faced each other. Peter later said that Dick and I had done that so we could watch their every movement. I wasn't even there! In the immediate foreground, 20 metres away, was the meteorological screen, erected on its pile of granite slabs and now equipped with barograph, thermograph, hygrograph, a hand-held

Fig. 22. 'Found it at b— last.' Barrie at the Upper Depot, on the southern shoulder of the western end of the Olympus Range. Wright Valley Hill (later Mount Fleming) is on the left skyline.

Fig. 23. The Lake Vanda Main Base. The dark figure between the tents is Colin. The white box in the background on the plinth is the met screen. Notice the New Zealand flag flown for the benefit of the American helicopter pilots.

anemometer and sundry thermometers. Close by were the food boxes, with Maurice's frozen blocks of chicken stew and cans of tinned fruit piled up at the side. We had covered the food with a small tarpaulin sheet at first, not that we were expecting rain. A kilometre away was the ice-covered lake; with a freshwater moat initially a few metres wide at its edge, but later in the summer maybe ten metres wide in most places. The lake was more than five kilometres long. On the north side, where the lake abutted the steep scree slopes, several benches were clearly cut by former higher stands of the lake. We wondered how long ago that had been.

Beyond the western end of the lake the valley divided into two, separated by a flat dolerite-topped mesa, and those we named straight away as the North and the South Forks. Obviously the valley floor rose to the west in the forks, but from the tents we couldn't see that area. But beyond that were two thin icefalls carrying a relatively small amount of ice from inland. At the bottoms of the falls the ice coalesced to form the apron glacier, just a few kilometres long, that we had seen on our recce flight.

Clearly lots of these features needed names but for the present we would name only the most pertinent. The glacier at the top end of the valley we called the Upper Wright Glacier, to match the Lower Wright Glacier at the other end. When bureaucracy ordained that they be called the Wright Upper Glacier and the Wright Lower Glacier we didn't object too much. How could we?

At Peter's suggestion we christened the flat-topped mesa with the name Dais, French for 'platform'. The previous year he had called a similar flat-topped feature, separating two valleys in the Victoria Valley system, Insel, German for 'island'. Now for the lake! Peter had called the two prominent lakes in Victoria Valley Lakes Vida and Vashka, so it was quite apparent that we needed another 'V' lake, and thus it became Lake Vanda, named after the lead dog in the only dog team I had ever driven seriously, in Greenland during the dark of winter 1952–53. I told the others the tale of how Vanda showed herself to be less than fully wired when she led the team, in the complete dark, within ten metres of the tent and didn't either smell or see it, but they couldn't think of another 'V' animal, and Vulcan, Viper and Vole did not seem appropriate, so Vanda stuck. At that point we had exhausted our imaginative powers, so for the moment the peaks on the valley sides were named A, B, C, D, . . . and even I knew that the next one along the range was E., as Guyon had done on his sketch map.

In the other direction, eastwards towards McMurdo Sound, far in the distance we could clearly see Mount Erebus, 150 kilometres away or more. Constantly we were amazed at the clarity of the atmosphere. Barrie said,

Fig. 24. View southeast across flat-topped Dais to Asgard Range, from the shoulder of Olympus Range, near the Upper Depot. Mount Odin is on the skyline, left of centre.

Fig. 25. View west from Main Base with Dais prominent in the middle distance.

Fig. 26. View east from close to Main Base, with *King Pin* landing. Mount Orestes and the entrance to Bull Pass are beyond.

Fig. 27. From near Mount Odin looking 35 kilometres eastwards to the Lower Wright Glacier and coast beyond. Mount Newell (1920 metres) is on the right skyline. Denton, Goodspeed, Hart, Meserve and Bartley Glaciers descend from the Asgard Range. Onyx River channels drain inland.

'Down here, you can see forever, but it's even further than that to walk.' From the tents we couldn't see the Wilson Piedmont Glacier or its offshoot, the Lower Wright, or Wright Lower, Glacier, because of the bend in the valley. However, we could see the cliff-sided hanging glaciers, extending halfway to the valley floor on the south side and, somewhat imaginatively I thought, we called them Glaciers 1, 2, 3, 4, and − go on, guess! − 5, and later after professors at Vic, not knowing that they had already been given names. Bob Nichols, a geology professor at Tufts College, Massachusetts, and a great old Antarctic explorer (he held some record for the longest unsupported dog-sledge journey, with Ronne's expedition in 1947), had been working at the Marble Point airstrip site in 1957, with a bunch of his students. One day they crossed the Wilson Piedmont Glacier (I don't know how) to the end of Wright Valley, which Bob called 'The Grand Canyon of Antarctica' and named the hanging glaciers for his students, Denton, Goodspeed, Hart, Meserve, and Bartley.

Our first full day in the valley started when the alarm woke me at 7.45 a.m. for a radio schedule with Peter Yeates, the friendly radio man at Scott Base, call sign ZLQ. Both the official radio, which belonged originally to the Trans-Antarctic Expedition, and the ship-to-shore ones that we had borrowed from the makers, worked well, surprisingly well for the little ones, considering the distance. We sent them a message thanking them all for their tolerance and helpfulness. We meant it, too, but Peter Yeates did seem to appreciate our saying it. After our conversation Peter 'patched' me into WWV, the radio station that transmits time signals 24 hours a day. I needed to know the time within a second in order to calculate our position from observations of the sun. Peter always managed to send us the time signals but once, when Peter wasn't at the radio, I asked his 'stand-in' for the time, and he replied 'Oh, in a little while it'll be ten past eight or so.' Both Dick and I carried 'deck watches' in leather pouches around our necks to keep them at a constant temperature. They worked amazingly well as long as we remembered to wind them.

We found the charts for the recording met instruments and after adding the ink to their pens, my first task was to take dozens of sun sights with the theodolite, throughout the day, to work out our position. It was warm, 4°C, but still a bit windy at the exposed instrument. Dick was luckier: as my 'booker' (for angles and times of observations) he built an armchair in the rocks and sat there, out of the wind, chewing his pipe, and reading a book when I had to stop to adjust the levelling of the theodolite. I then tried setting up the subtense bar to measure the baseline, but the bar was shaking too much in the wind.

Fig. 28. Colin inking the pens of the meteorological instruments. Note the letters in the screen, to be collected by any passing mailman!

Fig. 29. Dick booking for Colin while trying desperately to keep moderately warm in gale conditions.

Meanwhile Peter and Barrie had been sorting out the gear for their first exploration, which was to be a traverse of the range above the south side of the valley, starting from the most imposing peak visible from the valley floor, which was marked on our maps as Peak 105, and which we later called Mount Odin. Eventually they set off, with 35-kilogram packs, at five p.m. At eight p.m., on the radio, they said that the scree was so difficult that they had to relay their loads. Well, if those superbly fit 20-year-olds were having problems, how would Dick, aged 29, and I, overweight and all of 30, manage? I looked again at Dais with its wonderful central position and flat terrain but accessible, as far as we could see, only by steep scree slopes followed by vertical dolerite rock bluffs, thought about the weight of the tripod and theodolite, and put a line (for the time being, at least) through Dais on our list of planned survey sites.

Wearing his four-point instep crampons, Dick walked across the rough surface of the lake to build a cairn and plant the inevitable Day-Glo flag, near the end of the peninsula that extended more than half of the distance across the lake. He tried to walk back without crampons, fell heavily, decided to walk round the lake edge, and found a mummified seal. Back at the tent he announced 'No fall without profit!' and extolled the beauty of his wretched seal!

I'd just gone to sleep when, at two a.m., the crunch of boots on granite shards woke me up. Peter and Barrie had taken five hours to carry half of their loads up to 1300 metres, to an old glacier cirque between two peaks that rose another 600 metres above them. We had selected one of those peaks as a possible survey point. I wondered if we should delete that one as well. Peter said that carrying the packs up those steep scree slopes in near-gale conditions was pretty close to purgatory. They came back down in two hours, but rather than face carrying the other half of their load up to the top, they walked back to camp with just their sleeping bags. Barrie was particularly effervescent and equally full of pains and puns – even after that gruelling trudge. Peter seemed to be most concerned with what Bob Clark would think if he knew his precious Exacta telephoto lens was buried in sand and snow at 1300 metres. Ah, youth! We fed 'em and went back to bed.

Everywhere we looked there were interesting questions. Take the lake for example – ah yes, Lake Vanda. A stream flowed inland all the length of the valley from the Lower Wright Glacier; not a big stream. Just before it flowed into the lake it was confined to a channel about three metres wide and there it was 30 centimetres or so deep. There were a few other, and much smaller, streams flowing in to the south side of the lake, but I bet there was no outflow at the west end of the lake, because we could see the

Fig. 30. Mount Odin (approximately 2000 metres) as seen from Main Base (approximately 200 metres). Granitic rocks intruded by dark lamprophytic dykes (in foreground) are topped by the Peneplain dolerite sill.

land rising beyond the end of the lake. Yet the water level had gone down about a couple of centimetres on the bamboo marker I'd stuck in the lake edge at noon the day before. Evaporation?

Then, why wasn't there any moraine in this part of the valley? Over there in the South Fork there seemed to be something that looked like a lobe of moraine. Or maybe it was a rock glacier. But there was nothing at all in this part of the valley. Could fluvio-glacial outwash from some larger ancestral Lake Vanda have flushed the valley clear?

For a late breakfast I cooked egg for us all. It started as dried egg powder, the same stuff we'd lived on for two years in Greenland. There we discovered very many different ways to prepare it. All except one of them were disasters, and that one was almost delectable. After mixing the egg powder very thoroughly with lukewarm water, a dollop of milk or milk powder, if you have it, and a smidgeon of salt, you cook this mixture in a pound of melted butter. It is not possible to have too much butter. Anyway, it was very good and consequently, when Peter and Barrie left again in mid afternoon, after a lunch of Maurice's steak and kidney pudding (Boy! Those kids could eat!), they took with them quite a lot of dried egg, which they had previously rejected as inedible. (When Barrie read this he wrote in the margin: 'I vehemently protest! We only took a poultry (paltry) amount!' You can see that the man is still incorrigible, and can imagine what we had to endure on the expedition!)

The wind in the morning was cold and was from the east! Why was the wind from the coast colder, much colder, than the wind from the inland ice? Shouldn't it be the other way round? Nearly always the wind started to blow from the east at about five p.m., changing back again to blow from the inland ice at perhaps one a.m. With the easterly winds the humidity rose to about 80%, while the winds from the west were much drier, 40%, as well as being warmer. But whatever its direction the wind was usually strong and sand-laden, and we had sand in our diaries, our eyes, our food, the theodolite, and our noses – everywhere. No wonder the place was covered with sand-eroded rock.

It was too windy to survey the baseline, so we inspected the mummified crabeater seal that Dick had found partially buried in the sand just 40 metres from the tents. It was quite small, and therefore young, Dick argued. The upper part was eroded down to the bone, but there was still fur on the underside. This was the first of 99 seals, nearly all crabeater seals and nearly all young, that we found in the area. We wished we knew enough seal psychology to understand why they ventured so far from their natural habitat and into such an inhospitable place. Anyway, Dick photographed it, measured it (163 centimetres long), looked at its most recent dinner (granite sand) and wrote it all down, most assiduously, in his 'Seal Log Book'.

Supper was another of Maurice's frozen chicken stews, which were slowly melting despite our best attempts at insulation. After supper the wind dropped, so I started work on setting up and measuring a baseline for our survey work. Originally I was going to put the markers for the ends of the baseline on the lake ice because that was the flattest area around but then it occurred to me that since the ice was floating it might move in a heavy wind, so I put the markers on readily identifiable points on the southern shore of the lake, one where Dick had already built the cairn on the peninsula that extends most of the way across the lake.

Doing my own recording of angles was tedious but Dick wanted to do a first inspection of likely habitats for things that grow, whether plant or animal. Many of the local ponds, in the depressions between the dykes, were partly or completely thawed. In one of them, fully ten centimetres deep, Dick found the water temperature was 3°C and, to his great joy, he found some creepy crawlies, which, he said, were called nematodes. A bit later, when, dressed in a US parka belonging to 'POE', he had come down to the lake edge to see how I was doing with the survey work, he found some other things that moved, which he pronounced to be rotifers. He was practically ecstatic. He was equally joyful when, after dinner, we heard odd noises, which turned out to be a pair of skuas, disputing a discarded remnant down at the heliport. Apart from the nematodes and bits of algae and lichen, they were the first living things, other than our contubernial companions, that we had seen in the valley.

Ten days before Christmas, Dick and I set off to tackle our first surveying chores, hoping to establish three or four stations on the peaks on the north side of the valley before returning to the base for Christmas. Food for ten days, cooking gear, first-aid kit, tent, Dick's minimal collecting kit, sleeping bags, radio, Wild T-2 theodolite and tripod, cameras, film, down jackets, gloves, alarm clock, climbing rope, notebooks, all came to something ridiculous, more than 36 kilograms each. Fortunately we had excellent rucksacks, items called Mountain Mules, one of the results of my letter solicitations back in Wellington. One of their best features was the hollow tubing of their frames, which could be filled with kerosene. Dick filled his with Drambuie. I chucked out of the load all of my spare clothing and one of the two books, leaving me with *Gallant Gentlemen, Portrait of the British Officer, 1600–1950*, by E.S. Turner. Dick took John Masefield's *William Shakespeare*, a much better choice. When he tried lifting his loaded pack, he poured the Drambuie, most of it anyway, back into the bottle.

Fig. 31. Dick and his first defunct seal.

Fig. 32. Basic equipment for a two-week trek, most of the food still to be added.

We checked with Peter Yeates at Scott Base for a time signal and then talked with Barrie and Peter. The previous day they had climbed high on Peak 105 in temperatures around −8°C but hadn't quite reached the summit. They had mapped the geology, taken a round of carefully controlled large-format black and white photographs with a Rolleiflex camera mounted on a tripod and had then retreated to their tent, along with Bob Clark's telephoto lens.

But these words don't do justice to Peter and Barrie's exploits. The boys reported that they had been 'blown out' of their camp near Mount Odin. Peter's account of those three days is very instructive. He wrote:

> During the day (12th December) we assembled our gear and food for our first trip away from the main camp, and at five p.m. we departed, heading for Peak 105. Only a mile (couple of kilometres) out from camp we started to climb with heavy loads and the going became very hard work. Reality struck as it became clear we would have to drop weight. So we halved weights and carried on. I began to slow down but Barrie really started to get into stride and made much better time. At eight p.m., with the small radio, we joined in a sked with Scott Base, with ZLYO and Hamilton and Hayes over in the Taylor Glacier area. The only good thing to come out of today was when Colin relayed a message saying that we had both completed our BSc degrees. After a really rugged first day in the field we cached our half-loads around 11 p.m. at 4350 feet (1330 metres) and made a fast return down the wall to Mittelheim where we arrived well after one a.m. I felt pretty sick all day and during the trip down. Colin and Dick got up and brewed drinks.
>
> We surfaced at ten a.m. for breakfast and went back to sleep until four p.m. (!).

We left in higher spirits after dinner and headed back up the valley wall to the food cache left yesterday. Kept climbing up into the cirque just east of Mount Odin, hoping for a flat valley floor, which never arrived. At two a.m. (14th December) we stopped to camp at 4350 feet (1330 metres), and in a very exposed position. We were absolutely buggered and couldn't go any further. A fierce cold wind, more than 25 knots, came up and it was impossible to get the small tent properly erected on a considerable slope so we could get out of the wind. From 12.30 a.m. the air temperature had dropped to 18°F (–8°C). The tent was not pitched very well, was flapping and shaking, the wind was deafening and there was a small rip opening in the roof area.

The small tent floor sloped at least 20–30 degrees towards Wright Valley so we were literally hanging on the high valley wall and colliding as we tried to sleep. It was impossible to get two air mattresses inflated and organized in the jumble. But we slept despite the mess. This was my birthday and exactly a year since we departed Wellington on *Endeavour* during the first Antarctic trip. With characteristic foresight and good memory, Barrie delivered a birthday present in the middle of the storm and we toasted the day with some rum.

Our source of heat for meal preparation was a single fierce little Optimus (like a Primus), very noisy but super efficient. A heavy, loose, star-shaped disk is a flame-spreader and soon gets red hot. During a heavy gust of wind the tent wall flapped violently and we lost our balance in the tiny tent, and this red-hot disk became an airborne missile. The first job was to get the stove snuffed out so we didn't burn down the tent and then we wondered where the red-hot disk had gone. The question was soon answered when the windy tent interior filled with goose down and we began to cough and splutter. The disk had burned its way through my sleeping bag. There were down feathers in everything for days. I sewed up the hole in my Fairy Down bag and resumed life. (I recall seeing that bag and my rough thimble work in the VUWAE equipment store in Wellington for several years afterwards and always chuckled over that chaotic night on Mount Odin.)

We recovered our senses and resumed the climb at one p.m., reaching 6380 feet (1945 metres) where we had a spectacular panorama that extended from the edge of the inland ice plateau to the Ross Sea. Camped. Messed and in bed by nine p.m.

Dick and I arranged future radio schedules with Peter and Barrie, and then spent the rest of the morning sorting out the stuff for our own trip. After lunch, in a tiresome brisk wind we set off for the col leading from Wright Valley to the valley later named McKelvey Valley, part of the Victoria Valley system, to the north. As we walked across the valley floor, up and down across the swarm of raised dykes, in a rising wind, I regretted having lost the toss so that I was carrying the tent in its bag, more than a metre long, across the top of my pack and was being blown every which way. Dick had the tripod on top of his pack, also more than a metre long, but the wind could blow through that! It was obvious that I was being discriminated against! When we set out I thought of lots of pleasant things: Paremata and family, our canoe on Paremata Harbour and the like. Shortly I was thinking of John at Scott Base and his comment when changing reels on the projector, 'Only another ten thousand feet of this excruciating garbage.' That applied directly to us, now. Our first survey station, marked 'Peak 16' on the best photograph we had, was 'only' about 1900 metres above us. Obviously it was impossible to carry my load that high and that far, but I felt that with luck I could stagger to that big rock 50 metres away, couldn't I? And, with a little rest every few minutes, we continued.

Heading towards the pass we moved to the north side of the valley where we soon met the slopes of ancient, much subdued, moraines. Over thousands of years the relentless wind had concentrated sheets of sand in the depressions between bouldery hummocky crests. The sands and gravels were fairly well consolidated by the wind so that it would have been fairly easy walking if it hadn't been for those stupid packs. By now my only thoughts, on the sloping surfaces, were 'One, two three . . . twenty-five. Stop.'

At the top of the moraine blanket and just below the level of the entrance to the col itself, we sat for a welcome snack, biscuits and chocolate. We knew that that was good to eat, because we had been told so. One of us, playing with the sand on which we were sitting, unearthed a pecten shell, and then another, and a third. I arranged the shells on my ice axe and photographed them and then said, 'Well, I guess some skua must have brought these from McMurdo Sound.' (A pair of skuas had adopted us at the base tents.) It's not a good photograph but we're including it because some later workers have claimed that they were the first to find the pectens. It wasn't till later, much later, while we were working up our field notes, that we realized the significance of those pecten shells: at some stage a glacier, grounded in McMurdo Sound, was thick enough to plough up the sea floor bed and carry those shells, and many others, 50 kilometres or so inland. Peter and Dick disagree with this theory and insist that the shells are evidence that pectens lived in Wright Fjord in the early Pliocene, 3–5 million years ago, although I worry about the monstrous sea level change that this implies.

Along the col the sand carried by the persistent winds had eroded the granite boulders into the most bizarre shapes, utterly intriguing to us, even in our exhausted state, and the subject of quite remarkable photographs ever since. In other places the ground was covered with bits of dolerite, most of them about dinner plate size, but some much, much larger. These, known as ventifacts, had all been faceted and highly polished into neat geometrical shapes by the persistent wind-driven sandblasting machine. We stopped for a little rest under one particularly cavernous granite specimen.

Fig. 33. Three pecten shells from the moraine near Bull Pass.

We spotted another mummified seal, bringing my total to five, and near the highest part of the col (further north it slopes gently down towards McKelvey Valley) we found a very small lake, mostly frozen but with melt water at the edges. As there was a handy flat spot nearby and the melt water tasted fresh we decided to pitch tent among the eroded boulders, right there. We weren't in any shape to walk more than five more metres anyway. We just collapsed. Dick had a short air mattress; I made do with my down jacket on top of my rucksack. Pemmican never tasted so good.

The sand attrition continued for most of the night, but the sun shone so that the tent was warm. When the expedition was over, the col was named Bull Pass, and hundreds of people have walked through it, worked in it, put up seismic stations in it, and photographed those exotic, sometimes erotic, cavernous boulders. Nevertheless it gives me much pleasure to recall that Dick and I were the first people to camp there! Quite exhausted, we slept well until the alarm rang at 7.45 a.m., so that we could get a time check from Scott Base. After all we might have time to take sun shots for an astronomical position determination from our survey station at the top. Hearing Peter's cheerful voice along with the time pips was just about the best thing that happened all day.

I tried to explain to myself – Dick was too far ahead – why my pack was five kilograms heavier than yesterday. My 'immediate objective' fell from 80 metres to 25, and soon 20-centimetre-high boulders required deep concentrated thought lasting several exhausted breaths. Straight up the slope to the west was only 30° or so, and by judicious zigzagging we could keep to the finer scree, where we slipped back less. It wasn't difficult, merely exhausting. Dick was quite a bit faster but was very tolerant and took longer rests, every half hour or less. After five hours we found a moderately sheltered, moderately flat spot for the tent at about 1600 metres' altitude – the altimeter was one of the victims of the weight purge. There we dropped our packs and continued up the slope, with theodolite and tripod only, as the high cirrus cloud thickened and lowered. After another 150 metres or so of altitude we dumped the theodolite and tripod and continued the short distance to the top, unencumbered.

And from the top we gazed down on a minutely set out scene. There was our Main Base; two pyramid tents and the met screen all neatly laid out, the two ends of the baseline 1600 metres below – and just about nothing visible above 1000 metres. We piled invective on whoever was in charge of the weather, made sure the theodolite and tripod were tightly wrapped up for the night and returned to the tent, mumbling. That really was all very stupid. We'd have been so much better off making a dash – I wondered about that word – up the direct steep slope of the south side of the valley, with theodolite, tripod, camera and just a day's food, rather than lug all that clobber round the long, albeit entertainingly scenic, route.

It was snowing as we went to bed, before nine o'clock, being unable to think of anything else useful to do. It snowed all night, small and granular, pattering on the tent. When either of us woke we shook the snow off the tent and went back to sleep. We woke for the time pips, not that it mattered. It was still snowing and we weren't surveying. Breakfast, at 11 a.m., was half a bar of chocolate, the only food in the tent. After telling me that the chocolate was 'good and good to eat often', Dick went back to sleep. I read my book. It snowed. Around four p.m. Dick cooked a meal, lunch I suppose, starting from snow, always a slow process. I tried hard not to be a back-seat cook, and the meal was fine when it eventually arrived, porridge and scrambled reconstituted dried egg. I cleaned the pots, digging under the snow for some of that remarkably inefficient cleansing powder, 'Scratcho'. Dick wondered if we could market it, using some catchy jingle, 'Scratches without cleaning'. We played two desultory games of chess on Dick's diminutive board and went back to bed.

Fig. 34. Dick taking shelter from the wind in our favourite eroded granite boulder, Bull Pass.

Fig. 35. Our camp among much-eroded boulders, Bull Pass.

Fig. 36. Camping in snow on slopes of Mount Jason (Peak 16).

Fig. 37. '. . . mountains dressed in their wedding–dress white. . .' Mount Aoleus in the Olympus Range, from Dais.

Dick told me about Franklin and Coulman Islands, his work with the Forest Service in New Zealand, and of preparing for fieldwork on the west coast by first soaking shirt and socks in a bucket of insect repellent. Barrie and Peter, back on the floor of the valley, after being 'blown out' of their camp by Mount Odin, asked on the radio whether they should bring us extra food (always their highest priority), which was highly considerate of them, but we were fine.

When it wasn't snowing on the following day the visibility was distressingly close to zero at our elevation, although the boys said it wasn't bad in the valley. Dick and I discussed which way, and in what order the glaciers had moved in this complicated area. I started to read Dick's book, *William Shakespeare*, by John Masefield. Although we weren't supposed to discuss the book till we had both read it, Dick said he thought it just a bit too much of a chronicle, without illustrating Shakespeare as a man. I wrote a letter to five-month-old Nicky, complete with a plan of the chaotic tent, jumbled saucepans and sleeping bags. I started to write a deathless piece of poetry about our current state of decrepitude, of which I can now remember only four lines:

> And the beauty of that wind-swept land,
> For eons hid, but now revealed,
> That all may wonder and opine,
> On nature's puzzles all.

I decided it needed work. Perhaps after dinner. When P. and B. told us that they had found 19 seals in working the geology 13 kilometres along the valley, we congratulated them and asked them for the preferred treatment for bedsores.

And the following day made up for it all. It was coldish, −20°C, but no wind and no cloud. Underfoot, at the tent, there were 30 to 40 centimetres of fluffy, powdery snow. The glare off the snow was overwhelming and the sun so strong that I had to stop every few metres to wipe the sweat from the inside of my snow goggles, and after 400 metres, thanks to an insulating subcutaneous fatty layer, I was in shirtsleeves, although Dick still had on his anorak. I carried the light pack and Dick very slowly broke trail, trying to find safe footing on and among the deeply covered boulders. Tricky. Very. Far away we heard the helicopter droning slowly along the valley, with the gravity meter, I hoped, and maybe some mail. I wished I'd left a letter to Gillian to be picked up. Why couldn't we signal the chopper and get a lift to the top of this confounded hill? Three skuas seemed to be having a much easier time of it than we were.

Fig. 38. Lake Vanda and Main Base (marked by a red triangle) 1500 metres below the first survey station on Peak 16 (Mount Jason). The large number of black igneous dykes can be clearly seen.

Fig. 39. Victoria Valley stream draining a glacier in full mid-summer flow.

We should have left the tripod standing up but we found it fairly quickly and reached the summit, less than 300 metres above the tent, in two and a half hours, as the unfolding view grew more and more stupendous. It's a huge country. We could see Mount Erebus and beyond, 150 kilometres and more to the southeast; Mount Huggins, in the very impressive Royal Society Range, perhaps 100 kilometres southeast; some huge unnamed mountains to the north; and literally hundreds of minor peaks all around, all decked out in their wedding-dress white. Wonderful. And so exquisitely beautiful we had to pinch ourselves to be sure we were really seeing it all.

A few of the peaks had been given numbers on the aerial photographs, and a sub-set of these we could identify with certainty. Where do you start with a collection like that? We cleared the knee-deep snow from our intended tripod site, a bit back from the vertical northern face of the summit pile of Peak 16, overlooking Wright Valley, just in case I stepped back to admire our handiwork. Later the peak became Mount Jason, an impressive name to have next to Bull Pass! Dick fished out his camera, a cumbersome but efficient twin-lens Rolleicord, from under his anorak, where it was being kept warm, and took a round of black and white photographs from the tripod, levelling the camera and then taking a photograph every 30° of azimuth, using his fanciful automatic direction-fixing gizmo. That gave us enough overlap between adjacent exposures to be sure we had photographed everything.

I took a few Kodachromes of the most impressive peaks, wishing I had a telephoto lens to photograph Peak 105 across the valley. We took colour and black-and-white photographs of ourselves and especially our Anson boots, looking suitably intrepid, as requested. We selected just 19 'targets': peaks that were either identifiable on Guyon Warren's rough map, bigger than the rest, or of such an odd shape that we could be fairly sure to be able to recognize them from the next survey point. As usual I took six horizontal readings onto each target as well as the two ends of the baseline, three on each 'face' of the theodolite, and also two vertical angles to each of the targets.

I was thankful it was windless up there but even so my feet grew very cold in the four hours it took to measure the angles to all of the selected peaks. I stopped once to watch Peter and Barrie at Main Base. They seemed to take a long time over lunch. Down there the flags were showing a wind from the west. Must be a thin wind, because up here it was still calm. I hoped one of the boys had changed the met charts. While he was writing down the angles Dick had made pencil sketches of each of the target peaks. He took another round of photographs, the sun having moved round almost

75° since he took the first set. Last of all he built a cairn, and, heartily pleased with our work, we ate a couple of biscuits, hard and somewhat like unglazed ceramic tiles. Dick then headed back to the tent to keep the eight p.m. radio contact (he learned from Barrie at Main Base that indeed the helicopter we had heard had brought the gravity meter and some mail) while I collected a few oriented specimens from close to the top of the dolerite sheet, for the proposed paleomagnetic work. I managed to break the handle of my geology hammer, which ended that particular collecting episode. My spare hammer was down in the tent at Main Base. Above the dolerite was sandstone and there were bits of it lying around. One of the very light-coloured porous pieces had a dark line just under the edge. 'Odd bit of weathering,' I thought, tossing it away, and thereby missed yet another important discovery, for the colouration was actually a weird endolithic bacterium, as Imre Friedman from Florida pointed out a decade or more later. Breaking off the rock samples had been nearly as hard as the tombstone biscuits but, to make up, by the time I had reached the tent Dick had coffee ready and also dinner: pemmican and onions, followed by apples, sultanas and more coffee. Great!

When the next morning turned out to be windy, with a low overcast, we realized how lucky we had been the day before, that surveying was out of the question for that day and that we might as well return to Main Base. The packs were heavier than ever – rocks are denser than food – but gravity was now on our side, and the snow depth lessened as we descended. It was still sufficient to bury any dead seals that might have been around but it did accentuate the terminal moraines along the bottom of the col, laid down, we presumed, by ancient glaciers flowing from the north, and the snow showed up the edges of the huge frost polygons, five- and six-sided and 20 metres or more across.

Under our favourite cavernous granite boulder we made a cup of coffee and ate lunch – cheese and those obdurate biscuits. Eating them, Dick drew blood, cutting his gum, but he was pleased to find that he could use the jagged edge of a biscuit to cut hard frozen butter and cheese.

At the junction of the col and Wright Valley we spent a couple of hours trying to make sense of it all, without much success. Was the moraine deposited by a glacier coming along the col or up the valley from the coast, or both? There were miles of sand, one stretch in the bottom of the main valley long enough and flat enough to be an aircraft landing strip, except for some frost heaving. Elsewhere were sand and shingle piles that had been wind- and water-sorted, and a few little lakes, domed at the surface because they were frozen solid. Utterly fascinating – and weren't we lucky and privileged to be the first people ever to walk on it?

Fig. 40. Dick making lunch under 'our' boulder, Bull Pass.

Fig. 41. '. . . footsteps in the sands of time . . .'

Down in Wright Valley again Butcher Barwick found a bunch more seals, two of them still with strokeable fur on their upper sides. He examined them closely, inside and out, though what he did, other than remove the penis bones of both and the head from one, I don't know. We dumped our packs at an obvious place by the stream in Wright Valley, took out the sleeping bags and plates and eating utensils and trundled back to Main Base, cursing the 35-knot wind that was continuing to erode us and our happy, tolerant natures. We hated that wind! As I was the cook I planned what I'd cook – based on that TAE tin of ham I'd been thinking about for the last several hours that we'd liberated from Scott Base. I know it sounds strange to have such a fetish for food, but when you are being sandblasted as we were, can you imagine anything better to think about, with the tent door closed? However Barrie and Peter had waited dinner for us – good kids – so we ate mushroom soup, bully beef hash, tinned fruit and limitless coffee. The soup was incredibly strong and Dick's investigations revealed why. We had two kinds of dried soup packages: the usual ones, made in New Zealand, which held enough for about four servings; and a few khaki-coloured jumbo-sized packages, from the USA, which would make 20 or more portions. Barrie had used all of one of the big ones. He thought it was marvellous. So did I.

In the tent, and therefore out of the wind, everyone was very high-spirited. Peter and Barrie reckoned they had seen a great deal of interesting geology and, although they hadn't managed to sort out all of the country yet, their enthusiasm for everything except the wind and sand was remarkable. We talked till very late.

I asked Peter and Barrie what they made of the col – which they hadn't seen properly yet. It was ten kilometres long and more than three kilometres wide. From the high point, near which we had camped, the pass sloped down both north and south, more steeply to Wright Valley than to McKelvey Valley. And there were obvious watercourses here and there, most prominently down the steep slope to Wright Valley, although it carried no water during Dick's and my trip. And those moraines – we hadn't really managed to sort out anything yet! We blamed that failure on the snow cover, rather than our incompetence.

We'd all made some horrible boo-boos with our first trips. Peter and Barrie had selected Mount Odin as their first objective, for good reasons. They needed panoramas from prominent high points for their geology map-making and they wanted a complete view of Wright Valley. In addition, the basement crystalline granites and dyke swarms were well exposed along their route and they felt that once they had seen the basic rocks it would assist the geological map-making over broader areas. Finally, there appeared to be a basal succession of Beacon Supergroup – mainly sandstones – just above the Kukri Peneplain on the north face of Mount Odin. Despite the disastrous treatment of Peter's sleeping bag, it was all very much worthwhile.

However, although the boys' science planning may have been inspired, their bodies were not yet ready for that sort of treatment. They would have been better served perhaps by doing a low-level traverse first. Still, they had learned their limitations and they had learned not to camp where the fierce and dreaded katabatic winds can get you. Dick and I had learned not to try to carry all our living essentials up to great heights, but to live low and only carry the surveying stuff and a bar of chocolate up to the peaks. After all, according to Dick, 'It is good, and it's good to eat often!'

Barrie brought me breakfast in bed: completely delicious bacon, not from a can, but cut slices from the slab, and baked beans. 'Colin, Sir,' he said, 'here's the results of your literary efforts,' referring to my begging letter to the bacon man. Was it Kiwi Bacon Company? Anyway, it was so good we had a second breakfast immediately, and altogether consumed ten days' ration of bacon.

Peter and Barrie were heading down valley; Dick intended to bring his log of the panoramic photographs up to date and then to molest some more seals. I had to start the gravity traverse down the valley, and, of course, by the time I had made the flagged bamboo poles to mark the gravity stations, the wind had unleashed itself again. Six hours later a very disgruntled and sandblasted Bull decided that enough was more than enough. I'd made only eight gravity stations, a kilometre apart, in a straight line down the middle of the valley. The dozen three-metre-long bamboos across the top of my pack caught the wind every step of the way. How could I expect to walk in a straight line? When there wasn't sand in my eyes I could line up the flags at the last two stations, so that aspect wasn't too bad. But every time I was about to read the gravity meter a particularly vicious wind gust blew it off level. Less than six kilometres in six very uncomfortable hours!

The only worthwhile diversion all of that sunless day was the skua, at lunchtime, near the moraine at the entrance to the col. It had been flying around me, complaining, for 20 minutes when I sat down. Wisely it declined the piece of ceramic tile, aka biscuit, I threw to it, preferring to eat something fresh from the 15-centimetre-deep stream. Solely for my benefit, the bird did some nifty aerobatics and I took some absolutely breathtaking photographs of it, with the snow-clad majesty of Peak 105 as background, only to discover I'd left on the lens cap. I stamped my foot and said rude words. The bird flew away.

I sang belligerent songs all the way back to the tents, or rather hummed, because I could do that without opening my mouth. Dick was equally bad tempered. 'This something wind!' he said, 'I could cheerfully throw all the something seals into it! It even tore a page from my something notebook.' He'd found only two new seals to abuse. (I'd tripped over eight of the damned things, bringing my total to something close to 20.) He'd brought one of them back into the tent to examine, on my sleeping bag, I swear!

To cheer us up we opened the TAE ham and ate half a kilogram or so each, with spuds, resurrected dried onions and tinned peas. Our meals, the wonderful vistas and the knowledge that we were the first people here were the main reliably positive things in our lives. Sometimes we couldn't see the views, which put even more emphasis on the food. And, of course, the wind dropped to zero when we closed the tent door!

In the morning, Peter Yeates, on the radio, read us a telegram from Bob Clark congratulating Peter and Barrie on passing their final exams, and declaring that they were now fully certificated geologists. Dick and I were also included, although we hadn't passed any exams recently. Scott Base couldn't hear us on voice, so in my unpracticed Morse code I sent the very brief cable that Peter had left with me, addressed to his father in Sydney. It read, '-.. . --. .-. . . --.. --- -- .--. .-... - . -... .-... - . .-.' ('Degree completed. Peter.') Somehow I concluded that he had assumed that the exams would have a successful outcome! I sent four other Christmas telegrams – telegrams were one of our expensive but much-appreciated 'perks' – and was gratified when Peter reported that my Morse code was 'a bit slow but very readable', all thanks to Dixie's lessons at Northice.

It was a beautiful morning – very little wind and no cloud. While I changed the met charts, it being Monday, Dick did something evil with his latest pet seal, which he declared was 'only recently deceased' – within the last century I presumed. For no good reason we had all agreed to be at Main Base for Christmas Day – I had already planned several celebratory competitive activities: who could stand on one leg longest, on a lump of ice in the moat of Lake Vanda; a hands-and-knees race across 100 metres of the incredibly slippery, newly formed ice at the edge of the old solid ice on the lake; a race (among the other three – I'd be the judge), fully laden, up the steep scree slope on the side of Dais. But Dick and I decided we should be able to knock off another survey station in the four days before Christmas. We'd selected Mount Orestes, perhaps 2000 metres high, to the east of the col, entirely because we had left the tent, much food and the survey gear at the camping spot near the high point of the col, Bull Pass if you please.

From the last survey station, Peak 16 (Mount Jason) west of the col, we had seen what appeared to be a fairly easy route up Mount Orestes. From the tent we'd walk up into the large, gently sloping cirque basin directly to the east, up to about 1200 metres. Then south, along the ridge that forms the side of Bull Pass, to the unnamed, unnumbered peak, at 1800 metres or so, that dominated our view from the tent site. Then east again along the ridge between the first cirque and the one leading down to Wright Valley, and up to the top of Mount Orestes. Voila! Simple!

Barrie and Peter intended to work northward from the col after Christmas, so Dick and I carried 15 days of food, mainly for them, as well as my spare geology hammer, up to the same exquisite campsite we had occupied a week or so earlier, among the distorted boulders by the small lake. That load amounted to 20 kilograms or so each, just enough to prevent us from breaking into a gallop as we trudged across the dyke swarm, the aerodrome, and up the sand and gravel of the moraine that was later called the Pecten Moraine by ourselves and by others.

We stopped, very briefly, for a drink of fresh water at the stream – we must give it a name – and for a longer rest at 'our' big cavernously eroded granite boulder. There we admired a smaller boulder, a short distance away. It was 60 centimetres high, and into the side facing up the col the wind had somehow cut two deep holes, resembling grotesque eyes. It also had a protruding nose and a 'cowlick' of granite hair over its forehead. Years later someone else must have been struck by the droll appearance of this lump of rock, for it is now in the Museum of Science in Boston. But we were the first to see it – and I wish that it had been left there, for this horrible habit of 'souveniring' has now become completely unseemly.

As before, the tent site was great: great views, great weather, almost great food. Dick said that only the company was inferior. We were at nearly 800 metres' elevation and northward the col lost height to the part of the Victoria Valley system that Barrie selected for his own, McKelvey Valley. We found we'd forgotten to bring the pemmican, but the alternative – that delicious bacon – was no hardship. We'd also forgotten the dried milk powder, but that was deliberate. The stuff we had brought from New Zealand didn't dissolve very well, especially in ice-cold water, and we wanted to try the brand that Maurice had given us at Scott Base, 'Pream'. I think it came from the supplies left at Scott Base by Bunny Fuchs's crossing party. Anyway, we were told that it contained a detergent called 'Teepol', and therefore couldn't be sold in New Zealand, but we found it to be first rate, dissolving readily and fine eaten straight from the jar. It seemed to have no deleterious effects on us, at least in the small quantities that we consumed.

Fig. 42. Colin transmitting on the Main Base sledge-set radio by Morse. The radio rests upon a Trans-Antarctic Expedition food box that presumably had crossed the continent and then been 'acquired' by VUWAE 2.

Fig. 43. Dick and his first cairn at east end of Lake Vida, 1957.

On the radio contact with Scott Base I sent five telegrams. Mine, to Gillian and Nicky, began 'Paremata paradise preferable but . . . Merry Christmas.' Dick's, to his family, started 'Fit, fat and filthy . . .' P. and B. asked if we would like to swap tents at their current tent sites, rather than carry them back to Main Base. That seemed a good idea, for their tent was part way towards the coast, in the bottom of Wright Valley – and our next trip after Christmas was to be to the coast. Then, on a gorgeous cloudless, calm morning we set off, with minimum loads. Mine was the theodolite, aneroid barometer, ice axe, crampons, notebooks, and spare clothes; about 20 kilograms altogether. Dick had the tripod, camera and its fancy azimuth-controlling attachment, the climbing rope, and, most important, the food; about the same total weight. Before we reached the floor of the cirque I'd taken off my anorak – too hot! Underfoot the snow from the last gentle storm was deeper than on Peak 16 – deeper and softer, especially among the wind-worn boulders. Dick, taking a step or two on top of a big boulder, broke through the one-inch-thick rock lip, not seeing the eroded cavern underneath. He landed in a heap in the snow, swearing liberally, and with a vocabulary that even Taffy, my profusely profane Greenland friend, would have admired. We continued, carefully and incredibly slowly. We reached the top of the ridge, 1500 metres, after three hours, which we thought not bad considering the conditions of the terrain and ourselves. We could clearly hear a helicopter far away, near the coast, and again thought how much easier our life would be if we had one right here, right now!

From Peak 16 I'd guessed that it would take half an hour or so to walk to the other end of the ridge, just where it starts to become the steeper slope up to the unnamed 1800-metre lesser peak. Dick complained that the ridge was 'unnecessarily undulatory'. I told him to eschew obfuscation and to hold on for a minute while I tried to catch up. It took two hours to reach the other end.

From there the view of Mount Orestes was quite different. The ridge between the two cirque basins looked about the same as the one we had just traversed, another half hour, or maybe two, or more. But then the route became decidedly steeper and the last few hundred metres were mainly snow covered, but with rock protuberances scattered throughout, and an average slope of more than 60°. Dick looked at me; I shook my head. So we sat down on our ice axes and admired the summit snow cone of 'Inaccessible Peak', with its very impressive cornice, and decided that we'd cut our losses and make a survey station on top of the neighbouring peak. The aneroid there showed 1823 metres, rather low for a survey station in this he-man country, but just in case the peak felt slighted by that remark, we called it 'Alpha', and from it we could identify a whole bunch of peaks in every direction. Dick built a meticulously crafted cairn on the survey point, while I sat in the sun and smoked a cigarette. Dick is the sort of chap whose every effort is 'meticulously crafted'. He added a little red flag to his handiwork. 'That looks nice,' he said as he brushed his gloves together and struggled into his backpack.

At 7.30 p.m. we headed for our temporary home by the little lake. As usual Dick was ahead, sometimes a long distance ahead, and his main objective as we went down the slope was to avoid that horrible stretch of huge eroded and corroded granite boulders, covered with snow. To do this he scrambled down the headwall of the cirque, where the slope was the slipping angle of flat granite slabs, 40-odd degrees, and all of the slabs were loose and snow-covered. It too was horrible, far worse than the boulders, but at least we had avoided them!

At the bottom, we looked back up the ridge and spotted a much easier route. I pointed out that this was all part of our education. We had learned that whatever we did, we couldn't win, and if the reader thinks that this is just negative thinking, I will just add that I'm positive that this is the case. However, we did look again at the route up Mount Orestes, and noted that indeed the top 60 metres or more was vertical dolerite. We'd made the correct decision on that one, to abandon all hope of a survey station on Mount Orestes. But the last ten kilometres along the bottom of the cirque and down to the tent was indeed a pleasant walk. The sun was still shining, it was calm and warm enough just for a pullover, and there were exactly enough boulders to provide convenient sitting places. After our mandatory bacon fix we turned in about 1.30 a.m., very tired and just a bit disappointed that we had made so much effort for so little gain. Still, we had accomplished something, even if it was only that lower-grade survey station.

We established very quickly that we weren't going to do another survey station on that day, and with a second cup of coffee after breakfast we toasted and congratulated each other. We sorted out and packed all the extra food, nearly 22 kilograms of it, which we reckoned should hold Barrie and Peter for one or two days. We made the food, our tent, the Primus and a bottle of kerosene into a heap beside a granite boulder by the lake.

Dick made another trademark cairn. By now he wouldn't let me do any of the cairn construction, although I was still allowed to carry candidate rocks to his building site and some of them were accepted. Again he added a red flag, and after another inflexible biscuit and chocolate, still 'good',

Fig. 44. Colin at survey station on Peak 'Alpha'.

though we didn't have enough 'to eat often', we set off towards Main Base. We parted at the end of the long sandy stretch near the Wright Valley end of the col, Dick heading back to Main Base and his beloved seals, while I climbed up the dolerite 'organ pipes' exposed above the western side of the col.

Leaving the contents of my pack at the bottom I had a successful couple of blustery and chilly hours collecting eight oriented samples, spread from the bottom to close to the top of the 200-metre-thick dolerite sheet, or rather from the top to the bottom, because dolerite has the peculiar property that it seems to weigh less when you are carrying it downhill. Altogether the samples weighed about ten kilograms, so by the time I had reloaded the theodolite and so on, I was back to the standard heavy pack, 30 kilograms or more. However, I concluded that I must have been becoming fitter, for I managed the eight kilometres home, mainly gently downhill I must admit, in less than two hours.

We'd expected P. and B. to be back about nine p.m., but on the eight p.m. radio contact they said they were still down at the coastal end of the valley, and wouldn't be home for hours yet. So we put aside our special meal − rehydrated dehydrated salmon (tastes very much better than it sounds), mixed veg, canned asparagus and ham, and jelly and peaches − and just had a hearty snack, cups of coffee, and another cigarette.

We spotted the boys when they were five kilometres or so away, and set out to meet them. We'd walked a couple of kilometres, by which time they were half a kilometre away, but they still hadn't seen us. So we sat down, out of sight, in the dyke swarm and wondered why it was taking them so long to reach us. They were horsing about in the stream! Ah, the energy of youth! In the morning they had geologized most of the way up Mount Loke (about 1500 metres) in the area of the hanging glaciers, and then had walked 19 kilometres, most of it with nearly 25-kilogram packs. They looked fit, very brown − or maybe it was just dirt − and very tired. Barrie complained that he had had to carry Peter and Peter's pack for most of the day because it had been Peter's birthday last week. Anyway we carried their packs and reached the tents after two a.m. While we cooked dinner they set to on everything that was visible and edible, and after dinner they resorted to eating vast numbers of Weetabix. I noted in my diary 'I've never seen anyone eat like P. & B. Horses!'

No one at Scott Base was awake to listen to our eight a.m. radio call, so I inspected the outer world and then returned to bed, to wake at two p.m. Christmas Day! It was calm, completely overcast and had been snowing, just a centimetre down at the tents, but more up the valley sides, up to cloud level. We'd saved all our Christmas presents until after 'breakfast' – cornflakes, scrambled egg au Bull, and Barrie's Christmas cake, vast quantities of sweet biscuits, chocolate penguins from Dick, and those dates, 'Loose packed for thrift'! We decided that the thrift was being exercised by the date-packers. The presents were all small; liar dice, a cribbage board, packs of cards, a book or two and, best of the lot, a little human-model building kit called Flex-o-Link, with which someone was playing all day.

We had decorated the tent with flags, and a few Christmas cards. One of those was from Judith White, the music teacher at the same school where Gillian taught art until Nicky came along. The envelope for Judith's card was addressed 'Colin Bull, Antarctica', the only time I've ever received a communication addressed to me by continent only. I still have the envelope, although the card disappeared long ago. I dug out my previously unused towel and wandered down to the lake, intending to have a celebratory swim in the moat. None of the others was interested. When I got there, however, I decided otherwise. It was chilly; the cloud was down to 600 metres; I decided to leave the swim until the sun was shining, and just had a perfunctory wash. However, instead of using our normal universal cleanser, called 'Gritto' by me and 'Sando' by Dick, I used soap – as a treat!

Fig. 45. The four of us at Main Base, Christmas Day 1958. Note the fancy footwear and parachute nylon accessories.

Back in the tent I told the others great lies about Greenland, and they all reciprocated in various ways while eating large quantities of sugary biscuits, slices of corned beef, and pieces of tinned pineapple. We played liar dice for a while and then went to bed at two a.m. – and that was our Wright Valley Christmas, 1958.

Boxing Day was equally tacky, with clouds at 1000 metres all morning. I was still cross with Larry Harrington, and told him so in my eight a.m. message ('for Pete's sake tell us what you propose to do before you do it!'), but I also asked a bunch of survey questions so that it was obvious, I hoped, that we would prefer to work with him than otherwise. Scott Base told us that they were going to be visited by Sir Raymond Priestley: another member of Scott's Last Expedition, the Vice-Chancellor of Birmingham University, and the Patron of my first polar expedition, the Birmingham University Spitsbergen Expedition, 1951. I sent Peter Yeates a message inviting Sir Raymond to visit us. When we returned to Scott Base a month later, I received his reply. He said:

> Scott Base. 1/1/59. Dear Bull, I am delighted to hear from you. Best wishes for the New Year. We got held up in the pack and did not reach McMurdo until December 29. [sic]. So I could not come to see you. I am promised a flight over the dry valleys and hope to wave to you, but the chances are not good. Then I am going with *Staten Island* to Hallett and Wilkes and then to Melbourne and she leaves on Jan 2 and so things are pretty hectic. However I have seen Cape Royds and Cape Evans and now Scott Base. All good wishes. To the re-seeing. Yours. Raymond Priestley.

I still have the note.

After lunch Dick cut the tongue from one of his tent slippers to make patches for his leather gloves. I darned my socks, brought the met log up to date, and worked out a bunch of survey calculations, which suggested that Lake Vanda was about 100 metres above sea level. With our fully qualified geologists I discussed the relative ages of the various rocks that looked as though they might be useful for the paleomagnetic work. The youngest useful rocks looked as though they were the dolerite sheets, hundreds of metres thick and clearly standing out on both sides of the valley. They were almost certainly Jurassic in age. Older than the dolerite were the rocks that formed the dyke swarms which cut through the granite of the valley floor, but how old those units were we didn't know. I also didn't know whether the granite would be useful because all of the accessible material seemed to be very heavily weathered, but I certainly had to collect samples from the dyke swarms, both the light and the dark coloured rocks.

By mid-afternoon the clouds had nearly all disappeared and what were left were at 2500 metres or more. A single-engined Otter aircraft flew up

Fig. 46. Barrie and Peter, always hungry, attacking one of Dick's mummified seals, after Christmas dinner. (Peter's caption was 'By early December Bull and Barwick had consumed most of their food supply, and all of ours, and requested that we just go away and learn to live off the land.')

Fig. 47. Winter Olympics, Christmas 1958. Peter was the clear winner of the Chariot Race (Peter's caption was 'On early expeditions it was customary for undergraduate students to be treated like dogs. Here Peter Webb pulls the overlord and leader Colin Bull across Lake Vanda. Although quite demeaning, the exercise kept me very fit and I learned to take commands.')

the valley, quite high, but ignored us. It flew round the head of the valley for a few minutes and then went back to McMurdo.

Peter suggested that we might usefully tell Bob Clark what we had been doing with ourselves, so we all sat down and composed a long telegram, outlining our results and plans. After dinner we sent the telegram. Reception was good so I didn't have to strain my Morse code. Bob soon spread the word, publishing our news around the University and in the Wellington newspapers. Good man!

Oh, isn't it a pleasure to work with colleagues of such high intellectual attainments, spectacular mental accomplishments, and dazzling intelligence? Dick's most recent seal was named Sam. In fact he named all his seals Sam, independent of gender. He said it avoided confusion. Anyway, Sam had been leaning against the door of our tent for all of Boxing Day. For reasons unknown, Dick moved Sam to lean against the door of the other tent. When Barrie emerged he tripped over Sam, and found himself eye to eye with him/her/it. For revenge, he hurled Sam, all 20 kilograms of skin, sand and bones, into our tent, belting Dick across the ankle, but without appreciable damage to Dick or to Sam. Barrie continued on his way towards the hills, toilet paper and spade in hand. When he was out of sight Dick stuffed Sam into Barrie's sleeping bag, only his/her/its nose showing. Peter and I were wondering what would be the next escalation, but Barrie clearly won the competition, by doing nothing, other than ejecting Sam and his/her/its accompanying sand. We all had another sweet biscuit and went back to bed.

CHAPTER 6

An enigmatic lake and a remarkable saga

All of us reckoned we had deserved those two days goofing off over Christmas, but then felt we must again take advantage of our opportunities. I think we all felt – certainly I did – incredible satisfaction in knowing we were the first people ever to step over these treacherous lumps of granite and wipe those penetrating sand grains from our eyes, nose and mouth. Peter and Barrie, comparatively lightly laden, their only food being the pemmican we had forgotten, left on December 27, on a warm, completely overcast morning, heading for the depot we had left in Bull Pass, and points further north and west. Dick departed in search of further Sams. He was amusingly enthusiastic about finding one that 'was almost new', Sam # 13. I made another cup of coffee, dug out my powerful little Curta calculating machine, and spent several boring hours reducing the survey data.

The noon weather record in the met log reads '8/8 Stratus cloud at 5000 feet (1500 metres). Calm. Snowing very gently. Temp 33°F (0.6°C). Humidity (hair hygrometer) 87%.' An hour or so later I nipped out of the tent again. If I hadn't read somewhere the statement 'It never rains inland in Antarctica,' I would have sworn that the gentle precipitation was rain, and it was as rain I recorded it in my diary. Dick, who was working nearby, also noticed the rain. Another myth squashed!

Later in the day the cloud cleared over both ends of the valley, and the wind on the valley floor started its usual rampage from the east. At the level of the mountaintops, however, we could see that the wind was blowing the snow from the west. How unusual! Somebody should come and study the weather properly down here.

During my first winter in northeast Greenland, 1952–53, at our main base by the side of Britannia Lake, I had rather little to do except to enjoy being the bread, cake and patisserie cook. Most of that baking I did at 'night' when the galley was quiet. In the 'daytime', especially when the moon was bright, I made a gravity survey of the lake, accompanied by my one-dog dog-team, Nuguak. I did this survey mainly to get out of the hut and to gain experience with the instrument, but I was intrigued with the results and pleased with my accuracy in estimating the depths of the lake at many points. Well, I didn't have enough time to do a detailed survey of Lake Vanda, and Nuguak, I hoped, was still at London Zoo, but I decided to make at least one line of stations, closely spaced, along the length of the lake, and then along the North Fork as far as I could manage.

On the radio at eight a.m. Larry Harrington sent me abject apologies for not discussing his plans before coming our way, which was nice of him, but he didn't answer my surveying questions, so I asked them again. While Dick went to examine more seals I set off with a trivial 15-kilogram pack for my gravity survey. I was lucky to find a dry-foot route onto the lake ice – the ice extended all the way to the shore at one spot on the peninsula. Elsewhere along the lake edge there seemed to be much more dried algae than I remembered seeing on earlier trips to the lake. I thought it might be a suitable substitute for tobacco if we ran out. For the first five metres from the spot where I left land, the ice was just refrozen melt water or water that came in from the stream. It was very elastic and clear enough that I could see the bottom and wasn't worried about breaking through.

The next 50 metres or so of ice looked as though it was one-year ice, neatly corrugated and with small crystals. I wondered if that was the limit of the melted moat last summer. And towards the middle of the lake from the one-year ice was the old ice. This came in two kinds; one kind was cut by the wind into cusped surfaces, ten centimetres from edge to edge, in stretches up to 50 metres long, and the other kind seemed to be a mixture of lake ice and thawed and refrozen snow. This second kind was very uneven, with ice pinnacles up to 50 centimetres high, but more usually 30 centimetres. It was obvious that my idea of using the lake ice as a landing strip wouldn't have worked. Very dirty clumps of ice, 20 centimetres or so in diameter, were in lines stretching nearly halfway across the lake, and five of the lines were about 20 metres apart – but were at about 45° to the prevailing wind directions, so the dirt probably wasn't wind-carried.

Every fourth gravity station I 'fixed' with magnetic compass bearings onto the ends of my survey baseline and a few of the prominent points on the southern shore of the lake. Nothing was 'prominent' on the north shore. I made a gravity reading every 200 paces, the main difficulty being not to allow myself to be distracted by all the fascinating and inexplicable things on and in the lake ice – like the unexpected patches of surprisingly transparent ice. How did they get there?

Fig. 48. Peter and Barrie, fairly lightly laden, setting off on their next traverse.

Fig. 49. Barrie and Peter's camp, with Mount Boreas in the background.

Fig. 50. Dried algae at edge of Lake Vanda.

Fig. 51. Rock-strewn lake bed, North Fork.

The entrance to the North Fork was just as fascinating. If the lake level had been 60 centimetres higher the lake would have overtopped the dyke, ten metres west of the end of the lake, and the lake would have then extended westward another kilometre. (Looking at a 1990s satellite photograph, I see that the lake has subsequently expanded that kilometre.) I spent an hour or so wandering through the gigantic tumps of moraine, extending up to 100 metres above lake level. However, I couldn't find any evidence of the former higher stands of the lake, either in the moraine or in the north wall of Dais. But I was sure that the moraine was older than the higher lake levels.

Come to think of it, the site of our Main Base was lower than those upper benches cut on the north wall. We hadn't found anything that looked like lake deposits in the holes we had dug there, but I wonder how long unprotected lake deposits would last in these savage winds.

I'd walked about five kilometres along the North Fork by my 'turn-around' time, four p.m., past a strange, rock-strewn, dried-up lake bed, and some fascinating moraine piles. By that time it was gloomy, completely overcast and with that unfriendly wind spoiling everything. No photographs, and that was a pity because I'd just reached the area where the best-developed frost polygons were displayed, on the gently sloping moraine surfaces. Many of the polygons were approximately squares, about 40 metres on a side, and were 'the wrong way round', the edges being marked by fine material, while the other well-formed polygons we had seen in Bull Pass had coarse material at the edges.

I marked my last gravity station with my last red flag, and made for home, pausing for a snack among those huge moraine piles, which extended up to 200 metres above Lake Vanda level, complete, I thought, with faint shore lines. Former lake levels? No, can't be. They were much higher than the benches around the present lake, and weren't very level. Taking off my pack at the edge of the lake, I climbed up the scree to measure the altitude of a few of those benches. The top one, best developed, was between 47 and 49 metres above current lake level. Had there once been a small lake up the valley, held in by those moraine piles?

Dick had returned half an hour before me and as I poked my head in the tent he pushed a cup of coffee into my hand. Good man! Apart from the wind he'd enjoyed himself with Sam (Dick said this was Sam #15, but I never found what he did with Sam #14). For me, too, it had been a good day and I reckoned that someone would be able to make sense of all that weird topography after just a couple of years' work. But I was pleased no end to have had the opportunity to have the first day there. While Dick

Fig. 52. Defunct crabeater seal, named Sam (by Dick). Typical of a 'recent' seal with no erosion of the exposed fur.

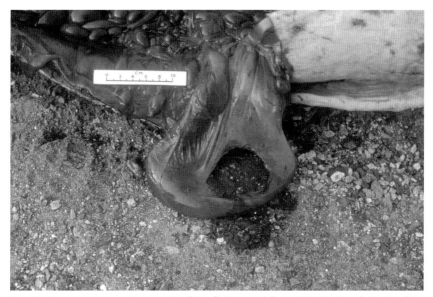

Fig. 53. The intestines and stomach of the freshest seal found, in the North Fork of the Wright Valley. On dissection the stomach was found to contain ingested gravel.

finished making dinner I made a quick and nasty reduction of the gravity numbers I had obtained on the lake. Ignoring the corrections for the local terrain and for the earth tides, and assuming the ice was three metres thick all over, I estimated that the lake was a bit less than 70 metres deep over a kilometre or so in the western lobe. Years later the New Zealanders made a very detailed map of the bottom of the lake, which confirmed my rough and ready findings. Trevor Chinn measured the greatest depth as 68 metres.

While Dick and I were engaged in all of these interesting and vaguely scientific pursuits, Barrie and Peter (on whom secretly we were relying for the scientific reputation of the whole enterprise) were trying their hands at much more difficult work, trying to sort out the geology of the high country. They've been reluctant to tell us all of the things that occurred on the first long, high trip, but eventually they did reveal some, if not all, of their adventures. This is how Barrie told their story.

> After our reconnaissance of the valley floor basement rocks east from Vanda, Peter and I needed to come to grips with the sub-horizontal Beacon Sandstone strata capping both the western Asgard and Olympus Ranges immediately above the big dolerite sill. To examine as much of the sandstone stratigraphy as possible we needed to push well to the west, towards the polar plateau. There would be time for us to examine the sandstones only in one range, and we chose the Olympus rather than the Asgard Range. It is less rugged, its crest essentially being a Beacon Sandstone platform from which isolated steep-sided peaks and mesas of younger Beacon strata rise. These spectacular but unnamed peaks we reduced for reference to dry letters of the alphabet, 'a', 'b', 'c', and so on. (Dick and Colin had named the same peaks 'A', 'B', 'C'.) We reasoned that the sandstone platform would allow us relatively easy movement in any direction about the crest and, most importantly, to the west. On the other hand, the crest of the Asgard Range is diversified by northeast-southwest trending cirque valleys, the steep walls of which deny easy westwards movement. When installing the Upper Depot, Dick and Peter chose a location about halfway along the Olympus Range west of the col, and immediately below the southern bluffs of the impressive mesa 'b'. Our plan was simple. Travelling lightly with small amounts of food and fuel, we'd climb to the crest of the range via the col, and move westwards along it as quickly as practical to reach the Upper Depot. We envisaged one or perhaps two camps en route. From the Upper Depot we intended to radiate in all directions through the sandstone country, in particular pushing and climbing to the west to gain access to the youngest sandstone horizons. From the valley floor and on paper it seemed a simple and straightforward plan but in reality it turned out to be disconcertingly difficult.
>
> Full of enthusiasm and an extra large breakfast, we sped off on the morning of the 27th, heading for the col where Colin and Dick had cached food and fuel. Travelling lightly we reached the cache by two p.m., snacked on some sledge biscuits, picked up the supplies, and were again on our way. The col scenery was new to us, and for the first time we appreciated that it was a valley in its own right. From

a high point about halfway along, the valley floor drained both northwestwards into the Victoria Valley system and southeastwards into the Wright Valley. But what struck us most were the spectacular contorted shapes of the sandblasted blocks of pink granite on the valley floor.

As we continued the going became definitely tougher. We were still well below the crest of the range, and to climb the steep, scree-draped walls of the col with our now fairly heavy packs we had to 'angle up' them in a northwards direction. We slowed, and became more conscious of a chill breeze as we started to encounter ever-deepening snow. The fun and novelty of the enterprise gently dimmed and eventually vanished as we plodded on, ever so slowly climbing. After about two hours, high on the northwest portal of the col at about 1300 metres, we stopped, cold, puffed and deflated and still well below the crest.

There we camped. The view from that campsite was remarkable. Below us, extending from the northwest around to the east, spread the Victoria Valley system. In the middle distance we could see Lake Vida clearly, and beyond it the individual peaks of the St John's Range, named from afar by the Western Party of Scott's *Terra Nova* Expedition in 1912. Far off to the northwest at the edge of the Polar Plateau we could make out the sheer and soaring curved face of Skew Peak (2537 metres). It was a remarkable view, for laid out before us was a complete cross section of the Transantarctic Mountains.

The following morning (December 28th) we headed straight upslope with rekindled enthusiasm, climbing the remaining 150 metres or so towards the range crest. The snow became deeper and we became wetter. Stops were brief, for otherwise our leather boots froze. We were climbing into a new environment, into a rather splendid (albeit chilly) new world. Boulders of cream and golden Beacon Sandstone became abundant in the scree. All was quite different from the drab valley-floor settings that we had trudged through the previous week, where we stared upwards at grey looming valley walls. On reaching the crest we seemed to be above everything, with vistas stretching in all directions. We ploughed on towards the southern side of the range and there took in the panorama of the Asgard Range, sweeping to both horizons. Very far to the east the faint profile of Mount Erebus could be made out.

There was no wind, all was still and silent, and we innocently camped on an exposed snowy sandstone platform, entirely devoid of shelter! Across the yawning gulf that indicated the hidden Wright Valley floor far below, we could make out considerable detail of the sandstone and dolerite peaks of the western Asgard Range. We could even identify, on the far side of the range, St Paul's Mountain and perhaps even Round Mountain, named by Scott's *Discovery* Expedition parties as they man-hauled up the Taylor Glacier to the Polar Plateau in 1902.

Next day (December 29th) was remarkable, with still conditions and brilliant sunshine under a vaulted deep blue sky. However snow was a very real problem as we trudged and floundered about the range crest seeking to understand the Beacon Sandstones. Useful rock exposures were minimal. And the range crest was nowhere near as platform-like as we had anticipated. Appreciable relief, snow-filled gullies and shallow cirques obstructed and slowed our traverses. We were delighted to be there, but we weren't achieving much geologically. And that night heavy cloud rolled in, visibility vanished and down came the snow.

For the whole of the 30th the snow continued and kept us tent-bound. We read, played cards and indulged as usual in sledge biscuits and chocolate. The calm conditions still persisted but visibility was really minimal, and that precluded both confident navigation and useful fieldwork. We were disappointed to say the least, and conscious that fuel was low. Furthermore we had no idea how long it would take to find the Upper Depot. So when the snow did let up a little, very early on the following morning, we broke camp and cautiously headed northwest through a gloomy cloud-draped landscape to the north side of the range. From there we dropped down long snowy screes into the unnamed valley separating the Insel and Olympus Ranges. Visibility improved and the amount of snow diminished the further we descended, and so near the valley floor we were able to pick a campsite and dump our gear in clear conditions. Then, unhindered by heavy packs, we sped down valley and around the corner into the col and back to the depot established by Dick and Colin. We quickly picked up more food and fuel, demolished a can of fruit and high-tailed it back to our new valley floor campsite. We were now becoming quite fit and moving about confidently, but our concern was that little of real geological significance had been achieved in the western Olympus Range over the last five days.

So came the New Year. The immediate priority was to return to the crest of the range and locate as quickly as possible the Upper Depot. Once that was done and we had an established base to work from, we'd be more confident about tackling the geology of the Beacon Sandstone. So in good weather we headed westwards along the valley floor for a couple of kilometres and then turned off and steadily climbed about 400 metres up to the snowy crest of the range. Continuing southwards we passed over the saddle between peaks 'b' and 'c' to reach the southern side, where we knew the depot to be. But its precise location was now the problem. From *King Pin*, Dick and Peter had cached the food and fuel in the middle of a prominent terrace just to the south of peak 'b'. It should be easy enough to find, we thought. However as we came through the saddle we could see a number of snow-mantled terraces that seemed to fit the bill, spread over a wide area! We ploughed up to and across several of the more promising pieces of real estate, but without success. Having been on the go with full packs for about ten hours, and not a little weary and disappointed, we settled for a charming campsite in the lee of huge tumbled blocks of golden Beacon Sandstone. The darned depot would have to wait until the morrow.

But that long hard day did have its own splendid reward. Amidst an almost tangible stillness, and with brilliant sunshine and that same vaulted deep blue sky, we took in a view we previously couldn't have imagined. To our right, a rock wall, perhaps 200 metres high, of sandstone capped by dolerite arced across to the Asgard Range and so effectively constituted the head of Wright Valley, abutting the Polar Plateau. Several icefalls draped the wall and at its base these coalesced to become the several-kilometres-long Wright Upper Glacier. From the top of the wall nearer its southern end, a broad undulating spine of sandstone and dolerite called Wright Valley Hill penetrated some kilometres further westwards before disappearing beneath the rising surface of the gleaming ice sheet. From beneath the terminus of the Wright Upper Glacier emerged a remarkable network of interlocking cliff-sided valleys cut in dolerite. These extended eastwards to merge below us with the whale-like ridge of the Dais. Both of us, knowing we were the first ever to observe this scene from the ground, gazed in silence for a long, long time.

Fig. 54. The Olympus Range Upper Depot. Mount Dido forms centre-right skyline, with bluffs of the mesa-like Mount Electra in the background. Southwest spur of Mount Boreas on right.

Fig. 55. Looking from the southern flank of the Olympus Range into the cliffed gullies of the Labyrinth. The Asgard Range forms the skyline.

Since leaving Lake Vanda communications with Dick and Colin had been poor or impossible most of the time. Either our two parties had been effectively isolated in separate deep valleys, or there was sunspot activity, or else heavy falling snow. In addition the radio batteries tended to weaken and fail in the lower temperatures, something which had not happened before. However, our growing sense of isolation was dissipated the next day by a really good radio sked to the others at the Lower Depot, more than 42 kilometres away. We felt we again had neighbours. We overcame the battery problem simply by taking turns to cosset them in our sleeping bags at night.

That day we located the Upper Depot within 58 minutes of leaving the campsite. Both the tea chests and the jerry can were partly buried by snow and it was the tattered Day-Glo flag that, while still far off, initially attracted our attention. Our relief was considerable. Confidence soared. We now had all the back-up we needed, in terms of food and fuel, to have a good crack at the Beacon Sandstone. Even before erecting the tent we celebrated with much laughter over a large tin of fruit and sledge biscuits heavily loaded with butter, honey, and jam. Life was very good.

Those next three days were magical. The weather held fine and we ventured far in all directions about the range crest. The thick snow cover continued to be a bother but if we dropped 100 metres or so off either side of the crest there were good exposures of the older horizons of the Beacon Sandstone. About the snowy crest a lacework of our intersecting tracks spread in many directions. At last we were getting somewhere, geologically speaking. However, the individual major peaks and mesas proved too steep to allow us to examine the younger Beacon strata. We accepted that, for neither of us wanted to risk a broken neck.

In addition to chasing the sandstones we were determined to sample right through the thick dolerite sill separating the basement granites from the overlying sedimentary strata. Accordingly on the north side of the range below peak 'a', we carefully picked, slid and scrambled our way 200 metres down a staircase ridge of the magnificently columnar dolerite until we reached its base. It seemed a long and somewhat daunting descent to us non-mountaineers. Once at the base we then slowly ascended with equal care, one person with the hammer belting off a sample every 20 metres and placing it into the pack carried by the other. The pack-carrier, with the aid of a Paulin aneroid barometer, called out the sampling intervals and entered the details in his notebook. Halfway up these roles were exchanged. By now, with heavy packs, it seemed even further going up than it had been going down. Eventually we got to the top and thankfully sat, yarning, taking in the view, and demolishing another two large cakes of chocolate.

Inevitably it became time to trudge back to camp and so we checked that both packs were of roughly equal weight, shouldered them, and bent to pick up the hammers for the return. But there was only one hammer! The consequent conversation was spirited and wide reaching but the controversy was never really solved. So we again carefully picked, slid and scrambled our way 200 metres down the staircase ridge. This time it seemed a yet longer and even more daunting descent. After retrieving the hammer, the final ascent was a rather silent one. Plodding slowly home into a freshening breeze, we agreed that some days were very much longer than others.

Next morning we awoke to a shrieking gale off the plateau, buffeting the tent broadside on, and to a world definitely closing in upon us. The tent's guys we'd simply secured by tying around boulders, none of which were in any way large.

Fig. 56. Peter playing hide-and-seek among massive fallen blocks of Beacon Sandstone.

Inevitably some of these started to drag and so our space gradually diminished between the wildly flapping walls. Outside the tent all was a howling white maelstrom in which visibility simply wasn't!

Our position was becoming untenable and by three p.m. it was clear we had to move, and move fast. The break-camp scheme adopted was for me to crawl outside and pass back into the tent the gear for Peter to pack. Half blinded by blowing snow, I groped and fumbled about in the blizzard locating the gear necessary for our retreat. I came across the small billy, half full and apparently frozen solid. Undeterred, I grabbed an ice axe and dealt several hearty whacks into the diminutive cryosphere. Only then did I discover the supposed ice block was more like thin sea ice. The generously punctured billy was never quite the same again. That it leaked copiously is a major understatement.

The struggle to pack continued until finally, enveloped in howling gale and swirling snow, we somehow managed to bundle up the tent and be off. The strength and direction of the gale forced us to travel north, and only north. The wind literally blew us up and over the southwest spur of peak 'b' and down into the valley beyond. With hoods up and begoggled, communications were restricted to signal thumps on shoulders, arm waving, and monosyllabic shouts. Swirling gusts of snow at times meant almost zero visibility, although directly overhead a blue sky and shining sun were just discernible.

We stumbled and lurched along the valley between peaks 'b' and 'c', still propelled by the funnelled wind. Several times the tent carrier (we took turns) was sent sprawling by particularly strong gusts and similarly we floundered many times into deep snow-filled depressions. However, conditions improved as we approached the northern side of the range and then slowly dropped down the long screes towards the valley floor. Above us spindrift continued streaming off the range. On the valley floor we thankfully dropped packs and, in still moderately windy conditions, made camp, and then in rapid succession several hot brews. It had all been quite a challenge.

Above us we knew the gale continued to howl across the range and very probably, we reasoned, also down into Wright Valley. That was a worry. Main Base had been unoccupied for eight days. Colin and Dick we knew to be far away, now almost across the Wright Lower Glacier and en route for Marble Point. We started to feel concern for the unattended tents at Vanda, and particularly for the safety of the meteorological records hung up and slowly drying inside those tents. Having experienced the violence of the gale our concern steadily grew.

There was nothing for it but to get back to those two tents and oversee the situation. So seven hours later, travelling via the col, we finally arrived with negligible pomp and circumstance back at the two wildly flapping tents. All was well, but that gale continued to lash the camp for two more days. Some wind blasts exceeded 50 knots and there was much blowing sand. We were kept tent-bound and took turns around the clock monitoring guy ropes and equipment, repairing gear and doing routine weather observations.

So ended the western Olympus Range enterprise. Ruefully we realized that although it had involved much activity and effort for ten days, the scientific return was modest. We had learned a major lesson. When working high, fair to good weather is absolutely essential. Down on the valley floors one can move about and achieve something useful even in inclement conditions, but not so in the ranges. High country data is not easily won. But we had had a great time!

CHAPTER 7

A trip to the seaside

Dick and I didn't know any of the details of the peregrinations of the other two, but they were sound, reliable people and we didn't worry. And we had our own tasks to accomplish. The readings one gained from the gravity meter, at two sites, told one the difference in the acceleration due to gravity between the two sites. In other words, I was merely measuring relative gravity. To convert these relative values into absolute values, which I needed for my traverse along the valley, at one of the sites I had to know the absolute value of gravity. Therefore our next task was to travel down the valley and cross the Wilson Piedmont Glacier to the coast, in order to make a linkage with the gravity station already established at Marble Point airstrip, the closest spot where the absolute value had been determined.

As we were going to a place of known elevation, namely sea level, if need be we could also use the trip to tie down the elevation of the occupied stations in our ground control survey. With economy of effort in mind (to save us from having to haul the surveying gear across the glaciers to the coast), I had asked Larry Harrington via radio if his surveyors had determined the elevation of the peak at the coastal end of the valley. He didn't answer that question first time, just apologized for intruding. So I asked again. 'Did you make a trigonometric determination of elevation? Can we use it to tie down elevations in our ground control network?' I guess that my Morse code wasn't up to scratch that day because his response was particularly useless: 'Anyone can use the data.' I said that, apart from that sort of thing, probably Larry was a very nice fellow. (He is.)

As we packed our bags for the trip to the local resort, Marble Point airstrip, we included the 21 kilograms of theodolite and tripod – we were sweating it to the coast, just to do the surveying from sea level at the coast to the mountains along Wright Valley – and it would all be unnecessary if Larry's people had already done it. Morse code was valuable but it didn't take the place of speech.

We were getting used to the ridiculous loads, 35 kilograms or more for each of us (and that was without the tent and things, which were along the valley where P. and B. had depoted them). However, that didn't make the loads any more sensible. In fact they were so absurd that we were somewhat hysterical, full of giggles and silly jokes as we packed. To discourage us, someone had left the valley door open; at noon the wind was blowing from the east at 11 knots; and by the time we were ready to leave, 3.20 p.m., the wind was up to 35 knots. At sea it would have been a gale. Here it was the usual sand-laden devastating storm, which we hated. By this time Dick's language had become particularly picturesque, such bits of it as I could hear through the wind. He had the tripod across the top of his pack, while I had a bundle of two-and-a-half-metre-long bamboos. We were both being twisted round like whirling dervishes. I wished that someone had told us to do this, because then we could have mutinied or rebelled, but it was all self-inflicted, and we were doing it all for fun!

For once I was no slower than Dick. We both spent too much energy cursing the wind and we merely oozed along the valley. We stopped in the dyke swarm after a couple of kilometres, for a piece of chocolate and a cigarette, merely to get out of the accursed wind. Dick complained that in addition to all the vicissitudes that I was suffering he also had to endure those from having changed into clean underclothes that morning. He missed the protective oils and greases. Reading the gravity meter was difficult indeed, and Dick had to be a windbreak for the instrument for me to have any chance of successfully reading it. 'This is quite horrible,' I thought, 'but in an hour we'll have passed the moraine by the col entrance, and we'll be able to see round the bend in the valley. It will all be new and different.' So I continued making my gravity stations every kilometre, 'fixing' every third or fourth one by magnetic compass, until we reached the bend.

Indeed the view from there was quite different, mainly with full views of the five hanging glaciers pushing halfway down the southern wall of the valley, but we looked at them through the same sand-filled eyes and we used the same swear words at the wind. And, damn it, the wind was stronger now and therefore so were the swear words. I wished I'd brought the hand anemometer, but it weighed a kilogram in its box! Here there weren't even decent boulders to sit on. Instead we sat on the sand, but then we had to get up again, camel-fashion. While we sat, we marvelled at the scale of everything and just how puny we were by comparison. The walking part was easy enough, lots of little ups and down as we crossed the dykes, but the sand and gravel that covered everything made for soft going.

Fig. 57. A seal with the upper surface eroded by wind-blown sand to expose the skeleton; a process estimated to require several hundred years.

Eventually we'd had enough of being blown to bits. I'd been walking down the middle of the valley, the windiest part, I'm sure, nominally in a straight line, for ease of locating the gravity stations. Because the stream also flowed in the middle of the valley, but not in a straight line, I crossed it perhaps 15 times during the day, a few times without getting my feet rewetted. Dick's diary description of the wind, our struggles, and his feelings, is quite poetic and decidedly unquotable. He did note that the south wall of the valley was less steep than the northern wall, and wondered why, since the geology on the two sides looked much the same. Why, come to that, was there a bend in the valley at all? As he said, 'We don't know nuffin.'

Again the sky was overcast on 30th December and it was still blowing strongly – we both guessed at 25 knots – from the coast. I didn't want another horror like yesterday, when our travelling conditions were so bad that I had very little confidence in the gravity readings we had made. Leaving the tent pitched, and carrying just the gravimeter, I returned to the last reliable station, back more than six kilometres below the col, while noble Dick carried the theodolite and tripod and other temporarily unwanted gear, 30 kilograms or more, another 11 kilometres or so down the valley. This, as ever, was into the teeth of a blizzard that penetrated every crack on his clothing, including his buttonless fly, in those pre-zip days.

On his way back he found four previously undiscovered seals and a happy bunch of red lichen. Of course he duly investigated them all, so from his point of view (as well as mine) his portage time was not wasted. In the blustery wind, I was very careful with the gravity readings, so that each one took up to 15 minutes, rather than the usual two minutes that they took in calm conditions. The distance back to the col looked like a kilometre. Instead it was seven kilometres or so, but with the wind behind me it was almost pleasant.

Returning, I stopped at the tent for a cup of instant coffee, and then continued along the valley eastwards, lugging the gravimeter along. It was easy walking; underfoot was either sand or shingle, disrupted only by the edges of the continual blanket of frost polygons. Very occasionally in this area the edges of the polygons were made of coarser particles, seldom more than a few centimetres high. But over huge areas they were 'the other way round', with the boundaries, up to two metres wide, of fine material, and coarser rocks in the middle. The boundaries of fine material were a few centimetres lower than the rest of the polygons. Over the following decades competent geomorphologists had a great time attempting to work out why.

I was still trying to walk in a straight line, for ease of mapping the gravity stations. At one meander of the stream (Why don't we give it a name?) I stepped into ten centimetres of water and 20 centimetres of mud, and got both feet wet.

I defy anyone to walk by those hanging glaciers without making as close an inspection as time will allow. My gravity survey straight line took me to the point where the stream cut into the outermost terminal moraine of what we learned later was called Meserve Glacier, a very handy spot to dump my pack while I had a closer look. The glacier, just a few kilometres long altogether, originated in a shallow cirque basin between two not-very-prominent peaks in the mountain range. From the valley bottom I couldn't see into the cirque. In fact the highest I could see was where the glacier spilled over the shoulder and started down towards the valley. Up there, on the shoulder, the eastern edge of the glacier was not very steep, but within a few hundred metres of its journey down towards the valley bottom, the side of the glacier became a cliff, which gradually increased in height until it reached perhaps 20 metres at the pointed snout.

The west side looked just the same. There wasn't much debris ice around the glacier edge and I concluded it must be moving very slowly indeed. On the east side there were four lateral moraines, fairly clearly discernible. The outermost one was nearly a kilometre away from the glacier edge, and stood above the general level by only a few feet. It continued down to the valley bottom where I had left my pack. When that moraine was deposited, the glacier was about three times as wide as at present, but only a kilometre or so longer. In that outermost moraine all of the boulders had been worn down to surface level. Incredible as it seemed, the boulders had been completely disintegrated by the wind-blown sand. Here and there were flat bits of basaltic lava, which looked out of place. It didn't occur to me to collect any of those volcanic rocks – I would have had to carry them anyway – but a few years later somebody did and found a radiometric age of three million years. At that time, back in 1958, I just wondered how long the wind had taken to wear down the boulders.

The lateral moraines closer to the glacier had progressively 'fresher' boulders until, at the edge of the glacier, they looked as though they had been deposited last week; some of them even had fairly sharp edges and corners. Droplets of water showered off the cliff to maintain a minuscule rivulet flowing down to the valley bottom to join the stream. With my ice axe I dug a shallow hole or two, to find that the weathering didn't go far beneath the surface, but the fine material looked approximately like soil. In my enervated state, I wondered if we could put a glass dome over the whole valley, with doors at the ends to keep the wind out, and raise sheep. (A few years later a colleague took some of the 'soil' and grew perfectly good grass in it, so I reckon my hallucination wasn't so mad after all.)

Seen from the side, the step-like surface of the glacier was most intriguing. Obviously I couldn't climb the cliff, and anyway Dick must have been wondering where I was. But the whole glacier was completely engrossing and I resolved, then and there, to come back sometime to investigate and perhaps fully understand it.

I finally made it back to Meserve Glacier in 1965–66, 1966–67 and 1967–68, in the company of my New Zealand PhD student and friend, Gerry Holdsworth, and many other fine young people. We dug tunnels over 150 metres long along the base of the glacier, with lots of side tunnels and holes from the top surface to the tunnel, and 'instrumented the heck out of them'. Gerry managed to work out the flow law of cold ice, to discover why the cliff was only 20 metres high, and many other fascinating things. But that all is a different story for a different time.

The following couple of days moving along the valley were so full of new country and new experiences that they were exhausting by themselves, let alone with lugging those ridiculous loads in those outrageous winds. New Year's Eve 1958 I spent continuing the gravity survey for a few stations beyond the easternmost of the hanging, or alpine, glaciers. Down at that

Fig. 58. Patterned ground, middle of Wright Valley, near Meserve Glacier.

Fig. 59. Meserve Glacier, from a low-flying helicopter.

Fig. 60. Outermost lateral moraine, east side of the Meserve Glacier. Note that the boulders are worn down to surface level.

Fig. 61. Innermost lateral moraine, east side of the Meserve Glacier. Most of the boulders are still fully upstanding.

end of the valley the pattern of moraines was complex indeed. Deep heaps of moraine, more than 50 metres high, were spread out on both sides of the valley, and terminal moraines cut right across, all evidently deposited by an extended version of the Wright Lower Glacier, discharging from a thicker piedmont. At one spot the still-nameless stream had cut a 'canyon' perhaps three metres deep through the moraine but I felt I didn't have time to examine the revealed section in any detail.

Dick in the meantime again took the theodolite and tripod ahead, and continued on for 11 kilometres, less severely wind abraded than usual, to the Lower Depot, where he liberated some goodies for our ceremonial midnight dinner.

The country is huge – real he-man country, as I've said. (Dick asked, 'What am I doing here?') On his return journey from the Lower Depot he dropped off a tin of pineapple, halfway along. And it was one a.m. before he reached the tent, with tins of peaches, peas, jam and corned beef. Dick was utterly exhausted – usually my prerogative – and dropped off to sleep while I finished making dinner. In my diary I noted that the peaches were divine. We really did relish those dinners in the tent – a wonderful respite from the horrible sandblasting.

Dick's account of this is all interestingly different. He wrote:

> At the chosen campsite near a small hillock we had a cup of tea and I set off about 6.15 pm to portage the theodolite and tripod and a bit of unwanted gear to the depot near the Wilson Piedmont Glacier, promising to get back by 2000 hours for tea. I hadn't been on the helicopter flight to place the depot and neither of us had a clear idea how far away the depot lay. I had only a rough sketch to guide me and little idea of the terrain but it was New Year's Eve and I was driven on by the thought of the food goodies in the two tea chests flagged with a small bamboo flag. It was about 1945 hours before I spotted the flag. Once there I devoured a can of fruit, placed others in my pack and grabbed a new book or two from the tea chest.
>
> I hurried back, conscious that I was beyond my nominated return-time, but on the way I cached and flagged the odd tin of fruit to be discovered for consumption next day.
>
> When I got back to the campsite at about 0100 hours I found the tent pitched and Colin up the adjacent hill looking for me up the valley. When we crawled into the tent for the by-now-overcooked dinner I remember being miffed when Colin scolded me for not rolling up the tent cords in the approved manner the last time I packed the tent. However, the first meal of the New Year was marvellous – with cold tinned fruit for dessert.

We seldom had matters of great importance to discuss over the radio, but the radios were obviously worthwhile for insurance – and they worked remarkably well. On New Year's Eve, Peter and Barrie reported that they had retreated to the campsite in Bull Pass, forced down by shortage of food and with 60 centimetres of snow covering nearly every rock in sight. They were headed north to look at the unvisited valley on the north side of the western half of the range north of Wright Valley. (After the expedition was over the New Zealand Geographic Board, of which Arthur Helm was the Secretary, invited the four of us to select one feature each to be named for ourselves. We all sat down in a room in the Geology Department and wrote our first-choice features, in secret, on bits of paper. All of us selected the same feature, the superb peak on the south side of the valley that was marked on the rough map as Peak 105. We decided no one should have it, but instead (later) called it Mount Odin and the range Asgard, the home of the Viking gods. And so we all tried again. Barrie selected that valley. It's now McKelvey Valley. There's also a Barwick Valley, a Webb Glacier, and I've already mentioned Bull Pass.)

Peter Yeates, at Scott Base, could hear us loud and clear so we all had a little chat, except Dick, who had dropped off again. We didn't have anything important to tell Peter, except to ask that he send any mail for us over to Marble Point, and we learned that if we could get to the US station by 5th January we might be able to send mail back to New Zealand on a plane leaving on 6th January.

On New Year's Day we reached the Lower Depot, having encountered a surprising tin of pineapple on the way, where we stopped for lunch. The depot was just as we had left it – the fibreglass sledge, a couple of tea chests with Maurice Speary's 'gifts' (frozen chicken stews and cans of fruit) piled up around them, the can of kerosene – all at the top of a small moraine, not far from the lake surrounding the edge of the glacier. We pitched the tent on a flattish area nearby and had another great dinner – tinned salmon, the penultimate of Maurice's chicken stews (saving the last for when we returned from the coast), stewed fruit, and New Zealand blue vein cheese, courtesy of that kind man at the Dairy Products Marketing Commission in Hastings to whom I had written asking for tins of butter. Dick said that apart from the company it was the best New Year's dinner he could remember, but he did suggest that I give up trying to be a scientist and just stick to begging food! We collected seven days worth of food – three days for crossing the Piedmont, one day on the other side (I think we were anticipating being invited out at the local restaurant), and three days back; 14 kilograms in all. 'Esmeralda' (Dick's name for the fibreglass sledge – he really did have an entertaining imagination, and he said that the sledge needed some distinguishing feature, to give it character!) was another 14 kilograms or so, making more than 100 kilograms in total – a monstrous load and obviously way beyond our ability to carry.

Fig. 62. Grass grown indoors at US station on soil from dry valley.

Fig. 63. Moraines in eastern end of Wright Valley, deposited by an enlarged ancestor of the Wright Lower Glacier.

Fuel was going to be our problem. Somehow we could only find a one-litre polythene bottle for kerosene, so Dick tried to make another container with a filled plastic bag, well closed with rubber bands, inside another plastic bag, inside another, and that inside an empty pemmican tin, which was to be kept upright until the fuel was all used up, or the sledge fell over.

On 2nd January 1959, unladen, we reconnoitred a route across the frozen lake to the steep but manageable end of the glacier, across a great mixture of ice, snow, silt and fine gravel. (We'd called the lake Wright Lake, but later it was renamed Lake Brownworth, for the fellow who did the aerial photography of the valley.) It was difficult to discern where the glacier ended and the moraine began – and that was just fine with us. We were lucky enough to find a main road of sorts with firm frozen snow from the end of the dirty stuff. We thought, after walking a kilometre or so, that this was as good a route as we were likely to find.

We returned to the depot site and packed up a first load, which in my case included Esmeralda, strapped across the top of the rucksack. By now, in the late evening, the wind had dropped from bestial to just positively infuriating, twisting Esmeralda and me like a puppet on a string. I had my crampons and had no difficulty with the lake ice but Dick's were somewhere else and he was having big trouble. In the end I pulled his pack at the end of a nylon line to the edge of the glacier. Fortunately I only had to carry Esmeralda for three kilometres, until we had reached the flattish part of the glacier, where it looked as though we might be able to sledge with the sledge, instead of carrying it. We unloaded everything, marked the site with a couple of flags, scampered back to the tent, and went to bed, quite exhausted.

Crossing the Wilson Piedmont Glacier was not as difficult as I had worried it might be. After the first few kilometres the surface was fairly flat, with just enough topography in the form of gentle rises, depressions and shallow streams to make it interesting. Most of the streams were covered with a few centimetres of ice, which sometimes broke underfoot and sometimes didn't. Although we hadn't seen a crevasse (the helicopter pilot said he had seen lots, but wasn't sure where) Dick, the lighter man, pulled on a longer harness than I did, just in case. I carried the gravity meter in my rucksack but everything else went on the sledge, and we found we could just about manage to keep it moving. To avoid the small ice hills and gullies Dick naturally kept changing direction, so that, equally naturally, I kept becoming entangled with his trace. Being separated we talked little, but each silently considered whether Dick was more inconsiderate (by changing direction) or Colin was more intolerant.

Fig. 64. Much-ablated terminus of Wright Lower Glacier.

The surface came in four varieties. Much of it was ice, either avoidable bumps up to a metre high, or fairly flat but cut by wind, water and sun into cusps just ten centimetres high. The rest was snow, either hard, which was good to walk on, or slushy – but fortunately not too deep – which was horrible to walk on and even worse to pull the sledge across.

Around six p.m. we experienced a minor phenomenon, the only time I've met it in Antarctica. However, I felt it once when we were surveying our way across the Greenland Ice Sheet. Then, in 1953, we called it a 'firnquake'. We heard a 'whooshing' sound that could have been a sudden expulsion of air from the snow surface, and the source seemed to move for a long distance across the surface. Dick thought it was the sound of a snow-bridge collapsing into a crevasse – but I stuck to the notion that it was the sudden sinking, or compaction, of semi-compacted snow, or firn. In Greenland our survey team heard it when we were about 100 kilometres east of our central ice sheet station, Northice, where the same quake was recorded by little 'blips' on the charts of the recording barograph and thermograph. On the Wilson Piedmont Glacier we merely continued to pull the blasted sledge.

We stopped at eight p.m. for our radio contact. Barrie and Peter had at last found the Upper Depot and contact with them and with Scott Base was very good. I sent an impromptu telegram to Gillian, which included 'lovely weather', as it was then, but very shortly afterwards a great layer of low stratus cloud started rolling across the Piedmont. First it obscured Mount Erebus, 110 kilometres away, by which we had been steering, and then Speary's Knob, five kilometres away, at the south side of the Piedmont, also disappeared. (We wanted to name this handsome little peak for our friendly and helpful cook at Scott Base, but unfortunately the name did not survive the hatchet work of the official place-names committee. However, the committee did accept our alternative name, King Pin Nunatak, named for the helicopter.)

Our route over the glacier was incredibly tortuous, as we (that is Dick, since he was in front) kept changing direction to avoid bumps and hollows, soggy spots and occasional small boulders. As long as we could see Erebus this was fine, but with Erebus cloud-shrouded we would have to keep our general direction by magnetic compass, which would have been an unbearably slow process. Being lazy and tired we quit soon afterwards and camped, sleeping on our pack frames, however uncomfortable, rather than on the cold snow. We'd only travelled a little more than eight kilometres, but it was a difficult part of the journey.

The next day's work (4th January 1959) was one of the hardest that I can recall. It was calm, sunny most of the time, and pretty warm, 2–5°C. For a couple of kilometres the going was moderate, but then we hit the rough ice coming down from Mount Newall, and that was distinctly unpleasant. Dobbin, the lead horse – previously known as Dick – was, in my judgment, still wandering all around the kingdom, tripping me up (deliberately?), while I either had to go back to heave the sodding sledge over some excrescence, up to my knees in wet snow, while trying to keep the gravity meter approximately upright, or had to wipe the sweat from my snow goggles. My shirt was sopping wet with sweat, too.

Eventually we reached the end of this rough stretch and in front of us lay an unbroken snowfield, stretching, it seemed, to the coast. Simple! Or at least it would have been if we had had skis and didn't have to haul that sledge. As it was, in boots, with a seemingly self-willed sledge, I stayed on the surface about one step in five and for the others stepped into wet snow foot-, calf-, knee- or occasionally thigh-deep. By now the sun had been blistering hot for several hours and both of us were growing more and more evil tempered, so, while I did a gravity reading, Dick scouted round and found some water and we made a brew-up of tea.

Feeling much better for that but disappointed that the Barwick-patented kerosene container was leaking – what else did we expect? (We admitted defeat and poured the rest into the tubes of Dick's rucksack, diluting the residual Drambuie) – we continued towards Marble Point. After all that's where Marble Point airstrip should be, isn't it? Wrong! After another stint of this foul-language-inducing surface, we gave up and camped, promising that we'd get up early, when the surface would be harder.

Well we did get up earlier and the glacier surface was a bit harder. After the first episode of sledge pulling, the surface was also growing steeper and steeper, as we neared the edge of the Wilson Piedmont Glacier. A helicopter flew past a few hundred metres ahead of us at a very low altitude, heading for the Marble Point US airstrip (at Gneiss Point!) and apparently away from Taylor Valley to the south. We were surprised the pilot hadn't noticed our contrasting black figures on the ice. A pillar of smoke rose in the direction we thought the airfield lay. About two hours later we speculated on possible reasons for the smoke when a Neptune aircraft appeared to be making repeated photographic runs over the airstrip, and later we saw two helicopters flying low over the sea ice to McMurdo. When we arrived at the airstrip we learned the reason for all this activity: there had been a plane crash. Many years later Dick learned that Larry Harrington had been aboard one of the rescue 'choppers'.

The slope increased and I went to the back of the sledge to restrain it while Dick pulled gently on a double rope, in case of crevasses. Eventually Marble Point appeared over the edge of the ice and slightly to the left, and then, 40 metres ahead, we saw that the ice ended in an ice cliff, 50 metres high or more. And no sign of any airstrip or buildings! Damn and blast the whole stupid set up! Let's go home!

But yesterday we had seen one of the helicopters land somewhere in that vicinity. We, like Marble Point, were near the southern limit of the Piedmont. From the airplane, a month ago, we thought we had seen that the cliff continued along the entire front to the north. Better to go south. Which we did, for two and a half hours along the ice edge, until we came across a fairly easy gully between the Piedmont and Hogback, the moderately sized mountain that marked the southern end of the Piedmont Glacier.

Down the gully we trotted, controlling the sledge with difficulty, but taking it all the way down, to the snow-covered solid ground. We pulled northwards, close, but not too close, to the cliff, until we reached a spot that I thought was about on the same line as we had been following on the ice, and I made a gravity reading there while Dick put up the tent. It was 11.30 p.m. so we had made about 200 metres of progress in the last four hours. Sixteen hours and 25 twisted kilometres and we didn't have enough energy left to traipse the hour or so up to the US base, creature comforts or not! But we had made it to our seaside lodging, and only a huge stone's throw from the sea-ice covered beach.

Fig. 65. Colin reading gravimeter on Wilson Piedmont Glacier.

In the morning, as we walked that last stretch to the US base, we noted that, as usual, we had excelled ourselves and had hit the edge of the ice in the worst possible place. On the Piedmont, if we had aimed three kilometres further south of where we did scramble down, or two or three or six kilometres further north, we could just have walked off the glacier.

Close to the station we passed a moderately sized melt-water stream, across which some wit had built a two-holer outhouse, which we patronized. Inside was a painted sign: 'THE SOUTHERNMOST FLUSHING W.C. IN THE WHOLE WORLD'. I took its photo to send to my father, who was a sanitary inspector in Herefordshire, England.

Dick's description of our arrival at our seaside lodgings runs like this:

> It was a bleak overcast day when we arrived at the neatly ordered array of Quonset huts adjacent to the airstrip. We wandered around looking for signs of life. Eventually a guy came out of one of the huts. On seeing us he reeled back with the query 'Where the hell did you come from?' We gestured vaguely in the direction of the mountainous hinterland, and his next words were 'I'll get the Commander.' He retreated inside to return with an officer who reached out a hand. As he shook my hand he circled around me until I was down-wind with the words 'Guess you boys would like a shower.' I realized Colin and I couldn't even smell each other. We then retreated out of the cold into the stuffy heat of the mess room. After all we had been in the field for a month, washless except for Colin's perfunctory Christmas splash.

We arrived too late for lunch and had to make do with steak (fried country fashion), corn, broad (fava) beans, mashed potatoes and gravy, followed by guavas, real bread and coffee. Marvellous! Eight of the 40 inhabitants (all hand-picked from 160 volunteers, we were told) came to talk to us. Jerry Whitehurst, the met man, compared the weather at Gneiss Point (which is where we were, not Marble Point) with ours, 60 kilometres or so inland. They never had a westerly wind, and none of our interesting high temperatures. Jerry, Lieutenant Commander Feinmann (the CO), Lieutenant Surko (Second in Command), the cook, a gentle-voiced chap named Elder and the first Afro-American with whom I'd ever had a long conversation, and a couple of others were all most interested in us and what we were doing.

They were just amazed that we had walked across the Piedmont, especially when we described the conditions underfoot. Why not by Sno-Cat? Or helicopter? The CO had a bright idea and walked outside, without saying anything. The rest of us followed him and shortly he reappeared from the storage Quonset hut (there were five such huts altogether, and a large orange wooden building) with two pairs of brand-new snowshoes, which he presented to us for our journey back.

Fig. 66. Our seaside home. Tent on coastal side of Wilson Piedmont Glacier, near Marble Point. The coastal face of the glacier is about 60 metres high.

Fig. 67. 'The Southernmost Flushing W.C. in the Whole World.'

The US Navy had invested quite a lot of effort into the area. They wanted to make an 'all-weather, all-season' runway, to service the McMurdo base, and felt that the flattish land between the Wilson Piedmont Glacier and the coast would be very suitable. During the 1957–58 summer the whole area had been very carefully 'geologized' by Bob Nichols from Tufts College and his students, and had also been surveyed. Lieutenant Surko dug out the survey data, and I was immensely pleased to see that it included a baseline near the coast and sight lines from two coastal stations onto Hogback and a few other peaks inland. We'd just saved ourselves at least a day's work.

We noticed that, even when we were outside, everyone was still standing upwind from us and somebody else asked whether we would like a shower – which I did just as soon as I had done the gravity linkage to the spot, a kilometre or so away, where gravity had been measured the previous year. Now I could make my 'relative' gravity measurements into absolute ones. Most of the heavy equipment used for making the airstrip in 1957 had been taken away, but the met man, the only one who knew where the gravity station was, offered to give the gravity meter and me a ride there in a jeep. On the way there he explained that the airstrip had not proved to be very useful because frost heaving was continually breaking up the runway. On the previous day, he also explained, they had had a fatal crash. An Otter had taken off, climbed to 25 metres or so, and then had side-slipped into the ground, killing both pilots: Harvey Gardner and Lawrence Farrell. When this happened, I calculated, Dick and I were approaching the edge of the glacier and had seen the plume of smoke, the rescue helicopters and the Neptune. Very sad.

After our showers we washed and put into the electric dryer nearly all of our clothes, retiring to a six-bunk cabin to read our most welcome mail as they dried. Talk about luxury! Dressed again, I felt uncomfortably itchy – the effect of undesirably clean clothes, Dick explained. Then I spent half an hour working out an approximate cross-section of the Piedmont, which had a maximum ice thickness of about 250 metres. Dick and I then composed a long cable to Bob Clark telling him of this result; also that we had found more than 50 seals, of which Dick had examined 26 fairly closely, had completed the first half of the gravity survey, and had made six survey stations (I must have adopted the two coastal US stations), and that his students, Peter and Barrie, were working hard and were very polite, usually.

We had taken our little one-mouse-power tent radio to the US base and, while drinking a cup of coffee, said to all and sundry that we were going outside to make our usual daily contact with Scott Base and to send the cable to Bob. The radio operator at the station, who happened to be in the mess room, averred we had no hope of getting a message through, for radio conditions were so bad he hadn't been able to talk to McMurdo for some days. He looked on in amazement when, once outside, we stretched our little dipole antenna between an ice axe and a stray packing case and connected it to our Collier and Beale valve-driven walkie-talkie. When we immediately got a clear connection with Scott Base he asked 'What the hell have you got in that box?' Those were the days before transistors and his amazement grew when we told him that our signal was about '0.2 of a watt'. Kiwi technology had the upper hand it seemed. Quite a contrast to his 200-watt transmitter and a formidable aerial array! Perhaps our weak signal was skipping across the ground to McMurdo while he was driving his 200 watts out into a magnetically disturbed ionosphere.

Dinnertime at six p.m. was also breakfast time for the second shift – everyone was on duty for 12 hours each day, seven days a week, so we had the opportunity to meet the other members of the station. Everyone was interested in what we were doing, and Dick found someone who was really intrigued with his seal studies. We signed the visitor's book and delighted in adding 'Your only visitors who arrived on foot!' After dinner we watched the beginning of a movie. It was excruciatingly bad and, despite the hard chair, I slept through most of it. This was just as well, for the cabin to which we had been assigned was very hot and there we both slept badly.

Breakfast was early, leisurely and full of cholesterol, although in those days we couldn't even spell the word. Eventually our audience decided they should go to work, so we did the same. In leisurely fashion, we went over and reoccupied two of the US survey stations, mainly to remeasure the vertical angles to Hogback and a few other peaks. Somehow we made the job last all day, a luxury to which we weren't accustomed, and then we walked back to the mess room for conversation and coffee.

The movie that night was *The Sign of the Pagan*. It was another real loser and so was the projector, which ran at about half speed, so the voices were only marginally intelligible. Not that they said anything intelligent! Still, the most impressive feature of the whole performance was the response of the audience. There was barely a murmur; no ribald remarks, and no guffaws, not even an emphasized groan. How different from the behaviour of a Scott Base audience to a similar event. Still, and especially in retrospect, it was all good fun, and after a shared beer we went to bed in our much-too-hot cabin.

On the following day, January 7th, in an 18-hour stint, we managed to do everything else we needed to do on that side of the glacier. It went like this: 0550. Get out of bed. Dress.

0600. Have breakfast: fruit salad, steak, fried potatoes, and coffee.

0645. Inspect the southernmost flushing W.C. in the whole world.

0655. Wake up.

0700. Check aneroid altimeter pressure against station barometer, and continue discussion of local climate with Jerry Whitehurst, the met man.

0730. Cup of coffee and farewells to CO and everyone else. Decline most of the goodies being thrust at us, eventually accepting two tins of shrimp, 100 Camel cigarettes, two small tins of fruit juice crystals, three tins of sardines and, of course, the snowshoes. They really were a generous crowd.

0800. Repeat farewells and depart. Walk to one of the survey stations we had occupied the previous day. Tie flags on survey station marker so that we can see it from Hogback.

0900. String aerial of little radio on bamboos. Talk with Barrie, who said they were back at Main Base, having been blown out of Upper Depot, with winds exceeding (guess) 50 knots.

0920. Leave Dick to flag other local survey station and ends of baseline while I return with gravity meter to tent to continue traverse to coast.

1030. Reach tent. Peckish. Snack of shrimp on 'ceramic tile'. Repeat gravity reading.

1045. Start towards coast, which looks half a kilometre away.

1200. Reach coast. Four kilometres. Three gravity stations. Nearly tread on skua nest with two fluffy chicks. Vigorously attacked by parent. Hit on head, fortunately not by beak. Erect two bamboos vertically on sides of rucksack to deter further aggressive acts by skuas.

1300. Reach tent. Very hot and sweaty. Wish I had brought shorts. Help Dick with tent packing, intermittently snacking on sardines and those indestructible biscuits. Quick cuppa.

1515. Leave. Sledge load as gargantuan as ever. Snowshoes on top, along with tripod and tent, feet soaked crossing stream. Still flaming hot in the sun. Laboriously haul sledge up gully between Piedmont and Hogback.

1700. Reach end of gully. Cigarette, American. Too strong.

1720. Start up Hogback, 750 metres. Usual agony caused by trying to overcome gravity, but fairly easy climb. Calm; incredibly hot. Sweating like a stuck pig. Shirt soaked.

1905. Reach top. Good views all round.

1910. Put up tripod. Level theodolite.

1912. Wind starting, gently at first but up to 15 knots within minutes. Put on anorak immediately. Barwick constructs windbreak for himself.

2135. Blowing quite strongly. Frozen stiff. Teeth chattering. Finish angles. Dick takes two rounds of photographs from tripod, one every 30°, as usual.

(We could see a storm moving across the Olympus Range 75 kilometres away. This was the storm that had driven P. and B. into retreating to Main Base, as their camp faced near-destruction. The gale was strong enough to pick them up and upend their ice-covered bodies, even though their packs were heavy with rocks.)

2145. Wind ceases. Curse our luck. Pack theodolite. Start down.

2230. Reach sledge. Pull it 400 metres to flatter area. Erect tent.

2350. Start eating.

0100. (8th January, 1959) Approximately clean dishes and go to bed.

0101. Sleep.

CHAPTER 8

And the walk back 'home' again

Well, that was our trip to the seaside. They didn't have any Marble Point Rock, sticky taffy, or even postcards. We hadn't had a swim, or even a paddle. In fact we hadn't seen any seawater in a liquid state. The natives all spoke peculiarly but they were just as kind, generous and helpful as they could be. Perhaps we'd come back another summer, but in the meantime it would be nice to get back home.

Most of the next day was devoted to education – ours! We spent far too long devising a method of attaching the snowshoes to our boots. Although the snowshoes were brand new they did not have straps; we used those from our crampons. They weren't long enough. The snowshoes fell off within five paces. We added bits of nylon cord from the tent guys. The snowshoes fell off within five paces. We added the auxiliary straps from our rucksacks. Left snowshoe fell off in five paces. Right one in ten. The snowshoes were one and a half metres long and 25 centimetres broad (they were 'Yukon' snowshoes), so that simultaneously with our 'attachment lessons and exercises' we were also learning how to walk, or at least to put one foot, with snowshoe attached, in front of the other – and not on top of the other. To do this, one needs to learn how to disarticulate one's hips, and move one's feet, still with snowshoes attached, in semi-circles. Unfortunately two other factors were working against us. Firstly, the snowshoes came without an instruction manual, and secondly, we found that some idiot had attached a heavy sledge to us.

Nevertheless travel was a bit easier than on our outward journey. When we had eventually passed the remedial snowshoeing exam we found we could stay on the surface for a greater part of the time; I didn't have to count steps and estimate distances for the gravity stations; and the wind was behind us. The wind was only moderate and the day was warm, 3°C, and sunny. I was making full use of my subcutaneous fatty layer of insulating material and was wearing only an open shirt with rolled up sleeves, while scrawny Dick had on a balaclava hat, a thick New Zealand tartan shirt, pullover, anorak and gloves, most of the time.

Our speed was controlled almost entirely by our growing ability to keep our legs apart and avoid stepping on the other showshoe and, after we had traversed the very soft snow close to Speary's Knob (where our snowshoes, very inconveniently, tried to travel several centimetres under the surface) and then the rough ice from Mount Newall, we progressed at perhaps three kilometres per hour. We pulled for 50 minutes and then sat on the sledge for up to ten. At the US station Dick had liberated a one-litre bottle, with screw top, which we'd filled with water at breakfast and refilled with snow, as required. It was a godsend.

By the late afternoon we had become accustomed to our conditions and the very slowly changing scenery to the extent that I started a mental list of improvements we could make to the snowshoes. My list started with a simple marine magnetic compass on the tip of one snowshoe, and continued with a crevasse detector and then a television set (this in 1959). Dick said he was working on a motorized track attachment.

In the evening it grew windier so I had to put on a pullover. Dick kicked me, inadvertently he said, on the ankle, which hurt. When I complained he offered to shoot me. We decided it was time to camp.

Our second day on the glacier was one of brilliant sunshine and no wind. The surface was very soft indeed and we really were grateful for our snowshoes, however inelegant they made our progress. Towards the end of the day we found our outgoing tracks and followed them back down the very steep and broken part of the glacier, where I, in crampons now, acted as brake to the sledge, down to the castellated arena, where we again left the sledge and the non-essential stuff to be collected on the following day. The ice on the edge of the lake had melted back considerably, and we had to wade more than knee deep to reach the firm ice. At the Lower Depot we again camped, and for dinner ate the last of Maurice's no-longer-frozen chicken stews. It was great and I got the wishbone.

The following day the only useful act we achieved was to collect the sledge and the rest of the gear from the dump near the end of the glacier. The sledge floated well on the thawed moat of the lake but we, now wading thigh deep to reach the firm ice, didn't like being ice-breakers. Otherwise we drank large quantities of coffee, had a little nap in the afternoon, did a few gravity calculations and sorted out the food for our return trip to Base. We included a heap of goodies, on the grounds that if we didn't eat them someone else would, tidied up the depot, and read. I was still working on

Fig. 68. Dick on snowshoes pulling 'Esmeralda', the fibreglass sledge, on Wilson Piedmont Glacier.

Fig. 69. Colin, much too hot for comfort, pulling 'Esmeralda' on Wilson Piedmont Glacier.

Fig. 70. Sastrugi encountered near Speary's Knob on the Wilson Piedmont Glacier.

Fig. 71. Dick paddling in Wright Lake.

The Adventures of John P. Wetherall, a sailor during the Napoleonic Wars, while Dick was reading John Masters's *Bugles and a Tiger,* from which he insisted on reading aloud the more salacious parts. We went to bed early with the tent door open because the tent was so hot.

And that lazy day was more profitable than the following day, when we walked 28 kilometres (through very interesting country I will admit), climbed up and down a total of 3300 metres, and all we accomplished was that Dick found some lichen growing on granite at nearly 1800 metres. We left the tent and all of our clobber at the Lower Depot, so that at least we were comparatively lightly laden. Well, the waste of this day and the following one was entirely Barwick's fault, as you'll see. To start with he didn't tell me it was a Sunday. I would have known better than to try to make a survey station on a Sunday on a 1829-metre peak with a name like 'Philosopher's Peak'. (The New Zealand Geographic Board did a hatchet job on that one, too. Now it is Mount Theseus.)

We started off at the crack of dawn, well nine a.m., on a brilliantly sunny, cloudless, nearly calm day. Dick went steaming ahead as usual, while I stopped every now and then to sketch the moraine patterns and to catch my breath. Intruding the granite on the north side of Wright Valley, for several kilometres east of the col, there is the same dolerite sheet as west of the col; several hundred metres thick, the lowest layers being at about 1000 metres' elevation. The dolerite forms a nearly vertical cliff, and the direct route up to Philosopher's Peak was not the sort of thing to excite lowlanders like Barwick and Bull, with or without theodolite and tripod. Fortunately the dolerite doesn't continue all the way to the east, so about eight kilometres from the Lower Depot, where we had left our tent, we started gently upwards on a long slow grind, on nicely decaying granite, and reached 1200 metres without having to use our hands at all, except to get up from our periodic rests. A few clouds were blowing up in the south and it was getting windier. At lunchtime, two p.m., we were at about 1500 metres and there were clouds in the north, too, obscuring the peaks. We might as well go back down. On the other hand, the going was easy. So we might as well go on, even if only to take the theodolite and tripod a bit higher.

Close to the peak we met the snowfield. It covered the ridge that was the next part of our route. The ridge started within inches of the sheer dolerite 150-metre cliff above the Wright Valley and, very narrow, continued off to the north. One side was the cliff over Wright Valley and the other side plunged down to the northeast and into the cirque holding the upper part of a moderate-sized northeast-flowing glacier that we later named for Bob Clark. We told him that we thought of him as soon as we saw the fat, smooth, decaying nature of the glacier – but in fact it was quite a handsome piece of ice. Near the terminus it divided into two lobes, one heading southerly towards Wright Valley, and the other northerly, towards Victoria Valley. Altogether it looked as though it offered an easy route through the Olympus Range.

The wind was rising and one look at the several-hundred-metre ridge stretching before us, combined with the slowly dawning truth that (although we had our ice-axe 'walking sticks' as usual) we had left our crampons and climbing rope behind at camp, made us stop and think. Dick said that only a bloody fool would tackle the ridge without proper gear, and besides, the Americans were responsible for air-sea rescue and national pride dictated that no true Kiwi would wish to cause an international incident. Well, I wasn't a true Kiwi but I didn't like the ridge much either. I thought there was a 99.97% chance that we would make it without trouble across the ridge but all the peaks, including Philosopher's Peak, were by now socked in, so there was no point.

Furthermore I was still carrying the theodolite, for which I had signed, and if I fell down the mountainside, I would still be responsible for the $3000 instrument. We found a convenient salient point to leave the theodolite and tripod, as an earnest of our intention to return. (Much, much later I came across Dick's comments on that same ridge. He'd written down that he thought that our chances of reaching the other side were about 50–50.)

We drew a little sketch map of the complicated array of valley-floor moraines visible from there, trying to make sense of them, without much success; rolled a few boulders down to the Clark Glacier, 1000 metres below, with more success, and headed for home. Five and a half hours wasted! (Over the next decade other workers managed to make a plausible history out of the moraines.)

And about 20 minutes later Barwick blew it. On a flattish bit of snow he wrote, with his ice axe, 'Damn and blast you, Huey'. Huey was, and presumably still is, the Australasian god in charge of the weather. He's apparently slow to react but is resentful. We reached the tent, and camped, pretty well done in. In the morning the alarm clock quit at 5.30, and we slept till 7.30 a.m., missing the seven o'clock radio schedule and the time pips. Not that that mattered, for one glance out of the tent showed that this was not a surveying day. Low stratus cloud covered everywhere except the coast, and the chill wind that blew 'blew no one any good'! We packed up slowly, tidied up the depot again, and weighted everything down, including Esmeralda, with a ton of rocks, then had a last ceremonial tin of guavas with a few Weetabix and peanut butter for lunch. We cursed the wind, the

lowering cloud and Huey, and walked westwards for 13 kilometres or so
to the old tent site, where there were still some bits of food, left by Peter
and Barrie. There was no point in going further. As it was we would have
to return a few kilometres to the long fairly gentle granite slope up to the
spot where we'd left the theodolite.

My pack was heavy. The wind was bitter. It was even snowing a bit.
My left ankle still hurt where Dick had kicked me several days earlier.
Maybe he should have shot me then and there. Drear and cheerless, as
I trudged along I wrote letters explaining exactly why I was resigning
from the expedition, but couldn't think to whom I should send them.
We stopped and I smoked a couple of cigarette butts in my pipe. We were
getting short. Why had we left those packets of Camels at the depot? Dick
wondered if the butt ends would go further as snuff. I asked him if he was
happy and he replied, 'Well, I'm here!' but half an hour later he came across
yet another mummified seal, which cheered him up no end. That was
perhaps the 25th one (I'd really lost count) he had examined closely, out of
about 60 we had so far found. I don't know what he found, because I was
digging through an interesting bit of moraine, but he was pleased, almost as
much as he was when Barrie had reported, a few days earlier, that they had
found a mummified Adélie penguin, fully 60 kilometres from the coast.
That apparently was a most significant find.

Fig. 72. Camp on Wilson Piedmont Glacier.

Huey had been at work with the stream, as well. It was in near-flood stage, fully 30 centimetres deep at its shallowest, so we walked along the north bank for a couple of kilometres, looking for a crossing place. The place we found was very close to our intended camping spot. There was a boulder in the middle of the stream, so that with two very long strides, not easy with a 30-kilogram pack, one could cross dry-footed. I didn't notice that the spray falling on the boulder had frozen. I didn't hurt my back much as I landed in the stream; not many of the things in my pack got wet and the gravity meter seemed to be still working.

On the following day Huey was still being resentful about Dick's impertinence. When we woke the sky was clear. We decided to 'do' Philosopher's Peak. Two hours later, clouds were descending. We decided that I'd take a load back to Main Base, including the gravity meter, while Dick continued to exploit seals. Then it looked as though it was going to clear up. We decided to give Huey half an hour to make up his mind. At midday, under a cloudless sky, we set off for the peak. At 2.30 p.m. I lost Dick but I knew where he was going and at five o'clock I found him, close to the theodolite cache. He was sitting in the sun, watching my arrival, wondering what he'd have done if I hadn't turned up. The weather started to deteriorate. I considered the merits of sending Dick to write 'Sorry, Huey' in the snow.

We tackled the ridge, roped together. It was a pig and much more tricky than we'd expected but in three hours we reached the summit to find that we could pick out about half of the peaks that we'd like to include in the round of angles. Good enough, I suppose. The survey was slow and damned cold and it was gently snowing, so I froze, despite my down jacket and windproofs. I stamped my feet while Dick built the cairn and we walked for half an hour afterwards to warm up before having a snack. Rather than face the ridge again Dick found a different route, down into the cirque west of the peak, and then, very, very carefully and slowly, down the steep snow and ice in the cirque, and the frighteningly steep gully below.

Next came the tramp over the much less terrifying moraine and miraculously we were back in the bottom of Wright Valley at about three a.m. Eight and a half hours to reach the peak, more than three hours on the top, and nearly six hours down. Well, that was the big advantage of 24-hour daylight. As long as we could stay awake we were fine. By then, of course, it was cloudless again but Dick was not the least bit receptive to my suggestion that we go back up and do the peaks we'd missed. To finish off the day, or to do penance, Dick slipped into the river. We reached the tent somewhat after four a.m.

At this stage in our lives, Dick and I were alternately having days of frenzied busyness and frantic inactivity. After our all-night session on Philosopher's Peak, we found excellent excuses to do nothing but deal with the radio schedules (Peter and Barrie were between Peaks 12 and 13), eat and chiefly sleep until five p.m. However, Dick was growing anxious to start his freshwater biology work, so we packed, as lightly as possible, even to the point of discarding the (nearly exhausted) batteries from the radio and leaving all the food, except the blue cheese, some very heavily buttered biscuits and four bars of chocolate for the journey home (and the dried egg because we were short of that at Main Base). Nevertheless, our packs still weighed about 35 kilograms. Must be Barwick's lichen samples, I concluded. However I noted that we were becoming even more adept at our camel-like mode of rising, unaided, to a near-vertical position.

We set off for home at 9.30 p.m., stopping for a rest after about five kilometres. The first few minutes of the next stint were sheer agony, from my raw thighs, until they had become self-anaesthetized. Another stop was called for at the Pecten Moraine (now known as Prospect Mesa). I needed a drink. The wind, as usual, was quite strong and very tiresome, so Dick suggested putting up the tent for some respite while we had a few cups of coffee. I then thought just how delightful a panful of egg, laced with blue cheese, would be. I scraped the butter from the biscuits and cooked the equivalent of about a dozen eggs. I had to ask Dick how to spell delectable. With snacks like that, it's not surprising that I was putting on weight. Perhaps I should take more exercise. Maybe carrying heavy weights up steep slopes would be the answer.

Then, home at last. I, for one, had a vague sense of satisfaction that I had covered the 23 kilometres to Main Base in less than eight hours, and that included the one-and-a-half-hour stop near the col. I changed the charts on the met instruments, but was too bushed to look at the differences in the weather between here and nearer the coast. Dick tidied up our tent, which the boys had left in a chaotic state. Dinner was tinned ham and dehydrated potatoes, followed by a small slug of Drambuie and an English cigarette – so much nicer than those Camels. Any sort of food would have made a memorable homecoming. We fell into bed at seven a.m., thoroughly whacked.

CHAPTER 9

Alone for a short while, maybe

I had really enjoyed Dick's company, continuous and almost undiluted, for the last month. He went too fast uphill, had brutally kicked me on the ankle, and usually put too much salt in the pemmican, but otherwise his disgusting habits, while different from mine, weren't too much worse. On one occasion, when he had been particularly considerate over some trivial matter, I thanked him and received his reply with no surprise: 'Oh, that's alright! I'm quite a decent sort of bastard sometimes!'

Fig. 73. Main Base. One tent from the other.

Nevertheless we had come to a parting of the ways, for a short while anyway. Dick wanted to start his freshwater biology work round Main Base, and I wanted to poke around in the North Fork, mainly looking at the moraines, and to extend the gravity survey as far up the valley as I could, maybe as far as the flat apron of ice that we were beginning to call the Upper Glacier, or sometimes the Wright Upper Glacier. I didn't intend to do any climbing, but just in case I broke a leg or Dick fell out of his little rubber boat into 30 centimetres of water we arranged to have two radio contacts each day, initially at nine a.m. and nine p.m.

My load was about 45 kilograms but I only had to carry it on my back as far as the edge of Lake Vanda, where we had left the second fibreglass sledge. In most places there was a three- to ten-metre-wide freshwater moat around the ice, and the water was too deep for us to make a causeway with rocks. However, I soon found a spot where the ice abutted the shore. The westerly katabatic wind made a change from the usual easterlies at the other end of the valley, and felt warm, almost hot. When I'd left Main Base half an hour before it was 7°C, and once, while we were at the coast, the temperature at Main Base had gone up to 10°C. However, the warm katabatic wind never extended very far eastwards, didn't normally last too many hours, and, as I noted earlier, was usually quite thin.

Anyway, I pulled the sledge into the pleasant warm wind, on the smooth one-year-old ice, for a couple of hours or so and found another easy way off at the western end. Soon afterwards I found a sheltered spot between two tumps of moraine – with a freshwater pool within five metres of the tent entrance, if you please. The westerly wind slacked off to nothing, and was replaced at nine p.m. by a savage, colder easterly wind that boomed across the lake and banged fiercely into the tent. I was pleased indeed that I had weighted down the valance with big rocks rolled down from the moraine pile. I had vague concerns that the tent, with me in it, would blow away, but, after dinner and a short radio schedule with Dick (he was calling 'Main Base to the other end of the lake') I eventually slept soundly enough.

The North Fork is utterly fascinating and such a complicated mixture of different landforms that I realized very quickly that there was little chance of making sense of it all in the time I had. I continued the gravity traverse almost eight kilometres westwards, through heaps of moraine, interspersed with scree lobes and flat sandy areas, some with very well developed frost polygons, up to the area, at 600 metres' altitude, where the valley bottom was carved into a maze of intersecting canyons, with walls more than 30 metres high in places. The canyons didn't look as though they had been cut by a glacier, but what else? Water? How?

I hadn't stopped for lunch but chewed one of those stubborn biscuits as I went along. I was still trying to count steps between the gravity stations, recognizing that that method of locating them was practically useless in the confines of the Fork. Consequently I was also taking magnetic resections at alternate stations, to position them. The biscuits were part of my downfall. I found it impossible to chew the unyielding things and simultaneously to count paces. I discovered I was counting chews instead, so that I had to fix every gravity station by sighting onto neighbouring peaks. And of course, due to Barwick and his imprecations on Huey, the weather then became impossible. It was snowing quite heavily, and the visibility was growing less and less and eventually was down to perhaps 50 metres.

From the east end of the maze (which we later called Labyrinth, a name that was approved) I thought I might get an occasional glimpse of the apron of ice at the foot of the icefalls from the ice sheet, but I couldn't see a damned thing. Apart from flat-topped Dais I couldn't distinguish any peaks at all. Perhaps I had carried the gravity survey far enough westwards to see whether the gravity results supported the idea that the mountains of south Victoria Land were indeed a horst, a block of elevated land forced up between two north-south, near-vertical faults.

That was 'the big picture' but the little pictures within it were even more intriguing. At the western end of the valley proper, where it became Labyrinth, the Dais, separating North and South Forks, is only a few hundred metres higher than the floor of the Forks. This was an easy way to travel between the Forks, and also to climb to the eastern end of Dais. That spot was beginning to look as though it might become our next survey station, Peak 105 still being snow covered and looking horribly inaccessible, despite Peter and Barrie having (nearly) climbed it. In addition, it looked as though this area, where the dolerite sheet became more deeply eroded as one went westwards along the top of Dais, would offer the easiest place I'd found for taking paleomagnetic samples from top to bottom of the dolerite sheet.

But then again, how on earth did those huge dolerite boulders find themselves sitting on top of a long low line of very fine moraine? Why did the northern moraine pile over there contain on the surface nothing coarser than a centimetre, while the southern one, which abutted it, have nothing much finer than ten centimetres across – and the overall composition of both moraines looks about the same admixture of dolerite and granite?

As I walked over one small hill between gravity stations 102 and 103, I spotted a little lake, maybe 30 metres across, and not ice-covered. Being thirsty, I went over for sippers, passing five mummified seals in the last 100 metres. I took one small sip and spat it out. Vile! Some kind of salt,

I supposed, which would be why the water was open, not ice-covered. The bottom of the lake was covered with fluffy stuff like the growths in an old bottle of vinegar. And now that I looked at it more closely there were lots of little maggoty things, a few millimetres long, crawling around. I wondered if the water was poisonous and that was the reason there were so many dead seals there. But what were the maggots doing in poisonous water? I must tell Dick.

I noted these things as I walked back eastwards along the North Fork. At one place there are two granite cliffs sticking through the scree-covered side of Dais, and at the foot of one of the cliffs, in amongst the large blocks of scree, I found the largest collection of mummified seals yet. Fifteen I spotted (Dick says it was only 14 – and I'm not going to argue) and goodness knows how many I missed, in the big blocks of rock. Why there? More intrigue for our resident seal psychologist.

What a great, exhausting day! I reckoned I'd walked more than 30 kilometres. I was completely pooped, my thighs were painfully raw and nothing in the whole world could ever have been so welcome as the sight of my little green tent. Oh, that cup of coffee! And the next one was nearly as good. Then it was time for the midnight radio schedule. ZLYO, or Main Base (Dick in this case), and ZLYO-2 (Peter and Barrie) both came on the air. The boys were back at Main Base, having walked 30 kilometres, half of it in snow. Dick couldn't have been more excited when I told him about the seals and the creepy crawlies in the bottom of the salty lake, and said he'd be at my little green tent at noon on the next day, complete with collecting bottles and so on. Food was often the highlight of the day, but I was so tired I cooked the simplest possible dinner – a mutton meat bar and dried onions made into soup. As I consumed it I thought how great it was that a grown and moderately sensible chap like Dick could go bananas over those sorts of things, bugs and dead seals.

Dick turned up the next day at 4.20 p.m., which, by our local standards, meant he was on time. The weather was piggy, 4°C and completely overcast with the clouds low and getting lower. Still Dick had brought me a large piece of Christmas cake, and when I had eaten that and had another cup of coffee we set off. Dick's first job was to expose a couple of sterile plates 30 metres or so up the local moraine – and then we took off up the valley. By six p.m. the cloud was down to 250 metres. It was snowing heavily and the visibility was about 150 metres. The snow was settling, which fouled up Dick's intentions with the seals. He needed photographs of the things 'in situ' before taking their previously vital statistics and so on, so I just showed him where I had found the specimens on the previous day. Well I've seen exuberance displayed by others many times. Previously my best example was shown by an amateur botanist in Greenland, who, spotting an innocent little flower by a stream, yelled 'Saxifrage' and dived on it from three metres. Dick didn't quite do that (because he's a professional?) but when he saw the crawlies in the little lake he admitted that he was 'impressed'.

Walking round to the other side of the lake we found another seven seals in a 100-metre stretch, one of which was still very fresh, with red blood at the mouth and the muscles still soft. That made a total of 37 I'd seen just in this part of the North Fork, and I too was becoming 'impressed'. Dick said that most of the mummified seals were immature, probably in their first year. They'd crossed the Wilson Piedmont Glacier into the Wright Valley and were trapped, unable to find their way back. Here I was, 80 kilometres from the coast, but I'd come by helicopter most of the way. These poor things had had to shuffle. When he had a raft of radiocarbon ages for the fool things, Dick calculated that the rate at which they entered the valley was probably about one every ten years or so.

By ten p.m. the weather was improving but I was growing hungry, so, leaving Dick to measure a seal that I had marked a few days earlier, I returned to the tent to make supper. The 0001 (one minute past midnight, standard met recording time) weather record read: 'Trace cumulus cloud, 5000 feet (1500 metres). Visibility 20 miles+ (30 kilometres+). Wind, 1–5 knots, Easterly. Temp. 29°F (−2°C).' Wouldn't it? Why couldn't it be like this when we needed it?

The weather in the morning was just wonderful. There was a bit of very high cloud but otherwise it was perfect. But the radio schedule with Scott Base was troubling. A couple of days earlier they had told us we might be evacuated at short notice on 30th January, 12 days from that date. This morning they asked what our evacuation requirements were and while Dick kept them occupied I calculated rapidly, in fact furiously, and then said 'From Main Base, 650 kilograms plus four persons. From Lower Depot, 100 kilograms.' Peter Phillips, the radio operator who had succeeded Peter Yeates, just acknowledged the message, without even saying 'Good morning'! We missed the humour and friendliness of the other Peter.

Anyway, after the radio schedule, Dick set off up North Fork to deal with his seals and collect the various obscure things from the salt lake, and I set off around the end of the mesa, along the South Fork and up to the spot where I knew I could climb up Dais to the dolerite sheet. On the way along the South Fork I passed another open lake, this one quite large but very shallow, only a few metres deep I guessed, and later known as Don Juan Pond (the water was saturated with a brand-new mineral, Antarcticite,

Fig. 74. North Fork of the Wright Valley.

Fig. 75. Barrie looking down South Fork of Wright Valley.

CaCl$_2$:6H$_2$O, which prevents it freezing). I then went along the strange glacier-shaped moraine that ended by the lake and that I thought was possibly a rock glacier. I'd have loved to go digging around on these features – but first things first.

As usual I took much, much longer to climb to the top than I had imagined possible. Vertical sections 15 metres high seemed to appear in my path, over and over again, while I was personally limited to 60-centimetre-high steps. Then, coming down, it was difficult to find bits of rock that, after marking horizontal lines and magnetic north on them, could be detached with only a finite number of hammer blows.

It took me nearly eight hours to collect 24 oriented samples (to annoy me, Dick always referred to the things as 'oriental' specimens), fairly uniformly distributed across the 250 vertical metres of dolerite sheet, and they weighed something like 20 kilograms, so I was careful scrambling down the slipping-angle scree into the North Fork and grateful that the walk back to the tent was fairly flat.

The instructions that we received from Lyn Martin on the following day, 20th January, were either frightening or ridiculous. All of the McMurdo helicopters had fallen to pieces. We were told to walk out to Marble Point, taking everything with us, all 650 kilograms, plus P. and B.'s samples stashed at the Lower Depot, and to be there by 1st February, to be collected by a US ice-breaker.

Dick's version of this panic-filled period is somewhat different and quite scurrilous. He wrote:

My memory of the first news that we might have to walk out was as follows: While you [that's Colin] were camping up at the Dais end of Lake Vanda and I was at Main Base, I fired up the large Main Base radio about 8.00 am to hear Peter at Scott Base calling us. After a wild scramble to find the Morse key in the clutter on the tent floor I found it, plugged it into the set and sent out our call sign in my rudimentary Morse. Peter immediately asked, 'Is that you Dick?' for I lacked Colin's suave Morse fluency. He then said that he had a long message, which I took down on a scrap of paper (I sent you a scan of the actual message). The message was from Lyn Martin informing us that we would have to walk out the 45 miles to the coast, since all helicopters were grounded for lack of spare parts and we were to be picked up by ship.

Dick, in his 2008 message to me, continued:

The helicopters in those days had about 100 hours of flight time before a major overhaul and parts replacement. The message was critical so I immediately started a call to Colin at the other end of the lake. Hallucinating, he tried to convince me that he could see a vision of Marilyn Monroe, beckoning to him from the other side of the lake. He refused to take me seriously when I said that I had an urgent 146-word message from Scott Base and he protested vehemently at the prospect of having to read 146 words of my Morse. Mercifully for us both, Peter and Barrie

Lyn Martin's (OIC Scott Base) radio message to VUWAE II
party as transcibed by REB - for retransmission to CB

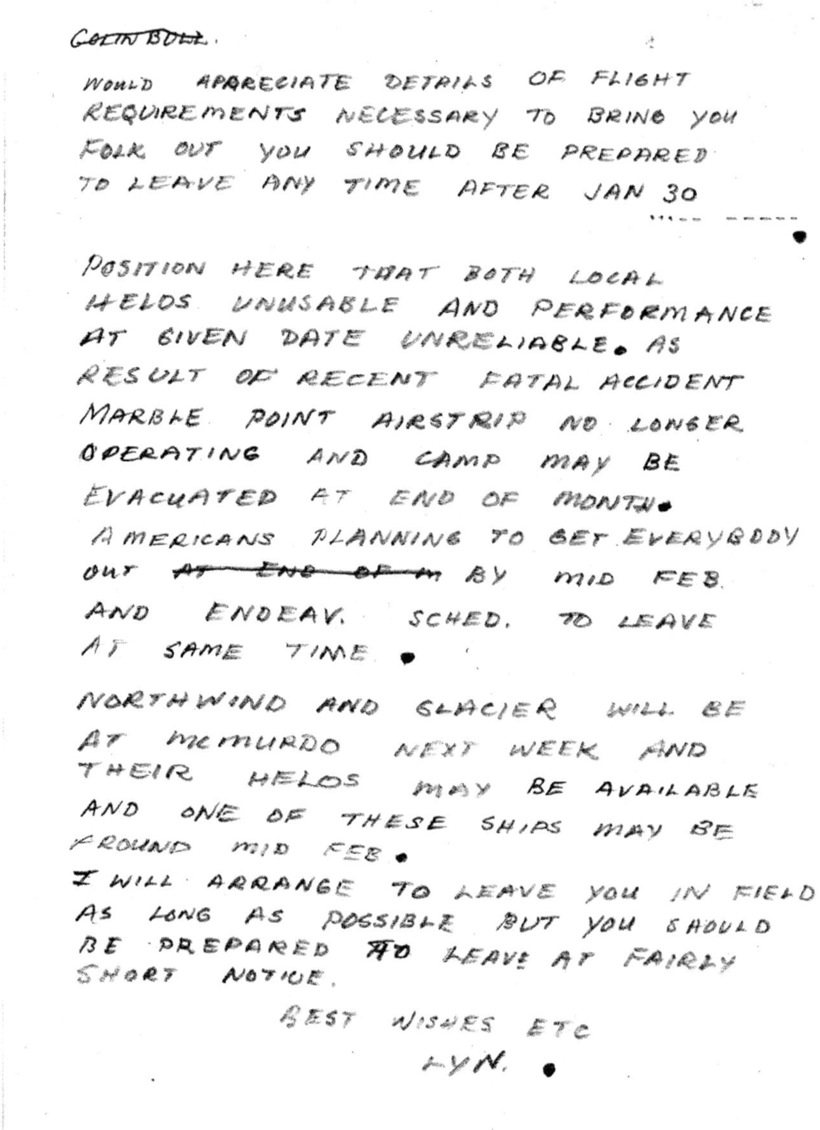

COLIN BULL.

WOULD APPRECIATE DETAILS OF FLIGHT
REQUIREMENTS NECESSARY TO BRING YOU
FOLK OUT YOU SHOULD BE PREPARED
TO LEAVE ANY TIME AFTER JAN 30

POSITION HERE THAT BOTH LOCAL
HELOS UNUSABLE AND PERFORMANCE
AT GIVEN DATE UNRELIABLE. AS
RESULT OF RECENT FATAL ACCIDENT
MARBLE POINT AIRSTRIP NO LONGER
OPERATING AND CAMP MAY BE
EVACUATED AT END OF MONTH.
AMERICANS PLANNING TO GET EVERYBODY
OUT ~~AT END OF M~~ BY MID FEB
AND ENDEAV. SCHED. TO LEAVE
AT SAME TIME.

NORTHWIND AND GLACIER WILL BE
AT MCMURDO NEXT WEEK AND
THEIR HELOS MAY BE AVAILABLE
AND ONE OF THESE SHIPS MAY BE
AROUND MID FEB.
I WILL ARRANGE TO LEAVE YOU IN FIELD
AS LONG AS POSSIBLE BUT YOU SHOULD
BE PREPARED TO LEAVE AT FAIRLY
SHORT NOTICE.

BEST WISHES ETC
LYN.

writing hand - REB

Fig.76. One of Lyn Martin's messages as transcribed by Dick, begining the 'difficult' time.

had heard the sked with Scott Base and they broke in, 'on voice', to convey the gist of the news. As soon as he could Colin beetled back to Main Base and we started to plan our retreat.

Of course all that junk about Marilyn Monroe was just the result of Dick sniffing too much formaldehyde. When I had understood the message I went out and collected a few more paleomagnetic samples from the dyke swarm near the edge of Lake Vanda, and then walked back across the lake to Dick, who had come back from Main Base to the little tent. There two of the most dangerous events of the whole expedition befell me. First Dick forgot to soak the dried apples before cooking them and the sulphur dioxide fumes from them nearly asphyxiated us both, and second, after I had snuggled into a sleeping bag Dick pointed out that I had chosen his bag! After averting serious consequences we discussed the order from Lyn and went to sleep before we'd solved it.

The following days saw many inane radio conversations with Scott Base. Lyn Martin, I'm sure, had our very best interests in mind but he seemed to have some real difficulties in understanding our situation. If we have to walk to the coast, I asked, may we leave behind all the items we had borrowed from Scott Base? These included the two pyramid tents (30–35 kilograms each), the first-aid kit (more than 20 kilograms), and the big radio (36 kilograms). Lyn's immediate reply was that we could leave the tents but we had to bring back the radio. Dick stopped my response: I was going to ask him if he would care to nominate which one of us should carry it, in addition to his own gear. However, I did ask Lyn to gain permission for us to leave behind the surveying gear, the meteorological instruments and the gravity meter. I knew that we would never be given permission to abandon the gravity meter, which was the only one in New Zealand, except maybe for one or two belonging to the prospecting oil companies. If we did have to walk out we would have to leave practically everything, permission or not, but I would prefer to have permission. 'What about a helicopter from one of the ice-breakers?' I asked.

Leaving Lyn to contemplate these things, Dick headed back up the North Fork for some more work on the seals. He was pleased indeed when one of the newly found carcasses turned out to be definitely a Weddell seal, though what it was doing among so many crabeaters he didn't know. Meanwhile, I took the gravity meter and a few other things back to Main Base on the sledge, returning with the theodolite and tripod. We were both very sorry that we were going to have to abandon the idea of climbing Mount Odin, but it looked as though there wouldn't be time. Instead we'd make a survey station on the top of Dais, our poor-boy cheap insurance

Fig. 77. View to west from Dais survey station.

alternative to majestic Peak 105 (Mount Odin). Dais was only 935 metres high, if that, but it was isolated, and central, and we could knock it off easily in a few hours from our campsite at the end of the lake. This we did on a gusty day (21st January) when the wind couldn't decide whether to be easterly or westerly. But we had a great view of the icefalls at the top of the valley. Dick estimated that they were 500 metres high. I thought they were a bit lower.

Dick and I were coming down the slope into the South Fork of the Wright Valley after surveying on Dais, when we saw a small, clear and limpid pool, just a few metres wide. We both knelt beside it, to scoop up water to drink. We both arose spluttering, and then we noticed the flattish crystalline deposits in the bottom of the pond. It was worthy of California's Death Valley. A saturated saline pool, it was much smaller than Don Juan Pond but the salts were probably the same.

Things were getting hectic. We were still facing the eviction order, with the threatened walk to the coast. Whether we carried the radio or not, it was absolutely essential that we take out the samples that B. and P. had collected, which were stashed at the three depots. The boys were near the Lower Depot and we had a long talk, at midnight, about 'the situation'. They felt that they must retrieve their rock specimens from the Upper Depot, on which their next year's thesis work depended, and with this thought to inspire them, they walked, fully laden, the 35 kilometres to

Fig. 78. View of western Asgard Range from Dais.

Main Base in six hours. When Dick congratulated them on this achievement, Barrie explained that it had only been possible by their careful choice of rest spots. They only stopped where there was a shallow puddle nearby and Barrie noted that when they sat in the puddle there was always a short, sharp sizzle.

At Main Base they ate and slept for six hours and then pressed on to the Upper Depot, another very long walk, as well as the 1600-metre climb up to the depot and then back down to the tent still standing at the western end of the lake. There they ate the meal I had left for them — stewed steak and vegetables, and then tinned pineapple — had a rest for an hour or two, and then sledged across the lake back to Main Base, with their specimens. Barrie asked us to excuse the smoke coming from his armpits.

While they waited for the meal that we cooked for them, they had a little snack, which started with ten Weetabix each and three quarters of a two-pound tin of golden syrup between them. Well, one Weetabix makes a rather skimpy breakfast, but two of them are enough for most folk. Dick and I watched, open-mouthed with admiration and astonishment, as they demolished the lot. And then they had dinner! Not only was it a remarkable walk but they also showed a totally commensurate ability to eat.

On the next radio schedule, while the boys were sleeping, John Gregory, in charge of surveying at Scott Base, told us that we should bring back all the survey gear, two tripods, theodolite, and subtense bar — another

45 kilograms. I told Dick that would be part of his load. He didn't say anything but he drew a wonderful cartoon of an intrepid but haggard explorer, himself, staggering towards the coast with a huge load, topped with the Stephenson screen. Richie Simmers, from the Meteorological Office, was much more realistic, bless him! He said, 'Abandon all met gear if necessary, but bring back barograph if at all possible.' Lyn said that he'd had no answer yet to the request for a helicopter from the ice-breaker.

Fig. 79. Dick's cartoon drawn in response to the request that we ferry all of our equipment to the coast.

Dick went off playing in his little rubber boat, collecting more last-minute stuff from the bottom of local ponds. I photographed him and suggested bringing him a book and a good woman. Dick said he'd prefer a bad woman. I reoccupied the two ends of the survey baseline, to take sights and angles onto those cairns (that Dick had erected at all of our survey stations) which we could see from the baseline. It was annoyingly windy, and I had to do my own booking (writing down the observations). That's always a slow task, and unpleasant in the wind. It wasn't a very good set of observations but unless somebody closed the door to keep the wind out, I doubted that I could improve on them very much. I also collected a few final oriented specimens from the dark dyke swarm near Main Base. Barrie had delighted in telling me that they were lamprophyric dykes.

Thus it was nearly eight p.m. on 24th January when Dick and I almost simultaneously arrived back at the tents. Barrie and Peter were still somewhere down the valley, finishing their work down there, and therefore did not hear Lyn tell us on the radio that VX-6 Squadron had undertaken to fly us out by helicopter. They couldn't tell us when, except that it would be before 10th February, perhaps many days before then. Consequently I didn't bother to send my message explaining that to carry the radio to the coast would occupy one man for at least eight days, there and back.

Fig. 80. Dick in his rubber boat, sampling small lakes near Main Base, Wright Valley.

For supper I introduced Dick to 'gravity soup', the meal that the four of us had eaten nearly every day for lunch on our record-breaking traverse of the Greenland Ice Sheet – the slowest ever crossing. You start with a large pot of soup, or stew, and at the first meal eat half. The next cook fills the pot, and again you eat half. In Greenland our most memorable lunches started when Malcolm inadvertently added a complete can of strong curry powder. We re-learned the meaning of 'exponential decay' and 'half-life', and that curry flavour continued for a month.

I'll leave you to imagine the reaction of P. and B. when they heard the news about the helicopter. Their mammoth two-day effort, while not wasted, hadn't been necessary. I hadn't realized that people that young could have such comprehensive vocabularies. There was only one thing we could possibly do: instead of packing our most precious possessions, notebooks, rock samples, met charts, Dick's bits of seal and his cartoons, and starting our wearisome trudge to the coast (with or without the radio), we declared a holiday. We sat, read, talked science, talked non-science. Dick, sitting in the corner of the tent and trying to make a family group out of the Flex-o-Link, uttered a remarkable 'I can't remember how the woman goes'. I made a rum trifle from the remainder of Peter's Christmas cake and the remnants of the minute bottle of rum, served with our version of whipped cream; an incredibly thick mixture of powdered milk, butter, sugar, and most of the rest of Dick's Drambuie. It was different.

CHAPTER 10

The End.
Wait for the applause!

At eight a.m. on 26th January Scott Base told us that we were going to be picked up, in two flights, on 30th January. What were the most essential things left to do? For Dick and me the most vital thing was to make a survey station somewhere to the north, in Victoria Valley. Barrie and Peter had spent a week in that area and strongly suggested we tackle Peak 13, later known as Sponsors' Peak, because it was very easy to climb, fairly high (1454 metres) and nicely isolated. There was a good campsite near Mount Insel, with a freshwater lake nearby. They, Peter and Barrie, would spend their last day sampling the granite-sandstone contact exposed on the south side of Wright Valley just below Mount Odin, and on the 29th would pack up the campsite.

So be it. Dick and I packed as quickly as possible. This time we didn't take the gravity meter nor the portable radio – it had developed problems which we couldn't solve with a pair of scissors and a tent peg – saving us 14 kilograms of weight. However, we must take the radio back to Collier and Beale in Wellington. The pair of tent radios had been invaluable.

It was a gorgeous day, just a smidgeon of cirrus cloud over the Piedmont, the lightest west wind, and a temperature of 4°C. I put a marker on the thermograph record at 10.25 a.m. and off we set. It soon became obvious that Huey, at long last, had forgiven Dick for being obstreperous, for it really was a nice walk, despite our preposterous packs. After about four hours, in the middle of Bull Pass, we photographed our very own eroded granite boulder yet again, but continued to the little depot we had made by the lake, a couple of kilometres further on. There we had a double brew of coffee, a couple of biscuits and a lump of cheese, sucked our pipes for a minute or two and thought to ourselves that this really had been a pretty good way to spend a summer.

Leaving our idyllic lakeside campsite we were in fresh territory, at least

I was. Dick had been in Victoria Valley the previous year. We had another snack after another couple of hours, by which time we were walking over the sands, gravels and frost polygons of Victoria Valley, and then, earlier than usual, we stopped at the campsite near Mount Insel, pitched the tent, made another mutton meat bar stew dinner and were in bed shortly after ten p.m.

Because it was going to be a long day, we were up early the next morning, another nice one. Following Barrie's advice we aimed west of Sponsors' Peak and gently puffed our way up the granite scree slope to the shoulder of the peak, and then up the north side of the final slope. Down below us was the Victoria Upper Glacier, looking much more like a conventional glacier than the Lower Glacier, which we could see off to the east, beyond the sand dunes. That, like the Wright Lower Glacier, was just an outgrowth of the Wilson Piedmont, flowing a few kilometres into Victoria Valley and ending near the ice-covered Lake Vida.

The ridge along which we were scrambling grew narrower and narrower, so that the flat part at the top of the mountain was very small indeed. From the summit we could see exactly why Barrie had sent us up from the north. The south side of the summit smacked of verticality, for several hundreds of metres, and the cliff continued down for a thousand or more. (In my diary I wrote: 'It starts off vertical and then gets steeper.') For the first time in my life I felt vertigo, and sat down for some minutes, had the biscuits and chocolate that we normally saved until we'd finished the theodolite work, felt better and erected the tripod several metres away from the edge. Dick tossed a rock over the edge and timed its fall – seven seconds till we heard it clatter into its mates below. The equation $h = {}^{1}/_{2} \, g \, t^{2}$ (space equals one half of gravity times the square of the time taken) gave us nearly 240 metres of verticality and, as Dick pointed out 50 years later, that was just the distance to the first bounce.

By this time the sky was completely cloud covered, but it was very high stratus cloud and didn't worry us at all – except that Dick took his round of photographs from the tripod before I put up the theodolite, in case the cloud thickened and came down. It didn't. Because this was to be our most northerly survey station, and Dickie Brooke, surveyor for the northern party of the NZ TAE, had made several stations on mountains beside the Debenham and Mackay Glaciers, further north, our round of angles from the peak contained 26 sights, more than usual, so that we could tie our survey very firmly into Dickie's. With the extra survey targets, it took more than four hours to complete. Hence I was pleased, for the sake of my hands, feet and nose, that the weather stayed calm and wasn't too cold, −7°C.

Fig. 81. Colin at the survey station on Sponsors' Peak (red triangle). He tells his grandchildren he climbed the face to get there.

Having to keep away from the cliff edge I continually intertwined my legs with those of the theodolite tripod, knocking it off level, and generating naughty words. Old Mother Barwick, from his nest in the rocks several metres away, kept telling me not to step backwards. (I still have daytime nightmares about that survey station, and feel weak in the knees when I recall the short distance between the cliff edge and the theodolite and tripod!) In the dry and calm conditions sound travelled very easily, and 'you could hear for miles', as Dick said. There wasn't much for him to hear, though, except the numbers I was reading out.

When we had finished the survey but with the tripod and theodolite still up, Dick scrambled a few hundred metres along the ridge to take a wide-angle photograph of me and the survey station a very few metres from the cliff. As he went I could hear him chime 'It's good, and it's good to eat often'. The photograph looks positively heroic, and would have been even more so if the tripod and I had both appeared on the same picture. I was happy to let Dick build the cairn, with his usual panache and skill, while I sat and ate the extra bar of chocolate that he had been proclaiming, and the biscuits he had sequestered about his person. Did I say he was a good companion?

On the way back towards the tent Dick found a gorgeous clump of red lichen, innocently living on a lighter coloured piece of rock quite close to the summit, so he photographed it, examined it, drew it, dissected it, drew it some more, and finally removed it from the rock and stuffed part of it into a bottle, probably with some foul preservative, and the rest into two paper folders. And then, damn it, he found another clump, and he treated that in the same time-wasting fashion. He called 'em 7a and 7b, and, bare-fingered, wrote it all up in his 'lichen' book. I told him time was precious but all he did was make an obscene gesture – he didn't hurry in the least. As we came down from the peak, the cloud did lower and by the time we were in the valley floor, near ten p.m., the sun was displaying a fine corona, just for us. We debated rather briefly whether to go straight back to Main Base, and maybe have an extra day to help the boys with the packing, but again we decided that the young are designed for suffering, as aforesaid. In any case we definitely weren't up to an extra 30 kilometres of walking with heavy loads.

The next day, January 28th, was our last day in the field. Walking back to Main Base was as good as we had any right to expect; better, in fact. It was almost calm and around 2°C all the time. We would have enjoyed our last trek through Bull Pass even more without those absurd packs, but we weren't in a desperate hurry, and Dick, always in front, found enough noteworthy bits and pieces to keep us amused. We had an interesting and barely controlled run down the steepest part of the moraine pile at the end of the col, and, best of all, when we reached the tents, Barrie had made us his favourite dinner, bully-beef stew. Great!

Peter told us that they had packed all their rock samples, and my paleomagnetic oriented specimens. If the weather was anything like reasonable I'd have time for the baseline remeasurements, as well as finishing the packing. As ever, the boys had done a good job.

For confusion Scott Base told us that we had confirmed passage back to New Zealand on the US ice-breaker *Northwind*. Previously we had been told we'd be going home on HMNZS *Endeavour*. It didn't matter to us which ship we were travelling on as long as we were leaving the valley by helicopter. After we had finished our dinner and were deep into our second mug of coffee, I tried to make Peter and Barrie give me an assessment of the work of the whole season, all 52 days. Barrie, true to himself, said, 'Well, Peter and I walked more than 500 miles (800 kilometres) and climbed up and down over 30,000 feet (9000 metres).' He pointed to his Anson boots, to prove it. He was going to discard them but I insisted on taking them back to New Zealand for Mr Foot to see. Peter, more prosaic, added that they had made sense out of most of the geology over 1000 square miles (2600 square kilometres) – except perhaps the youngest units, the quaternary deposits in both the Wright and Victoria Valleys.

Fig. 82. Barrie's boots, both pairs, one of them after some hard walking.

Most of Dick's time had been eaten up with helping me with the survey work, but he had made a good start on the freshwater biology, the high altitude lichens and, most of all, his horrid seals. I'd done a pretty good gravity survey along the valley and had made, I thought, a good collection of paleomagnetic oriented samples, although the value of those two pieces of work would depend on further analysis and laboratory work. We'd also done a bundle of survey stations for the ground control for map-making from aerial photographs, and we had the first long record of the weather in the ice-free valley region.

Then we started to talk about the things we hadn't been able to do: making some study of the soils, working on the chemistry of Lake Vanda and the ice-free lakes in the North and South Forks, and many many other topics. Barrie made us all a cup of chocolate (the man from Cadbury's was right; there wasn't much left) and we went to bed.

The next day, our last full day, started with Dick falling out of bed, falling off a full eight centimetres of air mattress. I'd previously woken up from a nightmare where I had fallen off Sponsors' Peak, much more serious. It was tidy-up, pack-up day. Dick and I tried to make a hole through the ice on Lake Vanda with his ice chisel, at a spot where my gravity survey suggested that the water was about 70 metres deep. We'd guessed that the ice might be as much as one and a half metres thick. We had taken down to the lake one of Mr Simmers's spare thermometers, having buried most of it in a piece of candle, and we were going to lower it to the bottom, leave it there for some minutes and then retrieve it.

We cut the hole 60 centimetres deep with a great deal of effort, but could get no deeper. All the chips of ice were clogging the hole and we were just disturbing them with each bash of the chisel. Why didn't I bring a SIPRE ice drill from Scott Base? We wished we had tried all this eight weeks earlier, when there would have been time to ask for the drill to be brought over. Then we might have found some way to sample the water down there, as well as measure its temperature. Ah, well! We had lots of other things to do, so gave up on the hole and the temperature measurement. And that was a huge pity, for the temperature down there was well over 25°C, as three people from Kansas, looking for algae, found a year or so later.

In 1961–62 Alec Wilson and Harold Wellman, senior members of Victoria University's Chemistry and Geology Departments (VUWAE 5) measured the temperature and chemical profiles of the lake, from which they also gained an understanding of the mechanism of the bottom warming. On VUWAE 7, working on another solar-heated lake in Taylor

Valley, Tim Shirtcliffe, a lecturer in the Physics Department, added to our understanding of the processes. The water of the lake is stratified, the surface water being nearly pure, and successively deeper layers more and more dense with various salts brought in by the stream flowing along the valley. The lowest layers are salt-saturated and also very dirty. A small part of the incoming solar energy penetrates the ice and the upper, nearly fresh, water layers and is absorbed in the lower, dirty, denser, salty layers. That heats the water. Because these lower layers are much denser there is no convection, even when the bottom layers are much warmer than those above, and because there is a layer of ice on top there is no mixing by the wind, so the bottom gets quite hot, and stays that way.

Well, we had failed to find the hot water, and I'd missed the endolithic bacteria, but we'd not done too badly for a little reconnaissance expedition. I decided I'd celebrate by going for a swim. The deep parts of the lake might be hot, but the shallow parts were distinctly and uncomfortably cold, as I found when I went for that first and last ceremonial swim. The other three, all native New Zealanders, refused to join me, so I became the first member of the Lake Vanda Swim Club, formed years later when the New Zealanders, intrigued with all the strange things we had found in the valley, built a semi-permanent station – Vanda Station – on the shores of the lake.

I dried off rapidly since it was 2°C. This was only the second time I had used my towel in seven weeks, except for drying the occasional porridge bowl. I then remeasured the baseline angles, only marginally better than the previous time, and carted the two tripods, the theodolite and the subtense bar up to the tent, to pack them. There Barrie and Peter were squashing tins, prior to burying them. Dick was off finding some 'fresh' algae specimens to take back to New Zealand. Very choosy, some folks. It all looked the same to me! Dick returned from the algae store, not particularly satisfied.

We collected all of the waste paper and other burnable material we could find, borrowed a couple of litres of kerosene from our small stock remaining, and made a conflagration, not a very satisfying one. Then we all stopped for a cup of coffee. There wasn't much more we could do.

We had to sleep in the tents. I wanted to leave the met screen behind for any successors and we might as well obtain the met records for the last day. Anyway, with our luck, plans would change and we'd still be here next week. But at eight a.m., 30th January, the new Peter at Scott Base confirmed that the helicopter would be here bright and early. It was. Peter and Barrie went out first, taking most of the material we were returning,

Fig.83. Barrie stoking the final bonfire. Peter contends that this was the beginning of global warming.

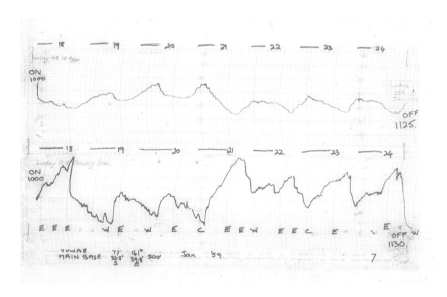

Fig. 84. Thermograph and hygrograph traces for one week. 'Highs' on the thermograph are close to 45°F. 'E' denotes an easterly wind; 'W' a westerly; 'C' calm.

except the tents. The pilot said they would be back in a couple of hours. We knocked down one tent, took the last charts from the recording barometer (12.10 p.m.), thermograph (12.30 p.m.), and hygrograph (12.37 p.m.) and packed them and all the thermometers, the sling psychrometer and the hand anemometer in the last tea chest.

The highest temperature we had recorded with a thermometer was 8.6°C (and 10°C on the charts). The lowest in the screen was −5.3°C. Years later, at Vanda Station, the temperature went up to 14.4°C. Positively tropical, I thought, compared with the −58.3°C I had recorded at Northice, high up on the Greenland Ice Sheet, early in 1954. That was the second lowest surface temperature measured up till that time, second only to one from Verkhoyansk in Siberia. I wondered if our Wright Valley high temperature might be some sort of record too. It turns out that the later Vanda Station temperature is the highest measured on the continent – at least until global warming catches up with us.

I was looking forward to analysing the wind directions, humidities and temperatures. We'd obtained a nearly complete set of records; only the records from 1st to 6th January were missing, when Dick and I were crossing the Piedmont and the boys were working in the high country.

We'd packed one of the big tents and all of our personal stuff. The only thing to do in such conditions was to have another cup of coffee and one final, tooth-breaking biscuit, with its accompanying piece of 'good, and good to eat often' chocolate. We'd just about finished when we heard the whap, whap, whap of the helicopter coming up, that is down, the valley from the coast. (The coastal end of the valley was higher than Lake Vanda, so that I often muddled up and down.) When he landed I noted the altimeter reading again. This time it was 149 metres, meaning the lake was at about 140 metres, encouragingly close to the most recent value I had calculated from our survey to the coast (123 metres). I decided not to recalculate our survey results! The official mapmakers eventually settled on 143 metres for the lake surface.

Dick and I piled in, with nearly all the rest of our clobber, and we flew along the valley, over the Piedmont, close to Speary's Knob and Hogback, and then over Marble Point. It was easier than walking! Much of the sea ice had gone out of the Sound. The helicopter pilots avoided flying over the open sea as much as possible, so we flew south from Marble Point, over the Dailey Islands, looking dark and sinister in the afternoon sun, and over the edge of the McMurdo Ice Shelf to the heliport at Scott Base. There seemed to be much less snow around, but the place still looked cheering and home-like. Maurice Speary came down to meet us and we had the following bizarre conversation:

Maurice: 'Co- Co- Colin. I'm so- so- sorry you've co- co- come back.'

Colin: (A bit miffed) 'Well I'm glad we made it, and I'm pleased to be back.'

Maurice: 'No, I di- di- didn't mean that. I'm ju- ju- just sorry yo- yo- you came ba- ba- back today.'

Colin: 'What do you mean Maurice? Why not today?'

Maurice: 'Yo- yo- you'll see.'

We unloaded the helicopter. Maurice invited the pilot and the AD2 up to Scott Base, but they refused, possibly because they had to retorque the head. We made a date for the following day when they would go back over to our Main Base site to collect the few remaining items. There had been room on our flight for the items, so we assumed they just wanted another trip over there.

At Scott Base, there were large numbers of new faces, including Larry Harrington's 'pyjama gang' from the New Zealand Geological Survey. We couldn't all fit into the sleeping quarters, and consequently we four slept in tents above the base. Out of consideration for the natives, Dick had a bath, and then I did, and we took the drastic step of putting on our cleanest clothes. We were told that Barrie and Peter had already taken baths and were washing their clothes and that the plumbing system hadn't failed. Comforting! We'd do the same.

Up in the mess room we all talked at the same time, to anyone who would listen. Lyn congratulated us on our achievements, without specifying them, and invited us to have a drink before dinner. I had a Scotch, much diluted and without ice, and felt I was settling back into civilization quite easily.

But dinner, when it arrived, was terrible! The meat was burned; the potatoes and other vegetables were over-salted and nearly raw. We threw nearly all of it away and later I said to Maurice: 'Why did you do that, Maurice? You're a good cook and that meal couldn't have been worse.' He said 'I said I was sorr- sorr- sorry yo- yo- you had co- come ba- back to- today.' He explained that once a fortnight he made an awful dinner, just so that everyone would really appreciate the other, excellent, meals he prepared. I'm not sure that Maurice, the psychologist, was entirely on the right track, but as a cook he was close to perfect, except once a fortnight.

After that dreadful dinner I asked Maurice if I could have a cold meat sandwich. Maurice's stuttered response was unprintable but the sandwich was fine! I wrote a telegram for Gillian in Moorabbin, Melbourne, telling her we were back from the field and were supposed to return to New Zealand on HMNZS *Endeavour*, leaving in a few days. Late in the evening

Barrie and Peter, true to themselves, cooked up a gigantic (and edible) meal of sausages and fresh eggs.

On the following day Dick and I went back in *King Pin* to collect the few remaining items, principally the banana boats from the Lower Depot and the Main Base. Dick could not resist the temptation to collect another seal for proper examination in New Zealand. We still had nearly two tea chests of food left there, and we made a list of the main items, to leave at Scott Base. I still had not read *The Affluent Society* but managed to leave the book with the remaining food. As we whapped back along the valley, the rotor blades started to make odd noises, very disquieting to the likes of Dick and me. However, our AD2 found a heavy wrench, leaned far out of the door, using the door lock as a footrest, banged away at something out of our sight, came back in a few moments later, smiled at us, and promptly went to sleep.

Back at Scott Base, Peter, along with Bob Henderson (DSIR) and Jim Wilson (Geological Survey), took a dog team 13 kilometres south across the ice shelf, to welcome back Bert Crary and his Sno-Cat team, who were just completing their geophysical traverse. They had been up the Skelton Glacier, turned left at the top and headed for the Pole. That evening we had a whale of a party, when VUWAE and the Geological Survey party cooperated in some lusty singing of Pete Seeger songs. The party finished at two a.m. with another huge cook-up of sausages and egg, inspired by you-know-who.

The *Endeavour* was now tied up at the edge of the fast ice, a few kilometres away, but before we started to help with the unloading, I wanted to prepare and send a cable report of our field activities and accomplishments, and this we did on Sunday, 1st February.

We repacked a few things, mainly rocks and seals, and did a whole heap of chores. One of the first items to be brought from the *Endeavour* to Scott Base was the marine magnetometer, with which Chris Christofferson, then an officer in the New Zealand Navy, but a future member of VUWAE, had been making a magnetic survey in the southern seas. Something had gone wrong with the instrument which Chris couldn't mend at sea. A few years later Chris joined the Physics Department at Victoria University, taking the position from which I had just resigned.

I helped a bit with John Humphries's ionosonde measurements and we all walked over to see the biologists at McMurdo. They had been doing a lot of work with seals, looking at their physiology, especially as far as deep diving was concerned. The team leader was the biologist from Stanford, Donald Wohlschlag, known to everyone as 'Curly' because of his billiard-ball baldness. He and Dick, talking about the peripatetic mummified seals, seemed to be getting on very well together, although neither, I fear, had any explanation of why the seals (and penguins) wandered into what we were all convinced was 'our' valley. I noticed that Dick refused Curly's invitation to go swimming with the group. So did I. Splashing about in 60 centimetres of water in Lake Vanda is one thing; swimming with seals under the sea ice of McMurdo Sound is quite another matter.

That evening we had a radiotelephone call from Bob Clark. We gathered, in a poor communication, that he was very pleased with us. We were already feeling rather pleased with ourselves, but it really was highly satisfying to have that call!

At Scott Base we had a steady stream of visitors from McMurdo, many of them being senior scientists from the USA. One of these was a glacial geologist named Richard ('Dick') Goldthwait from The Ohio State University. He had recently collected the responsibility for organizing the production of all the glaciological reports from the US IGY work in Antarctica, and had in mind the establishment of a polar science group at his university. Dick was most interested in all our work, but particularly the glacial geology work that Peter, Barrie and I were just beginning to tackle. However, he was also greatly interested in how we had organized ourselves, and how we had managed to carry out a two-month expedition for only $1000 or so.

Much of this conversation occurred in a beautiful cave that had formed in the deformed ice where the ice shelf abuts Ross Island; we sat on a pair of natural ice bollards, until our posteriors were thoroughly chilled. Just over a year later Dick offered me a 15-month visiting position at Ohio State to help him establish the Institute of Polar Studies, which I accepted – and stayed 25 years. Slow learner!

We felt it to be our duty at Scott Base to watch the absolutely awful Sunday night movie, but, as ever, we enjoyed and added to the crude remarks from the audience, and ate our share of the US popcorn. Originally we had expected to be in the field until nearly the end of February, so Gillian had arranged to stay with her wartime friend Ann in Melbourne until then. I was moderately happy to spend my time waiting at Scott Base, and then on *Endeavour*, our slow boat to Wellington. The four of us started to write the first draft of our Immediate Report while still at Scott Base.

After just two days of such work, during which we also spent time loading sledges and (Barrie and Peter) driving tractors out to *Endeavour*, we learned that she was leaving at nine a.m. on 5th February. A description of the party that everyone engaged in that last evening doesn't fit well with an account of a scientific expedition, but Peter, Barrie and Graham Caughley cleaned up the total shambles to which the mess room had been reduced, before Len Sales, the station mechanic, turned off the electricity generator at three a.m.

We said fond farewells to the wintering crew and hoped they would have as interesting a time as we had had for the last three months. We slapped our personal belongings into our kitbags, except for Dick's last seal, and with our boxes of rocks, specimens and records, were happily taken by radioman Peter on tractor and sledge to the ice dock. That was another chilly ride, but not nearly as cold as when we had arrived. *Endeavour* looked very small compared with the two US cargo ships and their ice-breaker, nearby, but we imagined no problems worse than seasickness with her. Anyway we spent most of that first day sleeping off the effects of the party.

The sleeping quarters for the four of us, and also for Mitzi, the husky pup that Dick Barwick was taking back to New Zealand for Murray Robb, was the floor of the mess room. We slept in our sleeping bags, which by now were becoming rather mature. With rather energetic seas outside, they slid easily across the polished floor, as did Mitzi. Somehow she avoided being squashed. The first few hours, while we were still in McMurdo Sound, with bits of interesting sea ice around and the coasts still visible, we pretended we were tourists, and, when not sleeping, just stood around on deck and gawked at the passing splendour. So much better than flying, we thought! But then, just north of Beaufort Island, we turned a bit to the east, to avoid the coastal ice, and we found ourselves in the rolling, open Ross Sea, with little to gaze at. We appropriated the mess table and went back to our Immediate Report, knowing that when we reached New Zealand there would be a rush of other things to be done.

Leaving Peter and Barrie to deal with their geological survey, and Dick to his seal studies and the freshwater biology, I started with the trigonometrical survey. Dick and I had spent most of our time with that, largely in struggling up those silly slopes. We'd seen large amounts of other interesting things while doing so, but we weren't going to have any part in making the map. Dickie Brooke and Guyon Warren, surveyors with the northern party of the TAE, had made survey stations on half a dozen peaks surrounding the Wright and Victoria Valleys, but with their dog teams and sledges, had not been able to penetrate the ice-free country, nor determine the altitudes of their stations. We had done that well enough. I was sorry that Dick and I had not been able to climb Mount Odin, for the second end of our expanded baseline, but Dais should do, since it was included in Guyon's 'targets'. Dick and I would be very happy to pass all our survey data and the panoramic photographs to him, when we reached New Zealand.

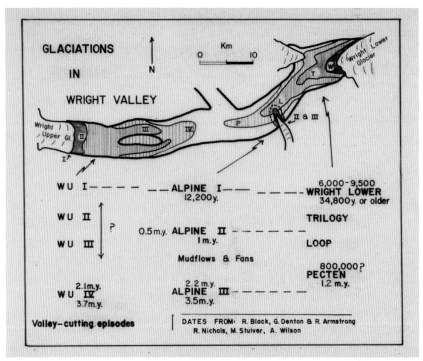

Fig. 85. Early attempt at unraveling the ancient extent of glaciations in Wright Valley.

Fig. 86. Colin, dressed for a party on *Endeavour*, plotting the profile of the Wilson Piedmont Glacier.

Dick had only been able to spend about ten days on his own biology work. His big find, of course, was the mummified seals: 98 in Wright Valley, including groups of 19, 14 and 12, and only one new one to add to the 1957–58 total in Victoria Valley. Why? Their condition varied from animals fresh enough to allow post-mortem dissection, to odd disarticulated bones. All of the identifiable carcasses, except one, were crabeater seals. The exception was the Weddell seal that Dick found in the North Fork near the western end of Wright Valley. In addition the geologists had found the remnants of four Adélie penguins, one of which Dick was taking back to New Zealand for further study.

Dick had mapped the distribution of such small amounts of lichen as we had found. Very nearly all of it occurred in sheltered spots on dolerite or granite at above 1000 metres. There was very little – or at least we found very little – in the lower parts of the valley, and none on exfoliating rocks or in sandblasted areas. Obviously, since it is very slow-growing stuff.

Dick had also made live cultures of algae and protozoa from the ponds by the coast near Marble Point, from the lake at the end of Wright Lower Glacier, and from several of the open water ponds and small lakes at the west end of the valley. He hadn't been able to sample the bottom of Lake Vanda, except very close to the edge.

I had made the gravity traverse mainly to look at the deep structure of the Transantarctic Mountains, and I couldn't do much with that for the Immediate Report. I could use the gravity readings to calculate the depth of the lake at a few points, and to draw a cross-section of the Wright Lower and Wilson Piedmont Glaciers. Elsewhere the Bouguer anomaly became lower westward along the valley, by about one milligal per kilometre, but with some odd wiggles at the inland end: there didn't appear to be any big changes in gravity at the coastal end. So it looked like the mountain range was more likely to be a tilted block, rather than a horst, as previous explorers had suggested.

While Dick and I were writing these bits, Peter and Barrie were spending their time trying to abbreviate their geology findings, except for periodic departures to find food. And every so often we all went up on deck, either to get a breath of fresh air or to play with Mitzi. Within a week Mitzi had been converted into a rather grubby shade of grey, so Peter and others, one sunny day, took her up on deck and converted her into a spotless white husky pup again.

Barrie and Peter started by drawing sections along the mountain ranges north and south of Wright Valley, and another section across the valley. Ancient limestones and greywacke sandstones intruded by granite had evolved over

Fig. 87. HMNZS *Endeavour* in McMurdo Sound.

Fig. 88. Our quartet on HMNZS *Endeavour*, during return to New Zealand.

geological time into a complex assemblage of gneisses, schist, marble and hornfels along the McMurdo Sound coastline. A younger sheet-like pink granite was intruded into the older granite, and then dykes of pegmatite, granite porphyry, and younger lamprophyres intruded the older rocks to produce the dyke swarms that had plagued all of us in the valley bottoms. About 450 million years ago, prolonged erosion had produced a near flat (peneplained) landscape upon which more than 1300 metres of Beacon fluvial sandstones, glacial strata and younger coal measures were deposited over 80,000 square kilometres of south Victoria Land. And then, about 160 million years ago, great sheets of sub-horizontal dolerite were intruded into both the crystalline basement rocks and the overlying sedimentary strata. It was the two oldest and thickest of these dolerite sheets that we spent so much time clambering over. All very simple? Well, perhaps.

For me the weather observations offered some of the biggest surprises. At our Main Base the mean temperature for the second half of December 1958 was −1°C, and for January it was 1.3°C − both about 8.3°C higher than at Scott Base and 5°C higher than at Marble Point airstrip. Wright Valley runs east-west and is deep and steep-sided, so that its direction controlled the winds at Main Base. They blew from the west, usually from midnight to ten a.m., or from the east for most of the remaining hours. (We were working on New Zealand Summer Time, 13 hours in advance of Greenwich Mean Time.) Westerly katabatic winds were warmer and drier, with relative humidities of around 40%, while easterly winds, from the sea, were colder and damper, with relative humidities of 60 to 80%. However, the westerlies, katabatic or föhn winds from the inland ice, were thin and did not extend far along the valley. On ten occasions when we were at 1200 metres' elevation or higher and could see the base tents, we were in light, variable winds and could see the flags around the tents being stretched by a westerly wind, but none of us ever felt a westerly wind when we were at the coastal end of the valley.

We felt we had done a good season's work. We really would have profited with a fifth person, who could have helped with the survey work while Dick made a full-time effort with the biology. I wished I'd been able to do a bit of proper glaciology on Meserve Glacier, though I couldn't think what I could do by myself in just a week or two. Lake Vanda had risen about 14 centimetres during December and January. We thought that somebody should do a proper water and energy study of the lake, and a bunch of engineers from the Department of Works, Christchurch, did so a few years later.

Fig. 89. The four of us back in New Zealand at the end of the expedition, 1959.

Then there were all the opportunities we had missed, though we didn't appreciate them till much later – the full significance of the pecten shells, the stain of the endolithic bacteria under the surface of the sandstone that I thought was some weird sort of weathering, the rain, and, of course, those high bottom temperatures in Lake Vanda that we'd missed by half a metre of ice. Ah well!

By 14th February we had done enough to that Immediate Report to feel that we could take part in the Saturday night party. Actually we didn't really have much choice, since the mess room, where it all happened, was also our sleeping quarters. It was a good party, although it didn't compare with the Scott Base affair. It finished by 11 p.m. and many people arose fairly early the next day as we cruised quite close to Cape Campbell and the Kaikoura Peninsula. We crossed Cook Strait and on a very pleasant summer's evening sailed into Wellington harbour. *Endeavour* anchored in the harbour, rather than tying up, and we spent the evening either lounging in the mess room one last time, or on deck watching the lights of Wellington.

I drew a line under the end of the report and dated it 'HMNZS *Endeavour*, February 1959', and the following morning, in exact naval fashion, we came in and tied up at the Clyde Street wharf at precisely nine a.m. Barrie's parents were part of the small crowd who had turned out to welcome us and, while Dick went off to his family, the other three of us went to Barrie's home in Island Bay, where we had an extraordinarily civilized breakfast, with a tablecloth, a teapot, saucers and normal sized portions. In the afternoon Peter and I went up to the University. Peter duly reported to Bob Clark and John Bradley, but I could find none of the faculty members in the Physics Department, so I just collected my mail and took the train out to Paremata.

Gill and Nicky were still in Melbourne, but the front door of our little cottage was unlocked and Bobby and Elsie, our landlords who lived next door, but in a 'proper' house, invited me for dinner. Did I say, earlier, that New Zealand was the best place to live in the whole world?

And the next day we all went back down to the wharf and the *Endeavour*, for one last visit to the wee wooden warship. Peter felt nostalgic about the wonderful times he had experienced on her during the past two summers, but admitted that she was no ocean liner, and the last ten days on our journey home from McMurdo hadn't been very comfortable. The trip south in 1957, he said, had been even rougher and there were times when he thought she would sink or capsize. Someone had organized a truck from Vic, so we unloaded all our stuff from the ship, and took it up the hill to the University. Apart from a year's very hard work, telling all of our sponsors and supporters what we had done, giving lectures and talks to all and sundry and mostly trying to make sense of the marvels we had seen and collected, that was the end of a very productive, exciting and adventurous summer. The Expedition was over.

CHAPTER 11

Aftermath

Although these fascinating events occurred 50 years ago, many of them still stick very firmly in my memory. I have a very vivid picture of Barrie, sitting cross-legged in the tent at Main Base, eating Weetabix biscuits as though they were going to be taken off the market. However my recollections of him bringing me breakfast in bed, and of Peter and Barrie carrying Dick's and my packs, when we were both exhausted beyond belief, are perhaps even stronger!

The 1957–58 adventure of Barrie and Peter was a remarkable, serendipitous event, and produced excellent scientific results. However, none of their activities were planned and Bob Clark was indeed incredibly lucky that the sterling character, cooperative nature, enthusiasm and industry of the two young men quickly gained for them the respect and support of all with whom they made close contact. These included Trevor Hatherton, Chief Scientist at Scott Base, Captain Harry Kirkwood, skipper of *Endeavour*, and Phil Smith, chief US IGY man in McMurdo. Phil Smith had made possible the helicopter flights and Captain Kirkwood the lifeboat landings that had allowed Peter and Barrie access to their study areas. And, of course, their very considerable ability as embryonic field geologists enabled them to produce scientific results worthy of a fully fledged and professional expedition, even if they just thought of themselves as a pair of footloose students having a great time, but taking advantage of all their opportunities.

Bob Clark was very impressed with Peter and Barrie's achievements, as is readily seen in his calling (two years later) their unforeseen successes 'Victoria University of Wellington Antarctic Expedition #1'.

Whether or not there could ever have been another equally unprepared and equally successful venture is a matter for speculation, but I imagine not. Among other considerations, the Ross Dependency Research Committee, formed in 1958 to take over from the Ross Sea Committee, did want to know that the University Council had approved my plans, and Dr Williams, our Vice-Chancellor, needed to be assured that I had sufficient experience to organize and lead a polar expedition, even a small one, before allowing me to attach the University's name to it.

My planning for our little expedition to Wright Valley had started before I knew anything about VUWAE 1, and I like to think that my experience as a chief organizer of that character-building ten-man Spitsbergen expedition (1951), and as the scientist of the section of the British North Greenland Expedition (1952–54) that crossed the Greenland Ice Sheet, as the winter leader and meteorologist of the Ice Sheet station Northice, and as the Chief Scientist of the Expedition for its second year, were strong enough credentials for Dr Williams. Among other things, I knew he had some confidence in me for he had appointed me to a Senior Lectureship in Physics when I had only applied for a Lectureship! However it was certainly both valuable and comforting to have the backing of Bob Clark, especially during the preparation and organizing phases of the expedition. Thus I delight in dedicating this little book to his memory.

Bob presented my plans to the Ross Dependency Research Council and to the University's Professorial Council, and thereby gained their absolutely essential approval of us, but he was not involved in any way with our work in organizing the expedition, or with my proposed scientific work. That work was very loosely planned, to include the collection of oriented specimens of Jurassic dolerite and other rock units for the paleomagnetic studies, the collection of meteorological surface data, the gravity traverse through the valley and some attempt at determining the glacial history of the area – and, because we were going to an area not previously walked on, we all had a responsibility just to keep our eyes open for anything of interest. Then we had such strong requests from both the US and New Zealand map-makers to establish a number of ground-control survey points that we felt we had to include that work. After all, we were depending on the US VX-6 Squadron for our travel into and out of the valley, and it would only be fair to help them out.

Bob didn't make any contribution to Dick's ideas of what biological studies he might be able to accomplish in the field. Indeed, Barrie, Peter and I, knowing that there was an area to be surveyed and mapped, rocks to be collected, air temperatures to be measured, had a much easier time in planning our work than did Dick, who didn't have a very clear idea of what might be biologically interesting in the area until we had arrived.

I was able to integrate my own work fairly well with the survey chore, but Dick, my constant surveying companion, suffered a considerable loss of time, and in the end spent only ten days (out of 52) engaged in his own work.

I don't know whether Bob played any part in laying out the work that Barrie and Peter should do, but because they were both planning to use their results for Master's theses, it is quite likely that Bob did decide which parts belonged to each. In the brochure that I produced for Dr Williams and for our sponsors I had merely mentioned the areas where the boys were likely to work, and had made no reference to Bob, except as a senior supporter.

Similarly Bob was not involved in any way with my efforts to raise our food and clothing by direct solicitation, in other words, by begging. In fact I don't think he really approved, judging by his reaction, after the expedition, when I gave him a tin of Capstan pipe tobacco, the last one from the gift we had received from W.D. and H.O. Wills. Nevertheless he did accept it, and graciously!

However Bob was highly supportive in many important matters. He certainly sold the idea of a University-approved expedition to the University Council, which saved me from having to try to do so. And Bob, being a respected member of that Council, could do that so much more easily than I could have done. He also supported me personally and even suggested that, if I would feel more comfortable, he would try to arrange my transfer to the Geology Department, as a geophysicist.

Consequently I did not feel the least bit put out when, a couple of years later, at the time of the next VUWAE in which I participated, 1960–61, Bob started to refer to our 1958–59 effort as VUWAE 2. I'd always thought of it just as the first proper University expedition to the Antarctic!

Life indeed was hectic in the months immediately after our return. We were all called upon to give scads of lectures and talks on our adventure. I had a heavy load of lectures to give, partly because Noel Ryder, the other Senior Lecturer in Physics, was very unwell, and I also had to thank all our sponsors for their help. In early 2008 I asked my colleagues for their assistance – and Dick came up trumps. He had, he thought he remembered, a brochure that Bing Harris & Co., the people who supplied our excellent Anson boots, had produced. He'd have a look for it in his basement. A couple of weeks later he reported that in looking through the mess down there he had found half a case of 1967 Seven Hills Cabernet Sauvignon (bought new, I expect, taken down to the basement and 'lost'), and not more than a week later he found the brochure. I'd love to see that basement – or maybe not! The brochure had photographs of Barrie looking down the South Fork, me at the theodolite on survey point 'Alpha', and this letter:

Physics Department,
23rd April, 1959.

R.A. Ford, Esq.,
Bing, Harris & Co., Ltd.,
P.O. Box 1299,
Wellington.

Dear Sir,

Now that the field work of the first University Antarctic Expedition is over, our major tasks are to work up the scientific data and to assess and record our experiences with equipment.

You will remember that when I wrote to you in October, asking for your support, we knew something of the conditions in which we would be working. We knew that in the predominantly ice-free Wright Valley even the conventional forms of Antarctic travel – sledging and mechanical transport – were ruled out, leaving us with no alternative but to man-pack considerable weights over great distances. We realized that solid, reliable boots would be essential items of our equipment and asked you for two pairs of Anson boots for each of our four members. These you most generously gave to the Expedition.

In the field we worked in two pairs. Peter Webb and Barrie McKelvey covered a total of about 500 miles in making their geological survey of the 2000 square miles ice-free area, while Dick Barwick and Colin Bull covered about 400 miles in the eight weeks, while carrying out their topographical survey, geophysical and biological work.

The conditions in which we worked varied enormously . . .

The Anson boots stood up to these conditions very well indeed. The two pairs we have returned to you were worn for 400 miles by McKelvey and Webb. [Note the mistake here. Peter and Barrie walked 500 miles, and I don't think they walked 100 miles barefoot!] By this stage the tread and heels were almost completely worn away . . . but the boot construction must have been very good, for no defects in workmanship appeared, as you can see.

The weather conditions which we experienced varied from a 'tropical' 47°F to . . .

In short then, we feel that our Anson boots served us excellently and in closing we would like again to express our sincere appreciation for the support you have given us.

Yours sincerely,

Colin Bull.

Bing Harris & Co. added five reasons why 'you should stock Anson Boots' and ended the brochure with 'This letter shows how well they wear'. Dick said he saw copies of it in sports gear shops for several years afterwards.

I wrote at least 30 more 'thank-you' letters to our other sponsors, and attached photographs of their products, or of Sponsors' Peak. We really did appreciate all the support – and I wonder if one could organize an expedition in that fashion, nowadays.

Both the 1957–58 and 1958–59 expeditions were so successful that Bob Clark and the University Council were keen to continue the work in Antarctica. To formulate the planning and organization of future Victoria University expeditions, a committee, called the Antarctic Research Committee, was set up by the Professorial Board. At first its members were Dick Barwick, Bob Clark, and myself, with Bob as Convener. For 1959–60 we decided that the most important work was to complete the geological survey, begun by Peter and Barrie, of the large Victoria Valley system. In addition, I wanted some reliable person to collect another suite of Jurassic dolerite rocks. The two main collections I had made, from Dais and from the dolerite sheet west of Bull Pass, had produced some spectacular results. When I told Ted Irving, in Canberra, what I had collected he was full of enthusiasm and invited me, and my samples, to visit him and his astatic magnetometer at Australian National University, where we could measure the residual magnetism of the rocks.

The South Pole at the time those dolerites were formed, or rather when they cooled through the Curie point, about 160 million years ago, was (relative to present-day Wright Valley) at about 55°S, and in the south Pacific Ocean. Together with the other paleomagnetic work from Antarctica, the Japanese results from Pre-Cambrian Ongul Island, the TAE results from the Whichaway dolerites, Gordon Turnbull's work on the recent volcanics from Cape Hallett, and my samples from the dykes in the basement rocks of Wright Valley, we had the beginnings of the polar wandering track for Antarctica. The South Pole had moved from equator to pole since the Pre-Cambrian. It wasn't surprising that there were fossil temperate plants near the Beardmore Glacier.

We also looked at the pole positions determined from rocks of the same age as the Antarctic dolerites, from Tasmania, from South America, South Africa and from India in particular. Of course, if all the rocks were the same age and if the earth's magnetic field had always been a dipole, then all the positions for the South Pole should be the same. So we juggled the continents around until this was the case, and produced a very satisfactory map of Gondwana.

Since then Ted had introduced a more refined technique of magnetic washing, to produce even more reliable results, and it would be wise to do it all again with a new suite of samples.

Because Gillian and I were expecting the arrival of Baby #2 (Rebecca) around Christmas 1959 I declined to have any part in the field work of the 1959–60 venture, but I did go with Bob in November 1959 for a week or so to Scott Base, during which we flew in a VX-6 Squadron Otter around the western half of Victoria Valley, selecting sites for the main camp – near Lake Vashka – and three subsidiary depots around the area. We also flew around the glaciers to the north, especially the Miller Glacier, but could find there no ice-free areas that appeared to be suitable for future expeditions.

Bob was away for much of the Spring Quarter, so I found myself with some other duties for the expedition that might have been momentous – but turned out to be just frustrating beyond normal endurance. The selection of the members for that next expedition started off easily enough. We had reckoned that we should have five members. The leader was to be Ron Balham, lecturer in Biology. Previously he'd been the over-wintering biologist at Scott Base, and a member, along with Dick Barwick and Peter Webb, of the group who visited Lake Vida in 1957–58. Ralph Wheeler, geomorphologist and Geography Department lecturer, took the position of deputy leader, and two final-year geology students, Tony Allen and Graham Gibson, made the number up to four. Then we waited and waited and waited for the fifth volunteer (we didn't pay anyone a salary in those days). Eventually a knock on my door in the Physics Department (Bob was away) produced an incredibly enthusiastic young MSc student, who asked, 'Do you think I could go to the Antarctic?'

The student had a good geology degree, held the record for the fastest ever crossing of the Tararuas, had made several first ascents in the New Zealand Alps, and was absolutely mad keen to go. Perfect!

Except that she was Dawn Rodley, female! Well, no woman scientist had ever worked in Antarctica. Why not? Here was our chance to make history in a big way! Because she was Dawn, and a remarkable person, male or female, we nearly made it. Dr Williams and the University were all in favour of such a momentous social advance. The other four members of the expedition agreed. So did the RDRC, and the New Zealand Navy agreed to take her to Scott Base. All we needed for Dawn was one miserable hour of helicopter time to fly her from Scott Base to Lake Vashka and back again at the end of the season. And that one hour US Navy Operation Deep Freeze refused to grant us! Adamantly!

Eventually Dawn withdrew and was replaced by Ian Willis, another geology student, one who had also taken my geophysics course, and he made a fine collection of oriented specimens of dolerite from Victoria Valley. Together with Ted we produced what turned out to be an immensely important scientific paper and, apart from the *Glossopteris* plants, provided one of the first conclusive bits of evidence that Antarctica was part of Gondwana. (Peter Barrett, who wrote the Introduction for this little book, made another huge step in pinning down Gondwana, by discovering in the

Transantarctic Mountains the fossil amphibian Labyrinthodont, and I've already mentioned Warren Hamilton's contribution – the similarity of the granites in the Taylor Glacier valley with those in South Australia.)

We all thought that the Deep Freeze refusal to accept the fact that women existed and were actually human beings was so asinine that for the next decade I tried nearly every year to include a woman scientist in at least one Antarctic party. I don't know whether Bob Clark tried again. From 1961, when Gillian and I moved to the Institute of Polar Studies at The Ohio State University, the National Science Foundation, who were required by law to approve and fund all US Antarctic activities, routinely denied every such proposal. Eventually, for the 1968–69 season, my friend Mort Turner from the NSF called me up and said that the US Navy had at last relented, and we could send a party of four women – and then he added, 'as long as they all have Antarctic experience'.

This I regarded as just another challenge, and we overcame it – but that's another story for a different day. New Zealand became the second nation to allow women scientists in the Antarctic, and Rosemary Askin became a member of VUWAE 15 in 1970–71.

I did take part in VUWAE 4, 1960–61, but not as the leader. Experience with the 1951 Spitsbergen expedition and with that first University-sponsored expedition, VUWAE 2, had shown me that the largest part of the leader's job occurs after the expedition is over, 'tidying up the bits and pieces'. Immediately after our trip to the ice-free area north of the Koettlitz Glacier, Gillian, Nicky, Rebecca and I were going to The Ohio State University, where I was going to help Dick Goldthwait set up an Institute of Polar Studies. (Dick was the visitor to Scott Base who had obviously been sounding me out, after the fieldwork of VUWAE 2.) Instead, Ralph Wheeler took the leadership role on VUWAE 4, and did a fine job. I made a gravity survey over as much of the area as I could walk, and some interesting measurements of the surface velocity of a small glacier, Radian Glacier, named for the family: Rebecca, Andrew (although he didn't arrive till the following year), Diana (Gillian's first name) and Nicky. Fortuitously the ends of my surveying baseline subtended almost exactly one radian at the first surveying point.

By far the most important single aspect of the VUWAEs has been their continuity. The 2007–08 expedition was VUWAE 52. It's about time that someone wrote the history of VUWAEs and their quite remarkable contribution to our knowledge of Antarctic science.

Of course everything, except Antarctica itself, has changed greatly in the 50 years since VUWAEs 1 and 2. Our expedition cost less than $1000 and involved four field members. ANDRILL, including many people from VUWAE, worked with a budget of NZ$45 million (spread over two years – and only part of it being spent by Vic), provided by the governments of Italy, Germany, and the United States as well as New Zealand. VUWAE 51 had at least 18 participants, many of them in the total of 60 or so international scientists and more than 20 others on ANDRILL working with incredibly sophisticated equipment. Others from VUWAE worked on different projects.

The idea of an Antarctic research unit within the University existed only in the mind of Bob Clark until 1960. When I told Bob late in 1960 that I was leaving for Ohio, he responded by offering me a position in his Geology Department, with the title 'Director, Antarctic Research Unit'. It was very, very tempting but I had already told Dick Goldthwait that I'd come to Columbus for 15 months. In the following 25 years, while I was there, we built up the Institute of Polar Studies, and then changed its name to Byrd Polar Research Center. Over the years we have maintained very close ties with VUWAE, and have accepted at least half a dozen New Zealanders as graduate students. One of those was Peter Barrett, who gained his PhD with the Institute of Polar Studies at The Ohio State University in 1968, returned to New Zealand, and became Director of the Antarctic Research Centre in 1970. It's difficult to produce a much closer relationship than that! As with VUWAE, I have watched and regretted some aspects of the changes at Byrd Polar Research Center, from 'small' science to 'big' or 'special' science.

The four participants of VUWAE 2 have remained good friends and over the years have met every now and again, most recently at 'The First and Last Reunion of the Former Inhabitants of Vanda Station' held at Twizel in 2005, and at a remarkable reunion held in June 2007 in Wellington, when Peter Barrett called for a meeting of members of all of the VUWAEs from VUWAE 1 through VUWAE 51. It was a wonderful affair! Several people called me 'Sir'. Julia Bull, VUWAE 51, and I discovered we are not related, but I agreed to loan her the use of the name of Bull Pass, for bragging purposes.

In the 'Recollections of the first 50 Years', prepared for the reunion, Warren Dickinson, VUWAEs 44–50, and Tamsin Falconer, VUWAEs 50–51, wrote:

> For most of us our first trip to Antarctica was a 'life changing' experience, for each of us was infected in unique ways. Antarctica has changed little in 50 years and still doggedly guards her scientific secrets. For some it may seem that the Dry Valleys have been 'done to death', yet nowhere else is it so obvious that the more we learn, the less we know.

Indeed the Dry Valleys have become the most intensively studied area of the continent. Knowing that the VUWAE members have generated over 400 published papers so far, I guess that well over 2000 refereed scientific papers have been published on aspects of the science of Wright and Victoria Valleys alone. Books of paintings and photographs abound and there are even several science fiction books about the area, some of them quite entertaining, even if not as good as the real thing.

When I first suggested writing this book, during the 2005 Vandals reunion, to which the members of VUWAE 2 were invited 'to provide historical perspective', two of the other three members suggested that we try to bring our story up-to-date by including an account of the scientific developments and discoveries in the valley since that time. I thought that was clearly impossible – at least for me to do. Just one small part of the valley's history, for example, is that as a consequence of the remarkable things we and our successors in the next few years had found in Wright Valley, the New Zealanders, with support from the US NSF, decided to build a small station on the edge of Lake Vanda, called, appropriately enough, Vanda Station. It was occupied for three winters and most of the summers between 1968 and 1991. David Harrowfield wrote an excellent summary of the life of the station, without mentioning an iota of scientific observation – and that alone took 50 printed pages. David dedicated the book to the four of us from the 1958–59 affair.

And just to mention one little bit of the science and the changes in 50 years: back in the 'good old days' we noted the air temperature and guessed at the wind speed a few times a day, although we often railed at it almost continuously. Some years ago somebody placed automatic weather stations in Wright Valley, near the entrance to Bull Pass, and in Victoria Valley, west of Lake Vida. Now one has hourly recordings of the air temperature, the 'soil' temperature at a dozen different depths, radiation values and lots more things, as well as the wind speeds. The wind directions aren't recorded, and neither are the relative humidities, else it wouldn't be difficult to work out the directions. I notice that the wind still blows strongly most of the time, and that they don't try to measure the quantity of sand carried by the wind at face height. Pity!

The thought of writing a 36-volume discourse covering all the science horrified me. I contended that the only important development that could be included in this book was the effect that our little expedition has had on the lives of the participants.

And here's what the participants have to say about that effect.

BARRIE

Barrie and Peter, over the years, have gained so much knowledge and experience of the geology of Antarctica that they are both known separately as 'The wise old man of Antarctic geology'. What they are known as collectively, I am not allowed to disclose. In any case, they had both been to that seductive place before I knew them – so I take no responsibility for their downfall. Barrie, like the rest of us, is just beginning to lose that first blush of youth, although he still has a long way to go. He was born on 4th October 1937 but although he admits to attending that event he says he can't remember anything about it, and in particular, at what time it occurred.

However, Peter can remember the time of another important event in Barrie's life. At 10.30 a.m. on 28th January 1958 the two of them climbed out of the helicopter (good old 'King Pin') near the Inland Forts at the top of the Taylor Glacier, on the Antarctic continent. And I'm pretty sure that in doing so he became the second youngest scientist ever to put foot on the Antarctic continent. Paul Siple, the Boy Scout who accompanied Byrd on his first Antarctic Expedition, was a couple of months younger than Barrie was in January 1958 when he landed at Little America, but that was on the Ross Ice Shelf, not the continent itself. Barrie's other competition for the honour might be John Marr, the Boy Scout with Shackleton's 'Quest' Expedition. Scout Marr was a year younger than Barrie, but the southernmost landing of that Expedition was South Georgia. That leaves Thomas Bagshawe, the Cambridge student who, at age 19, became a member of the oddest Antarctic expedition of them all. In the end Thomas and a somewhat older Charles Lester spent the winter of 1921 living in a slightly modified and very cramped boat, on an island a short distance – a hundred metres or less by memory – from the mainland of the Antarctic Peninsula. Well, I could dismiss Thomas's claim to be the youngest on the continent because they lived on an island, but I'm sure that they walked across the ice of the bay sometime in the winter. And it would be specious to deny the claim because they weren't even south of the Antarctic Circle. I guess that Barrie will have to be content with the Silver Medal.

I am just amazed at the amount of work that Peter and Barrie have accomplished over the years, together and separately, with VUWAEs, Byrd Polar Research Center, and otherwise. Even in 1958 it was quite apparent that they'd both go far, and Dick and I sometimes were prepared to suggest various remote spots for them. But all this is beyond a joke! – Colin

Returning, still rather hungry and footsore, to New Zealand and Victoria University, I spent the rest of 1959, like Peter, working on my MSc thesis.

Our theses consisted of joint manuscripts and one solo effort each. Peter worked up the sedimentology of the Beacon Sandstone strata and I fear I insulted the mineralogy of the Ferrar Dolerite sills. (It was my one and only foray into igneous mineralogy and is now properly lost and forgotten.) I was busy the whole year, but after the action and excitement of VUWAE 2, felt somewhat unsettled. Then in late November Bob Clark received a cable asking if he had a candidate suitable for a research assistantship in Geology at the University of New England in New South Wales. The position would allow study for a PhD. Although the New Zealand Geological Survey had offered me a position in sedimentary petrology upon completion of the MSc, the chance of an Australian adventure with a bonus PhD candidature proved irresistible. I obtained leave of absence from the Survey, which could perhaps see two advantages: I might learn something about sedimentary petrology in the course of the PhD and, probably more importantly, they would benefit by a two- to three-year salary saving.

In July 1960 I took up the assistantship at the University of New England, a charming rural campus situated at about 1000 metres altitude atop the New England Tablelands. Rural research was much emphasized and because of the University's farms and extensive campus, it claimed to run about a student to the acre (fewer during droughts). Signing me onto the staff the Registrar apologized for the smallness of my salary. I didn't tell him it was £50 more than my Survey position in New Zealand.

So started my international education. No longer a sheltered Kiwi living at home or in a polar tent, I plunged into University college life, mixing with a spectrum of undergraduate and postgraduate students. Perforce I learned a lot about life pretty quickly, and about other people's views from the banal to the bizarre. I acquired a large ancient Ariel motorcycle, and every one of my left shoes was soon covered with a film of blown engine oil. That rattling old machine and I explored much of the rolling New England Tablelands and the remarkable saw-tooth gorges.

The local gliding club was great fun but soon exposed my innate inability to soar like an eagle. Undeterred I joined the University's Parachute Club ('Plummet Airlines') and tumbled to that activity with natural ease. We packed our own parachutes – and I had never learnt to make even a bed neatly! It was a great time, and I thought I was maturing and improving considerably. Several of my colleagues weren't so sure.

As the Geology Department's research assistant (a position so lowly it no longer exists) I had to work only nine hours per week, with the rest of the time my own for pursuing the PhD. I was given a small research grant and access to a vehicle. A fellow student showed me how the gears worked and where the brake was. I had already spotted the steering wheel. And off I went, dispatched to the outback, to the rolling northwest slopes and plains of inland New South Wales. There in the catchments of the Horton and Gwydir rivers I started mapping several hundred square kilometres of a terrain that had never heard the ring of a geological hammer. I subsequently spent months in the field, in summer plagued by heat and flies and in the company of snakes and some big goannas, but absorbed by the geology and welcomed and encouraged by the remarkable people of the Australian outback. Again, I had fallen on my boots!

As time went by on-campus junior teaching duties came my way and so with the stroke of a pen I was metamorphosed into a Demonstrator. I discovered I liked teaching and students, and the Geology Department was dynamic and growing, so in 1962 I resigned from the New Zealand Geological Survey and settled for a life in academia, at least for the foreseeable future. (To my astonishment I also met, chased and married Jan, the most beautiful woman on campus – and promptly sold my parachute.) That foreseeable future proved to have an ever-receding horizon. I became a Lecturer in 1966 and only retired some 30 years later, as an Associate Professor. Over that time I steadily built up course components in sedimentology, sedimentary petrology and marine geology. I enjoyed the teaching, and especially thesis supervision of many students researching the Devonian and Carboniferous mysteries of New South Wales's northwest slopes and plains. I still totter happily about the campus as an Honorary Research Fellow.

Over those 30 years Antarctica continued to beckon and repeatedly interrupt a busy contented Australian way of life, centred about family, on 37 desperate acres of a hobby farm close to campus. In the austral summer of 1968–69, as a member of VUWAE 13, I returned with Peter and two postgraduate students, Michael Gorton and Barry Kohn, and two Italian mountaineering celebrities, Carlo Mauri and Allessio Ollier, to southern Victoria Land. We headed for the vast Skelton Glacier Névé, and then onto the Quartermain Mountains and western Olympus Range, to continue clambering over the peaks of Beacon Supergroup strata. What a contrast that season was with VUWAEs 1 and 2! No longer relying solely on dear old *King Pin* and our own foot power, we were grandly 'put in' onto the Névé by a ski-equipped Hercules and were supplied with three, albeit elderly, motor toboggans for glacier travel.

But it was the landscape that awed me. On VUWAE 2 we had struggled our way up interminable screes, scrambled up, down and along rock benches and slopes, or else plodded over carpets of hummocky moraine.

Peter and I had never once trod on glacier ice. For us it had been a world of rock and rock debris. There on the Skelton Névé we instead motored upon a glacial sea, the shores of which lapped against fringing islands of rock, small ranges and nunataks. On these we landed, Columbus-like, to search and document the Beacon Sandstone strata. We discovered much, including the deposits of an ancient continental glaciation that rested upon fluvial strata laid down by a turbulent and widespread river system. Coal measures succeeded the glacial strata and so we could witness the record of major climate changes in Antarctica's distant past. The glacial strata were the long-sought equivalents of the Buckeye Tillite, discovered by Bill Long, exposed far to the south in the Horlick Mountains. Within the fluvial strata we collected delicately preserved fossils of armored fish, some of which were up to a metre long. Even bigger ones had obviously gotten away. We were quite unprepared for the abundance of the fossils and so were forced to sacrifice precious spare underwear in which to pack them safely. (I suggested we utilized our used underwear, but was overruled.)

In 1972 I grabbed an opportunity to make my first foray into marine geology. I spent two months aboard the international Deep Sea Drilling Project's vessel, *Glomar Challenger,* spattered with deep sea ooze and logging endless ocean floor cores, whilst the ship slowly traversed submarine mountains and plains from Durban to Fremantle, in order to determine the origin of the Indian Ocean. No undertaking was ever too big for DSDP! The remoteness of the voyage was striking. For two months I watched the sun rise and set upon a featureless horizon. We did see one other ship, but only on the penultimate day of the voyage.

In 1974 Peter, then Chairman of the Geology Department at Northern Illinois University, pointed me towards the Antarctic Dry Valley Drilling Project (DVDP), a joint United States–Japan–New Zealand programme administered by his department's geophysicist, Lyle McGinnis. Still easily led and becoming interested in Antarctica's Cenozoic glacial record I took study leave and became the project's geologist for the first half of the 1974–75 field season, during the drilling of thick glacigene sequences mantling the eastern Taylor Valley floor. In the Thiel Earth Sciences Lab at McMurdo Station I logged the deeply frozen cores that were helicoptered in from the field, ever trying to warm my aching hands, and ensuring for the New Zealand drillers camped on site a steady supply of cigarettes. (Particularly fascinating in the lab were some amazing Japanese electric pencil sharpeners that produced a lead point sharp enough to pass through the eye of a needle!) After that drilling finished I moved to Northern Illinois University, to refine and prepare the logs for publication, and to thoroughly enjoy with my family the American Midwest way of life.

There had been some logic in my DVDP appointment, for my 1972 Deep Sea Drilling Project experience coupled with a knowledge of the Dry Valleys geology stood me in good stead for handling the cores. DVDP was a pioneering project that opened many surprised eyes to the considerable Cenozoic record of Antarctica's glacial history available through drilling. I was proud to be part of it.

In the summer of 1977–78 VUWAE 22 resumed the Beacon Sandstone studies that had been started on the Skelton Névé in 1968–69. Alex Pyne, on the first of his many trips to Antarctica, mountaineer Walter Fowlie and I helicoptered into the Kennar Valley/Mount Feather/Finger Mountain region of the Quartermain Mountains, close to the edge of the polar plateau. They were wonderful days, scree scrambling, climbing and walking ridges and taking in spectacular views across the 100-kilometre-wide belt of southern Victoria Land's mountains. We worked on the same ancient glacial strata we'd found on the Skelton and on the overlying Coal Measures, trying to determine which way Antarctic ice had flowed so long ago and the nature of the climate change that the two formations recorded. We recovered much detailed information about long vanished geographies. In Kennar Valley, and some 80 kilometres from the coast, we came across the bones of an Adélie penguin and idly wondered whether it had crossed Antarctica long before the Trans-Antarctic Expedition. Amongst many good memories I clearly remember Walter, sitting up in his sleeping bag, with one hand effortlessly turning out batches of scones on the Primus. Another recollection is suspect Primus kerosene repeatedly causing our carbon monoxide indicator to turn black.

On Mount Feather we were joined by Father Howard Brady, an Australian priest based at McMurdo Station. Howard is a delightful and unforgettable character, and a passionate geologist with unlimited energies. I'll never forget, when tent-bound by a howling blizzard high on the mountain, watching Howard hunched over his microscope (which seemed to appear from nowhere), coolly searching for microfossils, quite oblivious to the outside tumult. The microscope's light source was a battered flashlight jammed into Howard's even more battered sneaker.

During that field season my research interest unexpectedly changed, for high on Mount Feather we helicoptered onto an enigmatic and very much younger glacial deposit, loosely referred to by other workers as the 'Sirius tillite'.

That 'tillite' was simply too interesting to ignore and so with VUWAE 24 in the 1979–80 summer we pursued it northwards to the Coombs

Hills and Odell Glacier, bordering the huge Mackay Glacier. That was a memorable season in quite magical country, although once for three days in otherwise clear weather it was impossible to leave the tents without being blown over. There were just the three of us: myself and Howard, and Keith Woodford, our Himalayan mountaineer, who is now a Professor of Agriculture at Lincoln University in New Zealand. Field time was short so Keith cheerfully guided us up and down Mount Brooke (named for Colin's Greenland friend) by the most direct route and in so doing taught me the meaning of real terror. To top things off, just after we reached the summit platform a blizzard engulfed us. Back in the tent that night I was white faced and wide eyed, with clammy hands for hours afterwards! However, shattered nerves did recover, confidence returned, and a successful field season was accomplished.

In the 1981–82 season as a member of VUWAE 26, I searched yet further afield for Sirius deposits in the Rennick Glacier region, accompanied by Barry Walker, a postgraduate student from Victoria University. There we were a tiny component of the international (USA, Australia, New Zealand) Northern Victoria Land Expedition. This enterprise centred about a large Remote Field Camp on the Canham Glacier in the Freyberg Mountains. The camp was entirely supplied by Hercules aircraft and had its own support helicopters. Field parties were continually coming and going into the mountains either by helicopter or toboggan and so it was an exciting place to meet other workers. Between field sorties there were some great parties, as well as the luxury of hot showers and a laundry! Out in the mountains we tried hard but found no sign of the tillite, or certainly none in the places I was game to go. The lack of a supporting mountaineer made for some exciting times. Luckily one of our camps was close to spectacular and little-known exposures of that same ancient tillite we'd studied on the Skelton Névé and in the Quartermain Mountains. Close analysis of the outcrops made for a surprising and useful palaeogeographic contribution, and so saved the day. (Like Alex Pyne before him in southern Victoria Land, Barry worked on fluvial strata associated with the widespread Coal Measures overlying the glacial deposits.)

By now my Antarctic research was fully centred upon the history of the Ice Sheet. As a study the history was puzzling, controversial and attracted much international interest. So in the 1979–80 season, Peter Barrett at Victoria University organized us both to be the site geologists for the Dry Valley Drilling Project's successor, the McMurdo Sound Sediment and Tectonic Studies project, generally referred to as MSSTS, and very much Peter's brainchild. MSSTS was a remarkable project for its time as the drilling rig and camp was sited out in McMurdo Sound on two-metre-thick sea ice, over 197 metres of water. The operation depended on regular surface transport, often over rough and difficult sea ice from Scott Base. This involved a 60-kilometre drive each way, and took a heavy mechanical toll. At one stage, of the 13 vehicles available from the Scott Base fleet, only one remained serviceable! But the recovered core triumphantly demonstrated the ice sheet to have been in existence and dynamic for more than 30 million years.

In 1982–83 I spent study leave in the Geology and Mineralogy Department of The Ohio State University (OSU) in Columbus, Ohio. Peter had moved there in 1980 to become Chairman of the Department and with the assistance of Colin, then Dean of Mathematical and Physical Sciences at the OSU, a Visiting Professorship was organized and I taught the graduate sedimentary rocks course.

Then in 1985–86 I led a small Ohio State University party to the Reedy Glacier/Wisconsin Range region of the Horlick Mountains, the Harold Byrd Mountains near the head of the Ross Ice Shelf, and back to southern Victoria Land, ever questing for the Sirius 'tillite' or its equivalents. It was now appreciated that these scattered, obscure and less than spectacular deposits held a priceless onshore record of ancestral phases of the East Antarctic Ice Sheet. Originally OSU's remarkable John Mercer was to lead the party, but unexpectedly he withdrew because of ill health and so I stumbled into the breach. Our party consisted of PhD students David Harwood and Lowell Stott (now professors at the Universities of Nebraska and Southern California, respectively), Jim Leide, a soil scientist from the University of Wisconsin, and Carl Thomson, our New Zealand mountaineer. Encouraged by a wealth of fixed wing aircraft and helicopter support, that field season developed into one of the most challenging and exciting adventures I've had in Antarctica. Just about everything happened, and yet somehow everything worked out! I have many vivid memories. From where we were landed on the Reedy Glacier Névé, the half-buried Camp Ohio II Jamesway hut, abandoned in 1962, was visible. Tobogganing to it, we hurried with visions of loot and luxuries towards the entrance, only to discover, when two of us dropped into fissures up to our thighs, that glacier flow since 1962 had carried the site into a crevasse field. We immediately left, very cautiously and quite empty handed! The field plan required our crossing the ten-kilometre-wide and much broken Reedy Glacier. We tried, but the most we ever got was about 200 metres from the shore, and there a toboggan dropped several metres down into a bottomless blue-black crevasse, where it jammed in a vertical position. We got that toboggan back, but the Reedy Glacier defeated us. I returned home jubilant about the season and some six kilos lighter, verging on the skeletal.

Two marine geology voyages interrupted Antarctic activities. In May–June 1984 aboard the research vessel *S.P. Lee*, I sailed on Operation Deepsweep, which was a geophysical survey of the sea floors about Vanuatu and the eastern Solomon Islands. Before boarding in Espiritu Santo I had no idea how little of the submarine geography was known. This made for an often exciting cruise. Encounters with uncharted mountainous features rising from the sea floor several times caused abrupt changes in the ship's course and the frenetic recovery of geophysical arrays trailing astern. On one occasion the recovery attempt was too late. I also remember the time when several of us dived over the side to swim and float mid-ocean above the 7000-metre-deep New Hebrides Trench, whilst those on board maintained a shark watch. The rest of the world seemed wonderfully far away. I might well have been in space.

In 1986 similarly I participated aboard HMNZS *Tui* in a month-long marine geology survey about the northern Cook Islands, Niue, Samoa and Tonga. This project was to search for and dredge nickel-, copper- and cobalt-rich manganese nodules and crusts on the sea floor and submarine mountain slopes, and to assess their economic potential. Again it was fascinating to watch the submarine topography unfold on the chart recorder, with the huge Manihiki Plateau and many mountains rising almost mysteriously from abyssal sea floor plains. Several mountain summits do reach to within a few metres of the sea surface, to form mid-ocean reefs that must have been deadly threats to early navigators.

Berths on two more OSU field parties followed in 1985–86 and 1990–91. Both were led by Peter and were to the head of Beardmore Glacier, centred largely on the ice-free Meyer Desert of the Dominion Range. Here thick sequences of Sirius 'tillite' had been found by John Mercer back in 1964. The subsequent recovery of marine diatoms and exquisitely preserved leaves and twigs of Antarctic Beech (*Nothofagus* sp.) in these strata (now known formally as the Sirius Group), and what such data suggest about the history of the East Antarctic Ice Sheet, has led to vigorous controversy (stabilists vs dynamicists) that still continues.

At this stage the Sirius Group was known only from the Transantarctic Mountains. However, at the Fourth International Symposium on Antarctic Earth Sciences in Wisconsin in 1977, I had heard the eminent Russian polar geologist, V.I. Bardin, describe little-known Cenozoic marine glacial strata found far away in MacRobertson Land, in the Prince Charles Mountains bordering the Lambert Glacier, arguably Antarctica's largest river of ice.

I began to realize that these strata were probably equivalents, at least in part, of the Sirius Group, and so I decided to 'try' for the Prince Charles Mountains via the Australian National Antarctic Research Expeditions, or ANARE.

For me there ensued four very fruitful ANARE field seasons in the Prince Charles Mountains, run under a very different operational regime to those based from McMurdo Sound. Just reaching the appropriate Australian Antarctic base often involved lengthy sea voyages, because of en route marine science surveys or the delivery of cargo and personnel to other bases. ANARE at that time operated no fixed-wing aircraft on the continent and instead relied upon helicopter transport for putting in deep-field parties. This was achieved by en route refuelling from strategically located fuel dumps. My first three ANARE seasons were to the ice-free Amery Oasis and nearby Fisher Massif (1987–88, 1989–90, and 1994–95), and the fourth (1997–98) was to the Menzies Range, much further to the south and some 750 kilometres inland from the coast.

Just getting into one's field area was often a memorable experience. I well recall my first 'put-in' to the Amery Oasis. A big lumbering Russian Mil-8 helicopter, with a crew of four, including a radio operator using only Morse code, was our transport. En route we stopped briefly at the Russian base of Soyuz for refuelling. There we were courteously escorted to a small hut where an excellent Chicken Kiev, accompanied by bottles of vodka, awaited. The Russians wished us bon appetit and politely withdrew. A short while later, refuelling of both men and machine complete, we flew on.

The Prince Charles Mountains adjacent to Lambert Glacier are small rugged ranges and nunataks. Few exceed 1500 metres in altitude and the peaks only poke through the ice sheet because the latter's surface is remarkably pulled down by the enormous through-flow of the Lambert Glacier ice. Amery Oasis itself consists of about 1800 square kilometres of ice-free terrain. Within it the ice-covered Beaver and Radok lakes are joined by a steep-sided, river-cut Pagodroma Gorge. Although some 250 kilometres from the coast, Beaver Lake, remarkably, is tidal. The Amery Oasis holds many mysteries.

Another spell of marine science did intervene in the ANARE programs, for in 1992 I found myself logging cores for two months aboard the famous deep-sea drilling vessel *JOIDES Resolution*, the successor of the *Glomar Challenger*. The ship extensively drilled a submarine mountain range off Kamchatka and then swung south past the Aleutians to complete its drilling in the Gulf of Alaska. However, even in this maritime interruption of my Antarctic activities the research emphasis remained with past ice sheets, for in the cores I sought evidence of the somewhat speculative Siberian Ice Sheet.

My last ANARE season, to the Menzies Range, coincided with the 40th anniversary of VUWAE 1, and for me completed a full circle, as the geology there was as little known in 1997–98 as the geology of southern Victoria Land was to Peter and myself in 1957–58. The season was a challenge. It was the coldest and windiest I've experienced. Snow was a minor feature, the glacier surfaces being rolling or hummocky landscapes of blue ice. Never once did we see the smallest puddle of melt water, or any form of life. Much of the Prince Charles Mountains remain to be explored but we do now know a little about the glacial deposits preserved there on the floors of uplifted ancient fjords, which record advances and recessions of the ice sheet's edge over distances of hundreds of kilometres.

Since retiring in 1996 I've sailed on more than 20 voyages to and about Antarctica, aboard a Russian ice-breaker, lecturing to tourists on geology, glaciology and exploration history. One voyage was a 66-day circumnavigation with 26 memorable 'landings of opportunity'. More recently I've undertaken similar voyages to the Siberian and Canadian Arctic, tramping about the remarkable Wrangel, Baffin, and Ellesmere Islands, and twice have transitted the Arctic's Northwest Passage. Elsewhere in the world Jan and I have trekked in wild and wonderful places including Patagonia, the Kamchatka Peninsula, the High Atlas Mountains of Morocco, the Himalayas, and southwestern New Zealand.

Yet it's Antarctica and perhaps only Antarctica that continues to draw me, as it's done ever since those heady and funny days of VUWAEs 1 and 2. I still remember on VUWAE 1 scrambling about the sandstone and dolerite slopes of Beehive Mountain above our first campsite, near the head of Taylor Glacier close to the Ice Plateau edge. Still a fairly naïve third-year geology student, who had hardly travelled out of Wellington, I stared across a landscape of tumbled ice onto the sunlit flanks of the Transantarctic Mountains. That vast alpine panorama, vanishing over both horizons, captivated me as I stood in the near-audible silence. Fifty years later I hoard and treasure many such memories.

PETER

I experienced birth *(That's Peter's way of saying that he 'was born'. Probably Peter thinks he's a bit of Beacon Sandstone or a sheet of dolerite. You never know with geologists – Colin)* in Wellington (New Zealand) and spent most of my early years living on the northern slopes of Mount Egmont (Mount Taranaki) where I count myself as an alumnus of the Midhurst, New Plymouth, Urenui, and Inglewood Primary Schools, and later New Plymouth Boys' High School. My father was employed by an American oil company (Standard Vacuum Oil Company) and we moved all over New Zealand during the 1940s and after WWII, as the company drilled many holes in an unsuccessful search for oil.

For the polar explorer or scientist there is usually a moment in their past when he or she first becomes aware of the world inside the polar circles. For many, this comes quite early in life and is usually a chance happening. This was my experience. When I was ten years old, an uncle gave me two tattered old volumes of the 1913 edition of *Scott's Last Expedition*, suggesting that they might be of interest. The following year I must have done something of merit in school for I was rewarded with a copy of Frank Hurley's *Shackleton's Argonauts*. If I were superstitious, I might claim that these were prophetic and even divine moments, but I will resist this temptation. In 'colonial' New Zealand the average school boy certainly knew that the mother country or 'home' (that is, the United Kingdom) was the ancestral font of great British heroes, and that Scott and Shackleton resided in this pantheon of manhood, super-human excellence, suffering and even glorious death.

I laboured on through New Plymouth Boys' High School during the early 1950s but do not recall thinking again about the continent to the south that was to eventually claim much of my adult life. I do recall the Coronation Day parade of 1953 when the mayor of the tiny township of Inglewood (Taranaki Province) strode purposefully along its single street and proudly hollered to the several hundred cheering citizens that Edmund Hillary and Tensing Norgay had successfully scaled Mount Everest. However, Hillary's association with Antarctica was still several years into the future and I had little sense that I would join his Trans-Antarctic Expedition within four years' time.

I left high school in New Plymouth in 1954 and departed the rural serenity of Taranaki Province for Victoria University College, Wellington, where in 1955 I began my first year of studies for a Bachelor of Science degree. I had a vague idea that to become a secondary school teacher would suffice as a career and proceeded to enrol in Zoology and Botany, filling in the first year curriculum with a course in Geology.

I recalled at the time that when living in Greymouth (I am also an alumnus of Greymouth Main Primary School) and aged seven or eight, my father arranged for me to spend time with the oil company geologists in the field on the West Coast of the South Island, and also with the micropaleontologists who were using microfossils to provide age control during drilling. Given this flimsy childhood heritage, undertaking a first year course in Geology seemed like a familiar and natural fill-in course option. Within a few weeks of entering university my personal world came into focus as I encountered people who were to become life-long friends and mentors.

In 1955 the Department of Geology at Victoria University comprised just Professor Robin (Bob) Clark, Dr John Bradley, Dr Martin Te Punga, Mr Ross Lauder and a small number of BSc, MSc and PhD students. The atmosphere was family-like and access to staff easy and informal. The Department's facilities consisted of a small cluster of temporary huts that conveyed all the ambience of a deserted military post. Nevertheless, I felt very much at home and decided I had discovered my niche, albeit somewhat accidentally. Bob Clark indoctrinated us with daily doses of lectures based on his University of Edinburgh mentor Arthur Holmes's book *Introduction to Physical Geology*, and John Bradley began his onslaught on our uncluttered minds with revelations on continental drift dogma, strongly influenced by his recent close encounter with Warren Carey at the University of Tasmania. In the first week at Vic I made the acquaintance of a tall, urbane and always immaculately attired fellow classmate. Barrie McKelvey helped determine the eventual fortunes of the VUWAE enterprise and is one of the central characters of this book. Thus began a lifetime friendship and professional collaboration, which has survived these past 50 years.

By the end of the first year the idea of a career in geology had supplanted the idea of one as a secondary school teacher. However, I had one serious problem to surmount. I had accepted a bursary from the Department of Education and signed a binding contract to become a science teacher, forever and forever. I resolved to accept their miserable pittance, bank the proceeds in a separate post office account, and see how the flirtation with geology would play out. In the second year at Vic I decided to take action. I petitioned the Department of Education, convinced them that I was an exceedingly poor prospect as a future teacher and that I had lost all interest in the profession. I paid them back their pittance in full, and kept the interest it had been earning. I was liberated from a future career in the classroom but was now decidedly impoverished.

Having jettisoned my opportunity to become a secondary school teacher, I was now urgently confronted with the need for pay and temporary employment. In the summers of 1955–56 and 1956–57 I followed my family to oil company employment in Australia as a university vacation field assistant, first in New South Wales and Queensland, and then in Western Australia. While university was in session I had a variety of jobs, including gorse cutting, working in a bakery, a stint as a lighthouse keeper on Brothers Island in Cook Strait, and delivering new cars to dealerships in the southern North Island.

My most enjoyable and fruitful job over several years was as an unregistered Wellington waterside worker or, as we were known in the trade, a 'Seagull'. Through my university years I helped load thousands of wool bales, hundreds of thousands of frozen sheep carcasses and billions of apples on to all the famous P&O and Shaw Savill ships trading between New Zealand and the 'old country'. Perhaps the major bonus of this job was that even 'Seagulls' earned high wages and generous meal money, and I could work with the cream of New Zealand's highly educated post-war European refugees. I found myself in the company of talented doctors, surgeons, chemists, architects, writers, poets, and composers, and so on, mostly from Eastern Europe. They were not accredited for professional service in New Zealand at the time and whiled away their days as 'wharfies'. They accepted me as a 'good young seagull' and accorded me the title of 'honorary trade unionist'. I proudly carried a union card, which stated that I was a 'non-union registered waterside worker'.

This talented bunch taught me the art of 'working slowly', to spin out ship-loading into triple overtime at nights, and how to drop and break open boxes of cheese, butter, and apples from a sling at 12 feet to 'earn' free food. I was in effect a criminal in training. They also used me as a lookout while they played chess behind walls of wool bales. In other words, I was now part of the congenial waterfront world of sharing wealth by damage, and learning critical life skills from a gallery of New Zealand's most ardent socialists and even communists. The Trade Union Hall was located just around the corner from where I lived in Taranaki Street and I was invited to attend meetings, to help swell the crowds at demonstrations and to receive free copies of the *People's Voice*.

When I applied for a US green card visa at the US Embassy in Wellington a few years later, one of the many boxes that had to be checked yes or no asked if I had ever been a member of the Communist Party. As I stood with my right hand in the air, bowing in awe towards a velvet-draped and subtly illuminated large coloured photograph of President Richard Nixon, I could of course answer an honest no, but I had certainly worked with many who were members. I am not sure how this valuable experience equipped me for later life, but I still recall those several years among these wonderful people with a great deal of affection. I am sure that in later years they all went on to fit comfortably and constructively into New Zealand's evolving social fabric.

Jumping ahead in time, when later offered the job of cargo handler on HMNZS *Endeavour* during the Trans-Antarctic Expedition of 1957–58, I could honestly say I was very well-trained and possessed professional experience for the task.

During 1956 Antarctica started to make its presence known in the New Zealand psyche. The Soviet Antarctic ship *Ob* came into Wellington on a goodwill visit. Whereas the New Zealand government didn't quite know how to handle the diplomatic aspects of this unexpected visit, the New Zealand populace certainly did. The general public and government scientists swarmed to visit the ship. The entire Geology Department went aboard to talk with their geologists and oceanographers. The US Operation Deep Freeze ice-breaker *Atka* also came into Wellington on a goodwill visit. US Navy aircraft flew over Wellington regularly on their way to Christchurch. New Zealand Trans-Antarctic Expedition and New Zealand International Geophysical Year planning and fund-raising was a daily feature in the newspapers. New Zealand's foray into Antarctic exploration and research had arrived at last, and with a jolt.

By the time I arrived back in Wellington from fieldwork in West Australia in February 1957 and was about to start my third year at Vic, the first summer of the NZ TAE and NZ IGY had been completed, Scott Base had been built, the winter group had settled in, and the summer parties were returning to New Zealand. The US base (Williams Air Facility, later known as McMurdo Station) had also been constructed. News from Antarctica was commonplace in the papers and on the radio, and Antarctic workers from the US and other countries were visiting New Zealand institutions on their way home. The international Antarctic science and logistics community was largely prepared for the beginning of the International Geophysical Year (1957–58) by June 1957 and in New Zealand planning was underway for NZ TAE and NZ IGY activities in the summer season of 1957–58. This included Ed Hillary's support of the Fuchs-led UK TAE, dog-sled reconnaissance traverses in the Transantarctic Mountains, and geophysical programmes at Scott Base and at Hallett Station.

Two million other New Zealanders had become familiar with these events by February 1957 but I had not at this stage contemplated any polar role for myself as the year unfolded.

The year 1957 was a tumultuous one in many respects. Barrie McKelvey and I had progressed to the third year of our BSc degree studies. The academic year started in a routine fashion but this was soon to change very suddenly as we became increasingly involved in planning a visit to Antarctica during the 1957–58 austral field season. These activities spanned the period from March until our departure for McMurdo Sound on 14th December 1957 on the TAE–IGY support ship HMNZS *Endeavour*. Our first VUWAE venture to Antarctica during the International Geological Year in the 1957–58 austral field season has been documented in several publications, including this one, and so I will not dwell on these details here.

Let's now move on to the early 1960s and later years as I meander through my VUWAE 'aftermath' years. Much to my surprise and relief I completed my studies and graduated with an MSc degree in 1961. Barrie McKelvey and I had shared the results of the fieldwork in the Dry Valleys and wrote theses on our two seasons of fieldwork. Results appeared as several papers in the *New Zealand Journal of Geology and Geophysics*, the *Journal of Glaciology*, and *Nature* between 1959 and 1963. We also contributed our field mapping data from Victoria and Wright Valleys to the first reconnaissance geological map for the area between the Mawson and Mulock Glaciers, which was published as a NZ Geological Survey Bulletin in 1962 by Bernie Gunn and Guyon Warren, both of whom had been geologists with the Trans-Antarctic Expedition.

Barrie and I were pleased to share the award of the Cotton Prize (Victoria University of Wellington) and Hamilton Memorial Prize (Royal Society of New Zealand) in 1962 for our Antarctic work.

With the completion of university studies it was time to move on. The VUWAE foursome quickly went their separate ways in search of new opportunities, Barrie and Dick moved to Australia in 1960, Colin departed for the American Dream in 1961, and although I tried and failed in an attempt to follow them abroad I did make it as far as Lower Hutt, some 12 miles north of Wellington. Although I had been accepted into the doctoral programme at The Johns Hopkins University to work in paleontology with Professor David Raup, the fellowship offered was, in the eyes of the US State Department, too meagre for survival and I was denied a student visa. What were the alternatives?

During my first two undergraduate years at Vic I had developed an interest in micropaleontology under the tutelage of Dr Martin Te Punga. I had also spent two summers in Australia as an oil company field assistant, and was offered a summer internship at the NZ Geological Survey. These interests were abruptly shelved during the period of VUWAEs 1 and 2 between 1957 and 1959. With no immediate plans to follow my VUWAE colleagues overseas in 1960–61, I revisited my paleontology options and reported to the NZ Geological Survey (DSIR) in Lower Hutt as an assistant micropaleontologist, working with Norcott Hornibrook and Charles Fleming, amongst others. I was to work in the NZ Geological Survey for 13 years, from 1960 to 1973.

The desire for overseas experience and the completion of a doctoral degree was never far from my thoughts and the award of a NZ National Research Fellowship in 1963 provided this opportunity. Although doctoral studies at Cambridge or Oxford had been the traditional destination of earlier young New Zealand paleontologists, I opted for studies in continental Europe and arrived at the Rijksuniversiteit te Utrecht in the Netherlands in 1963. This choice provided an opportunity to study with Professors Cornelius Drooger, Ralph von Koenigswald and Reinout Willem van Bemmelen.

While domiciled in the Netherlands between 1963 and 1966 I wandered profitably around Europe, enjoying research stints at universities in Stockholm, Copenhagen, Berlin, Munich, Warsaw, Krakow, Paris, and Prague. Fieldwork, museum research, conferences, the liberal style of European education, and contacts with prominent geologists and micropaleontologists I met along the way were to impact the way I viewed the earth sciences and science in general over succeeding decades of my professional life. I often recall the events of my European meanderings whenever I pick up Griffith Taylor's *Journeyman Taylor*. His book provides an entertaining account of quite similar trips around Europe in 1908–09 while a student at University of Cambridge, and just before he enlisted with Scott's *Terra Nova* expedition in 1910.

Living in Europe and studying at European universities in the early 1960s was an interesting experience and much different from today. National borders and the cultures they encircled were sharply defined. Many universities were intellectual capsules from the past, where godlike professors still held sway over the then accepted geological dogmas and paradigms. The political division of western and eastern Europe provided further separation into western and Soviet ways of deciphering the earth sciences.

Fundamental earth science issues such as continental drift and sea-floor spreading were not part of the European curriculum in the early and mid 1960s, and universities were still well entrenched in traditional 19th century Eurocentric historical geology. This was not to change until the early 1970s, when general acceptance of plate tectonic theory obliged many European geologists to adopt a more global dynamicist-mobilist view of Earth's evolution. This was not the case in Soviet-dominated eastern European institutions where I worked. In them, mobilist notions were still regarded with strong disfavour and suspicion. My sojourn in Europe coincided, then, with the end of an era that extended back well before WWII and even earlier. However, I had made a fortunate choice in studying at Utrecht, for this was one of the more forward-looking European universities at the time. It was with some regret that in late 1966 I felt obliged to finish my PhD at Utrecht and return to a life in New Zealand, and the NZ Geological Survey at Lower Hutt.

I was, however, to launch off on one more profitable northern hemisphere journey before heading back to the Antipodes. I undertook postdoctoral research in Israel in 1966–67 with Professor Zeev Reiss at The Hebrew University in Jerusalem. I elected to drive overland from Utrecht to Jerusalem via Yugoslavia, Hungary, Bulgaria, Greece, Turkey, Lebanon, Syria, and Jordan. I certainly would not try this journey today and must have been quite naïve and very lucky at the time. Even in the relatively safe days of the mid-60s, this personal expedition through parts of eastern European countries, the Anatolian Plateau of Turkey, and Middle East deserts had its exhilarating, dangerous, slightly terrifying, and uncertain moments. As I passed through Istanbul and Ankara I reported my plans to the British Embassy. They suggested that I let the British Embassy in Israel know if and when I arrived safely in Israeli West Jerusalem.

The journey went as planned. My trusty Volkswagen kept chugging along although I needed the local peasantry to give me a push start from time to time. I travelled with long-distance truck convoys over the more lonely and dangerous stretches. At the conclusion of my stay in Jerusalem I departed Haifa for Cyprus by ship hours before the Middle East War of 1967, headed to London, and then departed again by ship for a six-week journey back to New Zealand.

The New Zealand I returned to in 1967 after my four-year absence had not changed at all and re-acclimatization was not easy. This was a common experience for the many returning Kiwis who tried the best they could to fit back in the deep groove of New Zealand life in the late 1960s. It was safe, slow, congenial, picturesque, staid and seemingly resistant to change. The sense of geographic isolation was palpable. The European and Middle East adventures of the past four years made life in New Zealand seem incredibly dull. These were still the days before air travel to the northern hemisphere was commonplace, fast, regular and convenient, although this was changing. My immediate sense was that two groups of New Zealanders had evolved: a majority who remained at home and were looking steadfastly to the past, and a minority who had enjoyed the benefits of an OE (overseas experience) and saw other ways of viewing a fast-changing world. The former were in charge and the opinions of the latter on enticing and progressive alternative directions were hardly heeded. I found the transition from Europe to New Zealand difficult, frustrating and at times demoralizing. My newly gained experience from abroad seemed to have little application and was often ignored or rejected.

Opportunities to break out, at least temporarily, came with a return to Antarctica to lead the VUW Antarctic Expedition of 1968–69 with Barrie McKelvey, work at the West German Geological Survey at Hanover for several months in 1969, visits to Thailand, Nepal, Afghanistan, Iran, Israel, the Netherlands, the United States and Canada in 1969, and another visit to the US in 1970. It was clear that I was not settling into the routine of New Zealand life.

In 1972–73 I participated in Leg 28 of the Deep Sea Drilling Project, then drilling in the Ross Sea and Southern Ocean. In the aftermath of Leg 28 I was invited to visit the United States in early 1973 and lecture at a number of universities and museums. In the course of this US visit I was offered the chairmanship and a full professorship in the Department of Geology at Northern Illinois University, DeKalb. The time to leave New Zealand again, and probably permanently, had arrived. I accepted the offer and moved to Illinois in December 1973.

There was an Antarctic motive behind this decision. Northern Illinois University (NIU) was the lead institution for the Dry Valley Drilling Project (1972–76), a venture jointly sponsored by the United States, New Zealand and Japan. This allowed me a return to full-time participation in Antarctic research. I had never taught in a university institution or led an academic department before, so this new environment was a drastic change of direction. The learning curve proved to be steep. The Department of Geology at NIU had recently developed an MS-level graduate programme; my main responsibilities were to develop faculty and facilities to doctoral degree-granting standards and to argue for accreditation before the Illinois Board of Higher Education. This venture provided sudden immersion in the world of US tertiary education and US state politics, a daunting experience for a new immigrant with no prior academic experience. We achieved these goals by 1979.

During the time spent in DeKalb, Antarctic programmes brought me back to the Ross Sea area between 1977 and 1979, where I helped guide the Ross Ice Shelf Project during two field seasons and also participated in New Zealand's (VUWAE) MSSTS drilling programme in McMurdo Sound. Barrie McKelvey spent his sabbatical year at Northern Illinois University in 1977 and we finally completed the Beacon Supergroup work of the VUWAE 13 (1968–69) trip to the Skelton Glacier/Boomerang Range region.

With my primary task at NIU completed in 1979, the arrival of offers of deanships and chairmanships at other universities convinced me that it was perhaps time to move on. The experience gained at Northern Illinois University had been both valuable and enjoyable, and it is still a source of satisfaction that their Department of Geology and Environmental Geosciences has continued to evolve into a very strong and active earth science centre since my departure in 1980.

A visit to The Ohio State University, Columbus, in 1979, during a regional meeting of the American Geophysical Union, brought me and Colin Bull (then Dean of the College of Mathematical and Physical Sciences) back together for a few days. The Department of Geology and Mineralogy at OSU was searching for a new Chairman; Colin was an excellent salesman. I became a candidate and in a short time I had elected to move eastwards to Columbus, to begin an 11-year stint leading the Department at OSU. Colin was Dean of our College and I reported directly to him. Any successes our Department of Geology and Mineralogy enjoyed during this period resulted from the excellent cooperative working relationship the two of us maintained. I relinquished the chairmanship in 1991 and returned to full-time teaching and research.

The award of a Humboldt Research Prize allowed me to spend 1991–92 at the Alfred Wegener Institut in Bremerhaven, Germany, where I caught up with long-neglected research. East European borders had recently dissolved and I took the opportunity to revisit East Berlin, Leipzig, Weimar, Dresden and Warsaw, all places I had known during my student days almost 30 years earlier.

Following the International Geophysical Year, The Ohio State University became one of the principal Arctic and Antarctic research institutions in North America and a mecca for polar research programmes and scientists. This environment promoted very active academic and research programmes for graduate students with polar interests. In the ensuing 28 years at The

Ohio State University I have been able to develop and maintain a very active Antarctic Cenozoic research group of MS, PhD and postdoctoral students, supported largely by National Science Foundation, United States Antarctic Program research grants.

Over the years we have been active in the Deep Sea Drilling Project, Ocean Drilling Program, the NZ-CIROS drilling project, the international Cape Roberts Project, and, most recently, the international ANDRILL programme. As has been the case with the VUW Antarctic Research Centre in New Zealand, the Institute of Polar Studies (later known as the Byrd Polar Research Center) at The Ohio State University has proved to be a superlative training ground for future polar scientists. One of the more rewarding aspects of my activities at OSU has been the opportunity to produce graduates who have gone on to successful academic and productive polar research careers. Already a number have attained Associate and Full Professor rank at major universities and now maintain their own stables of budding young polar scientists.

Barrie McKelvey spent another sabbatical in the US and based his visit in the Department at Ohio State University during 1983. Our days of working on the Beacon Supergroup of the Transantarctic Mountains were supplanted by a new research thrust – one that was to keep us and our students occupied in productive collaborative efforts over the succeeding decades. Interest in the Antarctic Cenozoic paleoclimate had been steadily escalating since the early 1970s and more attention was being directed to both the onshore outcrop and offshore drillcore records. John Mercer, a research scientist in the Byrd Polar Research Center, had published on the Transantarctic Mountains Cenozoic Sirius Formation (later Sirius Group) in 1972, and the presence of the three of us, along with my PhD student David Harwood, in Columbus during Barrie's sabbatical led to the launch of a new phase of fieldwork, centred on the Antarctic terrestrial record, with expeditions to the Reedy, Beardmore, and Shackleton Glaciers and the Dry Valley region. Controversies arising from this work have spurred continuing field and laboratory research at many institutions ever since. Barrie went on to mount a series of very successful Australian expeditions in the Amery Glacier/Prince Charles Mountains region of East Antarctica, studying deposits very similar to those of the Sirius Group.

Life has not been all Antarctica and university activity. When my wife Joan and I moved from Illinois to Ohio in 1980 we decided to expand our professional interest in German shepherd dog breeding and training, something we couldn't manage within the city limits of DeKalb. Through the 80s and 90s we gradually acquired dogs from Germany and established

Framhein Shepherds on our 25-acre plot of forested land in Pataskala, east of Columbus. Summers and autumns found us in Germany buying quality dogs, breeding our bitches to internationally ranked males, obtaining titles for them under the German registration system for 'protection' dogs, and attending regional and national German shepherd competitions. We built a barn and field on the property for the breeding and training programme. The many German shepherd progeny produced over the years went off into successful careers in hospital therapy, search and rescue, cadaver detection, the police, schools, and so on. At one time we had as many as 25 adult and juvenile German shepherds on the property. In recent years we have slowly reduced the population back to a much smaller pack.

Spouses and family bear the brunt of our long absences during expeditions. Some families adjust to these disruptions and some don't. During the 1984–85 season I was fortunate in being able to include Joan in the party as a field assistant, largely due the foresight and understanding of Mort Turner, then Earth Sciences Program Manager at the office of Polar Programs, US National Science Foundation. Being able to share the Antarctic experience with my spouse is a key reason why I was able to continue to return south over so many seasons. A couple who can live for two months in a Scott tent, survive the occasional blizzard for several days at a time, fight Coleman stoves, and endure a lack of hot running water will have a lot to talk about in their later lives together.

Communications back home during expeditions have seen one of the great advances over the years. In the early field days one would be fortunate to receive a couple of out-of-date letters in a single season. Nowadays we are in almost constant communication by e-mail and telephone. It is so comforting these days to learn about the latest domestic disaster within hours of it occurring! Why does the plumbing or air conditioning system undergo a catastrophic collapse within 24 hours of our departure from home?

I guess one could say that the initial VUWAE experiences have impacted my entire life to quite a considerable degree. Reflection on each and every expedition spurs specific memories. While the science was always exciting, as were the often complex logistical issues, it has always been the personal interactions that remain foremost in my mind. Expedition colleagues are the core around which the enterprise unfolds. Our groups were usually small and well chosen. Nevertheless, an expedition to a remote location is also an evolutionary process in human relationships and there is always the potential for surprise. On balance though, my experiences have been overwhelmingly positive ones.

Somehow, the scientific task at hand and the hardships associated with achieving it always seem to bring out the most constructive aspects in one's colleagues and in the total team. This seems the nature of the beast, and lessons learned in the polar expedition setting seem to provide excellent preparation for life in 'normal' society among apparently 'normal' people.

When Colin asked us to account for our lives after the VUWAE of 1958–59 I was prompted to tally up just how many years I had spent in Antarctica. I discovered that I had participated in 22 expeditions and spent more than three years south of the Antarctic Circle, either on the continent or on oceanographic ships in the Southern Ocean. I still regard my first two VUWAE ventures while a mere student as distinctly different and unique compared with all those that followed. First impressions of a new world of adventure are the last to fade. As I look back on the 50 years since the IGY I am extremely grateful for the formative experiences of VUWAEs 1 and 2. Somehow, I managed to stay active in Antarctic affairs for decades and was fortunate to be a member of one of the more dynamic and progressive fraternities/sororities in the world of science.

All this was brought home when I met again with Colin, Dick and Barrie in 2005 at the Vanda Station reunion in Twizel and in 2007 at the VUWAE 50th year anniversary celebration in Wellington. These were the first occasions we had all been together since 1961. The original chemistry, humour, enthusiasm and productivity amongst us had not dimmed with time. I find this a quite hopeful but curious outcome, given that my three colleagues often lacked the most basic and acceptable contubernial etiquette. We have survived the first 50 years and still communicate actively and even relatively coherently!

But perhaps the most rewarding aspect of our primordial expedition is the fact that Victoria University of Wellington is now home to the highly respected Antarctic Research Centre. Our legacy is safe and this is reward enough, I'd say.

In November–December 2007 I made what was probably my last trip to Antarctica. I worked with the international ANDRILL team and watched approvingly as my former students and their students administered and participated in this technically and scientifically amazing initiative. My former students were kindly and considerate, and allowed me to be their lab technician, cook for them in the field, and even carry their bags. I also assisted the visiting NOVA and National Public Radio crews with interviews and general guidance as they documented the history and advances of the past half century. At two a.m. on a bright, sunny, crystal clear morning in early December 2007, I stood on a promontory in the western Asgard

Range, in the shadows of gold-glowing Mounts Aeolus, Boreas, Circe and Dido, and just gazed in awe at this immense and magnificent landscape. My mind travelled back 50 years to the time when the spirited young McKelvey and Webb galloped innocently all over these great expanses. It was a very special and even sentimental moment. Hell, we must have been very fit and perhaps just a little crazy at the time!

Yes, life has all been an interesting journey after all. I thank my parents for being so far-sighted as to have provided me the opportunity to experience it!

DICK

Dick is the only one of the four of us who has not yet been back to the Antarctic continent. At the time we went, 1958–59, he had spent more time 'on the ice' and on the surrounding seas than the rest of us, but Dick was certainly not disenchanted with the place. And in his life he certainly found adventures, both scientific and topographical, that we could only envy. Now, in September 2008, he tells us that, all being well, he will return to the Antarctic in January 2009, as a lecturer and guide with an Antarctic cruise vessel. Don't you wish some people would grow old gracefully?

Dick told me that as a very young child he had once stayed with his grandmother in Christchurch when her doctor visited her. Well, there's nothing remarkable in that – except that the doctor was Dr Leslie H. Wetter, who had been the surgeon with Douglas Mawson's Australian Antarctic expedition, 1911–14. Dick wondered if he had become infected with something Antarctic, which had taken 30 years to wear off.

In the last month or two Dick has sent me a few photos from Victoria Valley that he took in January 1958. In one of them a biscuit-tin-sized dark rock looks very much like a meteorite. Dick is now idly suggesting that he might put together a little expedition to retrieve it! I'll go along very happily as long as he doesn't make me carry a huge pack. Perhaps we could carry a one-kilogram GPS system rather than that theodolite and tripod. – Colin.

How does one summarize 50 years of displacement activities? Zoologists define displacement activity as 'the performance by an animal of an act inappropriate for the stimulus or stimuli that evoked it. Displacement behaviour usually occurs when an animal is torn between two conflicting drives, such as fear and aggression. Displacement activities often consist of comfort movements, such as grooming, scratching, drinking, or eating . . .'

In my case the conflicting drives have taken many forms, usually as conflict between creative artistic inclinations and the discipline required by a working scientist. I have vacillated between the two, to the diminution of both.

Seeking to continue my academic career, in 1959 I applied (against the advice of my professor) for and obtained a Zoology lectureship in the newly created Science Faculty at the Canberra University College, which since 1930 had been a college of the University of Melbourne. Early in 1960 the college was amalgamated with the newly created and rapidly developing Australian National University (ANU) to become the School of General Studies.

As a resident of University House I glanced down the table at breakfast and asked 'Who is that attractive new student?' and thus I met and very soon married a Canadian anthropologist, Diane MacEachern, studying for her PhD. Early in 1961 I became the first deputy warden at Bruce Hall of ANU, the first mixed-sex residential hall in Australia. We occupied a convenient apartment that served as a hazard separating the male and female wings. That early period saw the growth and development of the Science Faculty at the ANU, and besides lecturing in many subjects I was also starting new research, on the ecology and life history of an Australian rock-dwelling skink. One of the highlights of that time was a visit by Griffith Taylor. During two long evening sessions I showed him many of the slides and photographs we had taken during the expedition. I remember him slapping his hand on his thigh and saying 'If only we had walked over the hill', by which he meant the Wilson Piedmont Glacier.

Eventually I submitted my dissertation in 1965, and received a PhD for my studies. Most of the fieldwork for that was conducted in the hills around Canberra, while Diane carried out her fieldwork on Aboriginal communities in Shepparton and Melbourne, Victoria, beginning her prominent career in Australian anthropology. Thus we spent much of our early married life apart (the opposite to most couples) – but marriage to Diane was the best move I ever made.

Diane finished her PhD in 1964 and became one of the pioneering researchers in urban indigenous studies in southern Australia. She was one of the initiators of the journal *Aboriginal History* and a member of the Aboriginal Treaty Committee – a body 30 years in advance of its time.

Our daughter Laura was born in 1973 – she inherited Diane's abilities and completed both a science degree in immunology and an arts degree in anthropology. Now she works in an educational role in the Commonwealth Public Service.

Tragically Diane died suddenly in 1986. During her career she completed some 75 publications, articles, books or manuscripts. A major archive of her work has recently been established at the State Library of Victoria in Melbourne.

In 1965–66 I spent sabbatical leaves in Berkeley, at the time of the 'Berkeley riots', Mario Savio and the 'Free Speech Movement'. The Berkeley campus was the centre of the Anti-Vietnam movement in the USA, a fascinating time of student ferment. Much of a 1973 sabbatical was spent in libraries at the University of British Columbia, with visits to the libraries of the University of Montreal and the British Museum of Natural History, exploring the world of natural history illustrators.

After initially encountering Stuart MacKay and animal radio-telemetry at Berkeley, I and my students explored the use of those emerging techniques in the study of feral Australian vertebrates. Other displacement activities included a four-vehicle crossing of the Simpson Desert in 1973 with a group including botanists, geographers and soil scientists. We followed the 1939 route taken by Charles Madigan, formerly a member of Mawson's 1932 British, Australian and New Zealand Antarctic Research Expedition (BANZARE).

Since the 1980s I have made many trips in search of Devonian fish; to southeastern Australia, to the Kimberly of northwestern Australia, to the low-rainfall belt of inland New South Wales, and to the Carboniferous of Queensland. The fossil finds, taking hours in the field, may lead to years of research, writing and illustrating! I have also gone on fossil hunts as part of paleontology conference fieldwork in Canada, China and New Zealand.

Over the years, I have supervised the work of about 50 graduate students, many of whom have had considerable success. As a means of intellectual renewal in 1975 I shifted my focus from ecological life histories to the evolution of vertebrates, commencing paleontological research with my tolerant friend and colleague, geologist Kenton W.S. Campbell. The work has used my neglected illustrative skills and revived my Dry Valley preoccupation with 'old bones'. The work, continuing to this day, has resulted in a long series of papers on Devonian fish morphology and evolution. Service on a plethora of University committees – for the ANU Press, Buildings and Grounds, Northern Australia Research Unit, the coastal field station etc, etc, confounded my pre-retirement time, as is usual.

I 'retired' as Reader in Zoology in 1996. Daughter Laura and I edited for publication *Rebellion at Corranderrk*, a major work Diane had just completed before her death. *Rebellion* is about to be the subject of both radio and TV documentaries.

Since retirement I have continued my obsession with 'old bones', in this phase, with 400-million-year-old Devonian fish, as a Visiting Fellow in the Research School of Earth Sciences at the ANU. I have published more than 25 papers since 'retirement', mainly on the evolution of fossil fish, with my esteemed colleague Ken Campbell. That and the intermittent production of assorted graphics, ranging from journal covers for Aboriginal History to historic maps and odd cartoons, thankfully, have kept me a healthy distance from the dangers of lawn bowls.

Although we have described fossil fish from Carboniferous deposits in the Drummond Basin of Queensland, the Lower Devonian of Burrinjuck Dam in New South Wales, the Devonian of Morocco, and Severanaya Semlya in Russia, the Mid Upper Devonian of Gogo in the Kimberley of North Western Australia is the main source of our fish fossils. Fossils from Gogo occur embedded in limestone nodules that can be etched in acid to prepare their three-dimensional bony skeletons. Every detail is preserved and in some cases the lower jaw still articulates with the skull, every pore and texture preserved as it was 385 million years ago. The preservation is so perfect that 3D tomographic x-ray scanning can be done. Now sharks, placoderms (the ancient armoured fishes), several groups of bony fishes, and particularly the ancestors of present day lungfish have been found. Over 40 species of fish have been described in the scientific literature. Gogo is regarded as one of the best vertebrate fossil deposits in the world. Ken and I are lucky to work on such material.

In my spare time I indulge hobbies such as photography, saltwater fishing and silver-smithing – mostly in a premeditated way to avoid housework. And now Colin has asked if I'd be good enough to produce the maps for this little book!

Our time in the Dry Valleys was totally challenging; we were faced with opportunities that we could only scratch at and in many instances we had no grasp of the intricate questions that were to be raised by the field context.

These opportunities were gradually exploited by following generations, as they did staggering amounts of research. At the time, for all we knew, other researchers would not follow immediately. In retrospect it is profoundly pleasing that over 50 expeditions from our little University have followed our fumbling efforts. What an immense privilege it was to initially explore the 'Grand Canyon of Antarctica'.

Of course I still regret the jobs not done; the opportunities not seized, as I followed another road. As a conservationist I have received great satisfaction from the designation by the Scientific Committee on Antarctic Research of Balham and Barwick Valleys as an Antarctic Specially Protected Area (ASPA 123) – in effect a closed internationally declared 'wilderness' area, where access is only granted after formal application, and access by vehicle is not encouraged. 'The Area contains examples of a wide variety of the environments found in this ecosystem, including desert pavements, sand dunes, patterned ground, glacial and moraine features, streams, freshwater and saline lakes, valleys and high-altitude ice-free ground. Some of the best examples of ventifact pavements and weathering-pitted dolerites are found on the valley floors, along with examples of chasmolithic lichens, layered communities of endolithic lichens, fungi, algae and associated bacteria, and populations of soil and lake microflora,' as it says in the blurb for ASPA 123.

I still don't know much – if I did I might have escaped from what is arguably 'the best sheltered workshop in Canberra' – and the company has been great!

COLIN

My first journey to Antarctica, and all our experiences during two months in the field, were most remarkable in so many ways. To start with, it was a most productive effort scientifically, so much so that I, Bob Clark and the University could see immediately the huge advantages of continuing the expeditions. Initially these advantages took the form of finding new areas and new problems for geology students and faculty to work on. I asked Bob once, in 1961 on our return from the Koettlitz Glacier area, if he didn't find it most satisfying to read a thesis that wasn't entitled 'A re-examination of. . .' or 'A reconsideration of. . .'.

One of the few good things to come from the 40-odd years of the Cold War was the political pressure that the USA and USSR put on each other by increasing the significance of their presence in Antarctica – and, most fortunately, they did this largely by their support of the scientific work that could be done there. This pressure, or competition, has continued to the present day. New Zealand's Antarctic research and, in particular, VUWAE has profited greatly from this continued US commitment. As a friendly spy in the US corridors of power, a few years later, I was delighted to hear the explanation of the plentiful US logistic support of the New Zealand science effort. A senior scientist-cum-politico said, 'Sure, we gain by supporting those Kiwis! They get so much more bang for the buck than we do that it makes our effort look better when we count them in with us.'

In addition, the Antarctic Treaty has controlled the military and industrial ambitions of all the signatory nations. The only worthwhile activities in the Antarctic are science and tourism. Inevitably, since so little of the Antarctic continent consists of exposed bedrock, and so many scientists have decided to work there – at least partly because funding and general support for Antarctic science has been relatively plentiful, in both the western world and in Russia – many of the 'easy' areas have been visited, and the first and inexpensive surveys have been completed. Nowadays, much of the cutting-edge earth science work is of the kind typified by the work of VUWAE 2007–08, as a major participant in ANDRILL: using expensive drilling techniques to drill deep beneath McMurdo Sound, to work out at least part of the glacial history of the continent for the last 20 million years, and possibly much longer.

That the Victoria University of Wellington has been able to take an international leadership role and has been able to adapt continuously from our days of 'small science' to the highly specialized efforts of today redounds to its credit – and the Antarctic Research Centre of Victoria University of Wellington certainly merits its forefront position in the world.

As for me, the visit to Scott Base by Dick Goldthwait, immediately after we had returned from Wright Valley, turned out to be most significant. In July 1960, I was holding a visiting position in the Australian National University in Canberra and working with Ted Irving, measuring the paleomagnetism of the suite of dolerites that Ian Willis had collected in Victoria Valley. We received a letter from Dick, offering me a 15-month appointment at The Ohio State University, to help him establish the Institute of Polar Studies. In the same week John Garlick, my PhD advisor, offered me a senior position at Hull, the university at which he'd been appointed Professor and Chairman, and an industrial physics laboratory in England offered me a job running the lab. I asked Bob Clark for his advice, whereupon he offered me a brand-new position as head of an Antarctic Research Unit in his department. So I asked John Jaeger, the head of the Canberra department where I held my visiting position, for his advice – and he offered to establish an Antarctic research unit for me right then and there in Canberra. We wouldn't even need to go back to Wellington.

It was obvious that I shouldn't ask anyone else for advice. Gillian and I quickly discarded the solid-state physics industrial laboratory position, leaving a choice of four. We'd lived in England, and New Zealand, and Australia. Perhaps we should try Columbus, Ohio. We unearthed an old 'cultural' atlas, which showed that Columbus was in the middle of the 'corn belt' and the 'pig belt' and just a bit north of the 'bible belt'. Surely no academic institution could survive, let alone succeed, in that sort of environment! Let's go and see! After all, it was only for 15 months and we could always return to Britain, or New Zealand. Having reached that conclusion, we tossed coins to confirm that we had made the correct decision. The pennies showed that we had.

I'd already agreed to be a member of the 1960–61 VUWAE, to the ice-free areas north of the Koettlitz Glacier, and shortly after making the Ohio decision we met Dick Blank, a US petrologist, who was also a member of VUWAE 4. He was spending a year in New Zealand on an NSF scholarship, studying ignimbrites, whatever they are. Dick and Glee, his wife, knew Columbus, and made encouraging noises about The Ohio State University but said much less about the city and its surrounds. We wondered what we had let ourselves in for.

Well, Columbus couldn't easily have been more different from New Zealand. The city was a huge village and the area was physiographically moribund, if not completely dead. The half-million population of the city had one department store, but at least they didn't have to wait six months before the next shipment arrived. On the other hand, the people in Ohio were wonderful and most welcoming, just like the people in New Zealand.

The University's undergraduate students when we arrived in March 1961 numbered 25,722 – and there were rafts of graduate students, of whom 12 turned up for my first class in glaciology. At least six of them were very good, with field experience on Alaskan glaciers or in the Antarctic, and they all challenged me. It was very exciting. Larry Taylor, Dick Cameron, John Hollin, Al Stuart, Bill Vickers and Kenji Kojima have all gone on to make names for themselves, many in glaciology. They were all members of the Institute of Polar Studies, as were many other interesting people who didn't take that first glaciology class, including George Doumani, a Lebanese paleontologist who had spent the previous year at Byrd Station, and Bill Long, a geologist from Nevada who enrolled as an MSc student but was afraid of the mathematics. Bill was very kind and loaned us his house trailer until we could rent a house of our own.

After a couple of weeks somebody asked me to give a talk on continental drift, which I did, based mainly on the paleomagnetic work I had done with Ted Irving. Most of the faculty members of the Geology Department turned up, as well as the young people from the Institute. I thought continental drift and polar wandering was all cut and dried and that there couldn't be any doubt. Perhaps that was because the people I had met and worked with in Cambridge, New Zealand and Australia were nearly all ardent 'drifters', but in Columbus there were many skeptics. The glacial geology people weren't sure; Jim Schopf, the United States Geological Survey coal geologist, didn't understand the mathematics but was on my side; but the structural geologists and the sediment people reckoned it was all a load of hogwash.

Bill Long had visited part of the Horlick Mountains, far south in the Transantarctic Mountains, the previous year and had measured the section up Discovery Ridge in the Ohio Range – full of *Glossopteris* and invertebrate fossils. Bill mapped a large part of the section as 'Greywacke', but when he gave a paper on his work another geologist, Ray Adie, a South African, suggested it might be a tillite, the solidified deposits laid down by an ice sheet. Bill took another expedition back to the same place, confirmed that the section was tillite and that it was analogous to another tillite in South Africa – and added this convincing bit of evidence of continental drift to the paleomagnetic material of a few years earlier.

Within weeks after my arrival in Columbus I had recommended that we invite two new people to join the Institute of Polar Studies. Fritz Loewe, glaciologist and hero of Alfred Wegener's German Greenland Expedition of 1930–32, was just retiring from the Meteorology Department at the University of Melbourne, and was happy to come to Columbus as a summer visitor. Fritz, of course, was an ardent supporter of Alfred Wegener and, although he had never done any geological fieldwork, was a confirmed 'drifter'. The following year he, Henry Brecher and I formed an expedition to the Sukkertoppen Ice Cap in southwest Greenland, which I had thought might be a good place for a long-term station. The logistics turned out to be too expensive for that, but at least I had crossed a Greenland ice cap with one of the great men of polar science.

The other new member was John Mercer. He had been with Bill Long in the Horlick Mountains. He was still compiling his atlas of northern hemisphere glaciers at the American Geographical Society in New York, but could come for a year. John, an unusual Englishman, was touched with genius, and soon after his arrival in Columbus he persuaded me to help organize a little symposium on global warming, or climate change as we called it in 1962. Our main concern in those days was that a few degrees increase in annual mean temperature of the Ross Ice Shelf would make it unstable. When the ice shelf broke up the ice sheet of western Antarctica would, in turn, become unstable and slide out to sea, raising worldwide sea levels by as much as six metres. The threat still exists. It really was all most exciting!

Of course, that first little warning of global warming was received with resounding silence but we have persisted with the message, and 45 years later, in 2007, I was gratified that my former PhD student, Lonnie Thompson, still at The Ohio State University, was awarded the US National Medal of Science for his part in bringing the evidence of global warming to the attention of all. Along with his wife, Ellen, he was also technical advisor on Al Gore's film *An Inconvenient Truth*, for which Gore won the 2007 Nobel Peace Prize.

If I were going back to New Zealand, I should have gone in July 1962, but that summer I was working with Fritz Loewe in Greenland, and was developing a batch of other ideas for glaciological studies. With many regrets I wrote to Dr Williams at VUW to resign my position. While New Zealand was clearly the best place to live in the whole world, it wasn't yet the best place to be a glaciologist.

One of my bright ideas was for a photogrammetric method of measuring the surface velocity of the ice sheet at spots that were remote from any fixed point, like a mountain peak. The place where we wanted to measure the surface velocity was Byrd Station, in the middle of the West Antarctic Ice Sheet. The idea didn't work because the US Navy pilots were unable to fly in straight lines down a row of markers that they couldn't see, but I did have the chance of working with Ian Willis and Jim Kennett in Taylor Valley with VUWAE 6, and to go with Charlie Rich, deputy leader to Ian, over to Lake Vanda for a few hours, to check on those bottom temperatures that VUWAE 5 had reported.

The northern summer of 1964 saw me in the Yukon, working with four graduate students – one English, one New Zealander and two American – on the Kaskawulsh Glacier. They all had thesis subjects, so I ended up being field assistant to two of them. I also did most of the cooking. And for summer 1965 I had three funded projects in Alaska as well as the second year of the Kaskawulsh studies. That was too much, along with my teaching responsibilities and an increasing amount of committee work, both within the University and in the polar scientific community.

In July 1965 Dick Goldthwait was persuaded to accept the Chairmanship of the Geology Department, and I was offered the job of Director of the Institute of Polar Studies. That didn't make the workload any easier, but it was all even more exciting to be able to try out an increasing number of glaciological schemes and other ideas.

One of these ideas, first conceived as I walked along the Wright Valley with Dick Barwick in December 1958, was to look at the mechanisms of flow of cold glaciers, and in the austral summers of 1965–66, 1966–67 and 1967–68 we dug tunnels under and into Meserve Glacier and 'instrumented the heck out of it', as I've said before. During 1965 Sir Charles Wright, for whom we had named the valley, was conducting ionosphere work at Byrd Station. We invited him to come over to see the kind of glaciological work we were doing in 'his' valley, but he was not able to do so. Instead he flew along the valley and waved to us.

Gerry Holdsworth, from Christchurch, who had been another one of the four students on the Kaskawulsh Glacier and was now my PhD student, did an extraordinarily fine job of determining the flow law of cold ice and of explaining many of the odd features of Meserve Glacier: the stepped surface, the orthogonal meeting of the sides of the glacier at the snout, and so on.

Another idea was to look at the developments of soils in the valley and relate it to the valley's glacial history. Part of this became the PhD dissertation work of Bob Behling, and during his time in the valley I walked along to see the new Vanda Station, to inspect their flow-gauging weir and have a cup of tea.

Following four years as Director of the Institute, I was asked to take the chairmanship of the Department of Geology. That, too, was an interesting challenge, because I had never taken for credit a single geology course. Some of my best friends pointed out that since I didn't know any geology and had a faculty position, the only possible job for me was as Chairman. During those three years I managed only one field season in the Antarctic, to Deception Island after its volcanic eruptions, along with PhD student Olaf Orheim and with Valter Schytt – which produced, among other things the renowned Orheim-Bull-Schytt scientific paper and my first acquaintance with a semi-luxury tourist ship in the Antarctic. That was the *Lindblad Explorer*, the first purpose-built Antarctic cruise ship. We were living at the Argentine base, on the west side of the bay that fills the centre of the island. As we travelled by Zodiac to our work area on the east side of the bay, we saw the ship looming through the fog. We boarded her, had breakfast, liberated two bottles of scotch whiskey, and left before the passengers returned from their trip ashore. However, the experience gave me some new ideas for a later day. As I write these words in November 2007 I am sad to report that the 'little red ship', now the *Explorer*, has recently sunk in the Antarctic, after colliding with an iceberg.

By 1972 my students had made a good start in comparing the histories of climatic change in the northern and southern hemispheres, as revealed in the ice cores from the Greenland and the Antarctic ice sheets. There were many interesting similarities and even more interesting differences. Wouldn't it be great if we could find an ice sheet in the tropics, to compare the climate record there with those at higher latitudes, both north and south? Obviously those would be rare and difficult to find. Well, good old John Mercer pointed out that the Quelccaya Ice Cap, very high up in the Andes in southern Peru, looked as though it might be thick enough to give us a few hundred years of climate record. We wrote it up as a proposal for funding to the NSF and, slightly to my surprise, the application was successful. The Quelccaya Ice Cap rose to about 5500 metres and knowing how I had puffed and blown in climbing Sponsors' Peak, 14 years earlier, I went along to see one of the doctors who were working with the NASA astronauts. He said I could do it, as long as I spent a month acclimatizing to the altitude.

Well I had just been appointed Dean of the College and there was no way I could take an extra month off, so in the end I asked my PhD student, Lonnie Thompson, whether he could lead the expedition. Of course he could – and he made a magnificent job of that, and of the countless other expeditions he has taken to examine ice in remote parts of the world in the succeeding 30-odd years. In 2005 Lonnie was awarded the Tyler Prize, the highest award in the Environmental Sciences, and sometimes compared with the Nobel Prize. And then in 2007, as I said before, Lonnie collected the US National Medal of Science. A kind-hearted colleague commented to me, 'That's absolutely typical of university people. If you can't do it yourself, you get one of your students to do it!' I still don't know whether he was referring to Lonnie's winning these high honours or going to Quelccaya in the first place. But good for Lonnie!

Ian Whillans, another former PhD student, took over my glaciology lecture course, although he did invite me to turn up to give a few lectures. As he so kindly expressed it, 'It'll show the students how far we have come since your day!' Ian didn't like committee work, so I continued with that – and, of course, the assignments grew in number. Gillian remarked that one shouldn't leave them alone in the dark. 'Leave two committee jobs alone overnight, and when you go back to inspect, there are three.' I still had a few graduate students to supervise, but travel for fieldwork in the polar regions was not possible. Still I did greatly enjoy the job, and was happy to ignore the few offers of promotion from elsewhere.

After five years as Dean I was re-elected to the position, presumably because no one else wanted it. Then came a situation which could have been very embarrassing, but wasn't. Charlie Corbato, who had succeeded me as Chairman in the Geology Department, decided he had had enough. Among the applicants for that position was a young lad from Northern Illinois University, named Peter Webb. I had visions of lines of protesting faculty, all carrying placards saying 'Nepotist', or worse. Unfortunately for me, Peter was clearly the best qualified of the applicants, for otherwise I could have had a beer with him when he visited and then appointed someone else. However, Peter was the strongest applicant, as all of the departmental Search Committee agreed, so I asked John Riedl, my Associate Dean, to deputize for me in the matter. Anyway, Peter was duly recommended as Chairman, and the recommendation was accepted by John and then by me. Peter still spoke with a subdued strange accent, but then, so did I – and, as expected, we worked very well together for the following six years.

In 1982 I was re-elected to a third term as Dean, but after a couple more years it seemed to me that, however good I might be as a Dean (I can immediately see Barrie making hay with that remark) the College, which to me was obviously the best and strongest in the University, could profit from a different leader. I'd resign, but what would I do? Two of my former students, Ian Whillans and Lonnie Thompson, both world-beaters, were on the faculty there and I didn't want to compete with them. After looking at a few university presidencies, including VUW, I had decided that it was a one-handed job: as president you were either glad-handing politicians and the like, or holding out your hand for alms of one kind or another. There was very little academic content in the sort of presidency that I could get. What, then?

I can't recall whether Gillian or I first mentioned the word 'retire' but the more we thought about it, the better it sounded as an option. There were a score of activities we'd always wanted to try and if we found we didn't have enough money I could always get a teaching job at a community college. Let's try it!

Having made the decision we became more and more enthusiastic about it. First we had to decide on a retirement site. Gillian said, 'Now I don't mind living in Columbus, but I certainly don't want to die here.' Which country? Back to New Zealand? After all it is the best place to live in the whole world! Or Canada, which combines some of the better aspects of Britain, France and the US? Or England? On the other hand, all of our material assets, that is three children, live in the US – and we rather like them, so there was no reason to move away from them to another country. For tedious reasons we picked on the Pacific Northwest and in particular, Bainbridge Island. It's half an hour by ferry from Seattle, which isn't a bad city, as cities go. There's a good art community, the university does good polar work, it's close to the sea and the ragweed pollen count is low.

Our first task was to build a house, which Gillian avers she had always wanted to do. That turned out to be a great pleasure, largely because Marc, our builder, was such an excellent teacher. He still is, but now as a professor of history at a local university.

My next serious task was to start again on a 30-year-old project to write an account of the Antarctic work of Charles Wright, 'Silas', after whom we had named our valley. I had met Sir Charles, as he was by then, in London in spring 1969, and learned from him that the diaries he had written while in the Antarctic were in the archives of the Scott Polar Research Institute in Cambridge, that no one had done anything with them but that he was planning to do so when he retired.

He did retire later in 1969 but didn't start his memoir until early in 1974, and he died in November 1975, before it had been completed. Soon after his death his artist daughter Pat started to prepare an account based on the memoir and the Antarctic diaries. She spent several years producing many hundred exquisite illustrations and generating a huge manuscript that, unfortunately, none of the 45 publishing houses she approached was willing to publish. In 1986 Pat invited me to undertake the editing of the work, and that took five years, in between building the house, and working on establishing a book business, buying and selling polar books. The Ohio State University Press eventually published *Silas* in 1993, and like everything else I tackle, it proved to be a most pleasurable undertaking – and perhaps one day I shall manage to break even on it, monetarily.

The book business slowly expanded, but so far has not become exactly profitable, merely enjoyable. Normally I refer to it as a 'Not-deliberately, not-for-profit' enterprise.

While I was conducting fieldwork in Antarctica, even after 1968, when we were first able to send women scientists to the continent, we were still not able to take or send women non-scientists. Gradually the rules became more and more relaxed, so that in 1984 Peter Webb took Joan, his wife, as his field assistant, and together they stayed at Vanda Station for a few days. Joan, then, had had a chance to see at least a small part of the area that has intrigued Peter for all these decades. Gillian has not.

However, I realized I now had an alternative way of showing her bits of the gorgeous scenery of that beautiful land. Accordingly I volunteered to be a lecturer and guide on the tourist ships (including the one I had seen in the harbour of Deception Island) and over the next decade and a half I made eight trips to the continent, most of them on *Explorer*. In all of them we crossed the Drake Passage, the usually greatly disturbed stretch of water between South America and the Antarctic Peninsula. On each crossing a few of the lecturers have suffered mal-de-mer, whereas usually I do not, and I have been asked to 'fill in' for them. Thus a whole bunch of Antarctic travellers have been subjected to my talks on 'Polar Cooking' and 'Antarctic Poetry', as well as the more usual 'History of Antarctic Exploration', 'Glaciology, the Queen of Sciences', and 'Mineral potential of the Antarctic'.

Gillian has been on three of these trips, so she has seen and painted just a little of the stuff that made up some of the peaks of my earlier life. However, she hasn't yet seen Wright Valley, or the River Onyx. Perhaps, when we travel there in our wheelchairs, we could manage a brew of tea at that cavernous granite boulder in Bull Pass – and we may even trundle over to Victoria Valley to help Dick find his iron meteorite again. That all depends on how heavy my pack is – and whether the door is closed to keep out the wind!

Fig. 90. And, finally, the aged four of us at the VUWAE reunion, 1 July 2007, Antarctic
Research Centre, Victoria University of Wellington, New Zealand.

> Though much is taken, much abides; and though
> We are not now that strength which in old days
> Moved heaven and earth; that which we are, we are;
> One equal temper of heroic hearts,
> Made weak by time and fate, but strong in will
> To strive, to seek, to find, and not to yield.
>
> – Alfred, Lord Tennyson, *Ulysses*

Publications

The following is a listing of the scientific papers that arose directly from our small seven-week expedition – well, two of Peter and Barrie's come from their remarkable jaunt in 1957–58 – just to show that Peter and Barrie weren't always eating, that Dick did something besides building cairns, and that I wasn't always asleep. I feel that we should also be able to make a reference to a map or two, but I don't think that any of the New Zealand or United States map-makers of the area ever acknowledged our work in helping with establishing the ground control, despite the large number of hours and the prodigious amount of puffing that Dick and I contributed in doing so. Such is life!

Barwick, R.E., Bull, C., McKelvey, B.C. and Webb, P.N. 1959. Immediate Report of the Victoria University of Wellington Antarctic Expedition, (1958-9). 15 p., five maps and diagrams (Lodged in Victoria University of Wellington Library).

Barwick, R.E. and Balham, R.W. 1967. Seal Carcasses in a Deglaciated Region of South Victoria Land, Antarctica. *Tuatara*, Vol. 15, Issue 3, pp. 165-180.

Bull, C. 1959. University Men Explore Victoria Land Dry Valleys, Antarctica. *Antarctica*, Vol. 2 (2), pp. 50–52.

Bull, C. 1960. Gravity Observations in the Wright Valley area, Victoria Land, Antarctica. *New Zealand Journal of Geology and Geophysics,* Vol. 3, pp. 543–552.

Bull, C. and Irving, E. 1960. Paleomagnetism in Antarctica. *Nature*, Vol. 185, pp. 834–835.

Bull, C. and Irving, E. 1960. The Paleomagnetism of some Hypabyssal Intrusive rocks from South Victoria Land, Antarctica. *Geophysical Journal of the Royal Astronomical Society*, Vol. 3, pp. 211–224.

Bull, C. 1962. Quaternary glaciations in southern Victoria Land, Antarctica. *Journal of Glaciology,* Vol. 4, pp. 240–241.

Bull, C., McKelvey, B.C. and Webb, P.N. 1962. Quaternary Glaciations in southern Victoria Land, Antarctica. *Journal of Glaciology*, Vol. 4, pp. 63–78.

Bull, C., McKelvey, B.C. and Webb, P.N. 1964. Glacial Benches in South Victoria Land. *Journal of Glaciology,* Vol. 5, pp. 131–134

Bull, Colin. 1965. Climatological Observations in Ice-free Areas of southern Victoria Land, Antarctica. In *Studies in Antarctic Meteorology.* Antarctic Research Series, Vol. 9, pp. 177–194, published by The American Geophysical Union.

McKelvey, B.C. and Webb, P.N. 1959. Geological Investigations in South Victoria Land, Antarctica. Part 2: Geology of Upper Taylor Glacier Region. *New Zealand Journal of Geology and Geophysics*, Vol. 2, pp. 718–728.

McKelvey, B.C. 1960. Geological Investigations in southern Victoria Land, Antarctica. University of New Zealand Thesis for MSc (Lodged in Victoria University of Wellington Library).

McKelvey, B.C. and Webb, P.N. 1961. Geological Reconnaissance in Victoria Land, Antarctica. *Nature,* Vol. 4764, pp. 545–547.

McKelvey, B.C. and Webb, P.N. 1962. Geological Investigations in South Victoria Land, Antarctica. Part 3: Geology of Wright Valley. *New Zealand Journal of Geology and Geophysics,* Vol. 5, pp. 143–162.

Webb, P.N. and McKelvey, B.C. 1958. Antarctic Vacation. *University News,* Victoria University of Wellington, pp. 3–4.

Webb, P.N. and McKelvey, B.C. 1959. Geological Investigations in South Victoria Land, Antarctica, Part 1: Geology of Victoria Valley. *New Zealand Journal of Geology and Geophysics,* Vol. 2, pp. 120–136.

Webb, P.N. 1960. The Development of Ice-Free Valley Systems in Victoria Land. Royal Society of New Zealand, 9th Science Congress, Wellington: p. 45.

Webb, P.N. 1960. Geological Investigations in southern Victoria Land, Antarctica. University of New Zealand Thesis for MSc (Lodged in Victoria University of Wellington Library).

Webb, P.N. 1963. Geological Investigations in South Victoria Land, Antarctica. Part 4: Beacon Group of the Wright Valley and Taylor Glacier Region. *New Zealand Journal of Geology and Geophysics,* Vol. 6, pp. 351–387.

Glossary

AD2. Aviation Machinist Mate 2.

Aka. Abbreviation for 'also known as'.

Alga (pl. algae). Mainly aquatic photosynthetic plants, unicellular and multicellular, that range from seaweeds to diatoms and dinoflagellates.

ANARE. Australian National Antarctic Research Expedition.

ANDRILL Antarctic geological drilling project. International project to drill deep into sea floor in southern McMurdo Sound. VUW Antarctic Research Centre is a major participant.

Anemometer. Device for measuring wind velocity.

Aneroid barometer. Instrument for measuring and indicating atmospheric pressure. Here the pressure is converted into an elevation of the site.

Astatic magnetometer. Sensitive device for measuring the magnetic field around a sample of rock.

Aurora. Phenomenon in upper atmosphere caused by interaction of solar particles with atmospheric gases, to form displays, arcs and streamers of coloured light.

BANZARE. British, Australian and New Zealand Antarctic Research Expedition, 1929-1931.

Basalt. A hard black, often glassy volcanic rock, produced by partial melting of earth's mantle.

Beacon Supergroup. Any or all of the sedimentary rocks, from Devonian to Jurassic in age, overlying the basement rocks of south Victoria Land and elsewhere in the Transantarctic Mountains.

Bouguer anomaly. Result of applying, to measurements of the acceleration due to gravity, corrections for all the known material above a set elevation, usually sea level.

Bully beef. Popular name for tinned corned beef.

Bushed. New Zealand slang for 'exhausted'.

Cirque. Steep-walled, often semi-circular hollow, caused by glacial erosion in mountains.

Col. A low point in a range of mountains, often a pass between two peaks.

Coleman stove. Common item of camping equipment. One- or two-burner stove, fuelled with kerosene or gasoline, under pressure.

Continental drift. Movement of continental blocks of the Earth's crust by tectonic forces.

Cornice. Here an overhanging mass of snow and ice, caused by wind action.

Crevasse. Crack in glacier, usually its top surface, caused by differential ice movement.

Curie point. The temperature above which the remnant magnetization (of a rock) disappears.

Dolerite (Diabase). Igneous rock, usually fine-grained.

DSIR. Department of Scientific and Industrial Research, here of the New Zealand government.

Dyke (Dike). A vertical or near-vertical mass of igneous rock that has been forced upwards through overlying strata.

Endolithic. Literally 'inside the rock'.

Erratics. Rocks that have been carried from their source by ice and have been deposited when the ice retreats.

Fast ice edge. Edge of sea ice that is frozen to shore.

Firn (Névé). Old, compacted granular snow

Frost polygons. Approximate geometrical shapes formed in surface deposits by movement of particles under action of freezing of moisture.

Glacigene. 'Having its origins in a glacier.'

Glossopteris. A woody, seed-bearing shrub or tree, found in the Permian rocks of Gondwana, that resembles primitive conifers.

Gneiss. Coarse-grained metamorphic rock, in which light and dark mineral constituents are separated into visible bands.

Gravity meter (gravimeter). Portable device for determining the (relative) value of the acceleration due to gravity, essentially by measuring the extension of a coiled spring bearing a small weight.

Greywacke. Variety of sandstone, with poorly sorted grains of quartz, feldspar or rock fragment in a clay-fine matrix.

Hornfels (pl. hornfelses). Fine-grained metamorphic rock composed of silicate minerals, formed by the action of heat and pressure on shale.

Horst. Elevated block of the earth's crust forced upwards between near-vertical faults.

Ice cap. Thick and extensive permanent covering of ice and snow, not sufficiently thick to hide completely the form of the underlying land.

Icefall. Glacier, the surface of which is so steep that the ice breaks into blocks.

Ice sheet. Very thick and extensive permanent covering of ice and snow, sufficiently thick to hide the form of the underlying rock. As in Greenland Ice Sheet, West and East Antarctic Ice Sheets.

Ice shelf. Thick mass of snow and ice, floating on sea, and largely formed from coalescing glaciers moving from the land. As in Ross Ice Shelf.

Ignimbrites. Volcanic rock comprising droplets of lava and glass, coalesced under action of intense heat.

IGY. International Geophysical Year. Period from 1 July 1956 to 31 December 1957, when many nations made concerted attacks on geophysical problems, worldwide and in space.

Intrude, intrusion. Geological process whereby an igneous rock, usually in liquid form, is forced between layers of sedimentary rock or into weaknesses in overlying units.

Ionosonde. Apparatus designed to investigate properties of ionosphere.

Ionosphere. Layers of the Earth's upper atmosphere, in which incoming radiation creates ions and free electrons that can reflect radio waves.

Jamesway hut. Transportable hut, often used in Antarctica for construction of temporary bases.

Jurassic. Period of geological time from about 210 to 140 million years ago. Time of dinosaurs and first mammals.

Katabatic wind. Wind that blows down a slope, usually caused by cooling of air at higher altitudes.

Labyrinthodont. Extinct amphibian, resembling the crocodile, that lived in Late Paleozoic and Early Mesozoic eras.

Lamprophyre. Igneous rock, usually occurring as an intrusion or dyke and containing large crystals, especially of biotite and mica.

Lichen. Complex plant consisting of fungi and algae growing in symbiotic relationship.

Marble. Dense metamorphic rock, formed from limestone under action of heat and pressure.

Mesa. Relatively flat-topped erosional feature, usually with steep sides.

Mesozoic era. Period between about 250 and 65 million years ago, when dinosaurs, birds and flowering plants first appeared.

Met instruments. Meteorological instruments: thermometers, barometers, anemometers and the like.

Micropaleontology. Study of the micro-organisms that exist as fossils in sedimentary rocks.

Moraine. Earth and rock debris carried by a glacier and deposited at its front and edges.

Mukluks. Cold-weather footwear, often with rubber soles and canvas uppers. Designed to accommodate multiple pairs of socks.

Nematode. Worm with cylindrical unsegmented body, usually microscopic, protected by a tough outer skin. Ubiquitous in freshwater, marine and terrestrial environments.

Névé. Compacted granular snow.

NSF. United States National Science Foundation.

Nunatak. Mountain peak protruding through glacier or other ice mass.

Operation Deep Freeze. Name given to operations by US Navy in Antarctica in support of IGY and later programmes.

Otter aircraft. Light, single- or two-engined aircraft, used in the Antarctic mainly for reconnaissance.

Paleomagnetism. The polarity and intensity of the residual magnetism in ancient rocks.

Paleozoic era. Geological time about 600 to 250 million years ago, when fish, insects, amphibians, reptiles and land plants first appeared.

Paraffin. Kerosene.

Pegmatite. Coarse-grained igneous rock, usually granite, characterized by large, well-formed crystals.

Pemmican. Man's best attempt to stuff a whole cow into a one-pound can. Powdered lean meat, mixed with perhaps 40% fat. Delicious when consumer is famished.

Peneplain. An area of nearly flat, featureless land that is the result of a prolonged period of erosion. Here Kukri Peneplain: peneplain surrounding Kukri Hills, on which thick sediments, mainly sandstones, were deposited.

Perks. Slang for perquisites.

Phenocrysts. Any of the large embedded crystals in a porphyritic rock.

Photogrammetry. Making measurements from photographs, especially using aerial photographs in the construction of maps.

Piedmont glacier. Low-lying glacier, formed by coalescing of valley glaciers flowing from adjacent mountains.

Polar wandering. Path of the Earth's pole through time, relative to a particular land mass, caused by continental drift.

Porphyry. Any predominantly fine-grained igneous rock that contains isolated large crystals.

Primus. Portable cooking stove, burning kerosene (paraffin oil) under pressure.

Protozoa. A single-celled organism, like an amoeba, that can move and lives on organic compounds.

Quid. Slang for a pound. Sterling and New Zealand monetary unit.

Quonset hut. Transportable prefabricated semi-cylindrical hut, common on military facilities.

Radiosonde. Instrument carried aloft by balloon, for transmitting meteorological data.

RDRC. New Zealand Ross Dependency Research Committee. In 1958 this was the body responsible for the overseeing of New Zealand's Antarctic operations.

Recce. Slang for reconnaissance.

Reefers. Refrigeration units used in New Zealand's meat industry for storage of carcasses.

Remnant magnetization. Residual magnetic properties of a rock, often after it is subjected to a procedure like heating or randomization of particular components of its magnetization.

Rotifer. Small invertebrate that has a wheel-shaped crown of cilia at its anterior end, and usually lives in freshwater habitats.

Sastrugi (sing. sastruga). Ridges of snow formed on a snowfield by wind action.

Schist. Any rock whose minerals have aligned themselves in one direction, in response to deformational stresses, so that the rock can be split in parallel layers.

Sill. More or less horizontal layer of igneous rock forced between layers of sedimentary or older igneous rocks.

SIPRE. Snow, Ice and Permafrost Research Establishment. Cold regions research branch of United States Corps of Engineers.

Sirius Group. The formations associated with the Sirius Glaciation.

Sked. Slang for schedule, usually a radio schedule.

Skua. Large gull-like seabird, common around penguin rookeries in the Antarctic.

Sling psychrometer. Instrument for measuring the relative humidity of air.

Sno-Cat. Tracked over-snow vehicle.

Spindrift. Snow, blown by the wind.

Subtense bar. Surveying instrument, whose length is known accurately so that the angle it subtends at a fixed point is known.

TAE. Trans Antarctic Expedition.

Theodolite. Surveying instrument for measuring accurately the angle between two points.

Tillite. Hardened deposits left by ancient glaciers.

Trimetrogon photography. Photographic system used in aerial mapping. One camera points vertically downwards and two others point off to the sides at pre-set angles.

Tump. English (Herefordshire) slang for clump, heap, pile, deposit – a very useful word, available for adoption.

Ventifacts. Wind-faceted, usually fine-grained rocks.

VX-6 Squadron. Squadron carrying out most of the aerial operations of Operation Deep Freeze.

Vic, VUW. Abbreviations for Victoria University of Wellington, New Zealand.

Weasel. Light tracked vehicle, sometimes amphibious, and also snow-capable. Invented in WWII for use in European and Pacific theatres.

Wharfie. New Zealand slang for dock (or wharf) worker.

Wheatstone Bridge. Simple instrument used in elementary physics classes to measure electrical resistances.

Place-Names

Amery Oasis. Eighteen hundred square kilometres of largely ice-free terrain in northern Prince Charles Mountains, bordering eastern flank of Lambert Glacier.

Beacon Heights. Ridge of peaks between Beacon Valley and Arena Valley in south Victoria Land, 77°50'S, 160°50'E.

Beardmore Glacier. Very large valley glacier flowing from East Antarctic Ice Sheet to Ross Ice Shelf through Transantarctic Mountains at 83°45'S.

Beaver Lake. Lake of smooth ice, about 11 kilometres long and 5 kilometres wide, in Prince Charles Mountains, at 70°48'S, 68°20'E.

Beehive Mountain. Peak at north side of Taylor Glacier, at 77°40'S, 160°33'E.

Byrd Station. US scientific base, 1957–63, on West Antarctic Ice Sheet, at 80°S, 120°W.

Canham Glacier. Glacier flowing through Freyberg Mountains, to Rennick Glacier, in Oates Land, 71°49'S, 163°E.

Cape Adare. Cape at 71°17'S, near northern end of Transantarctic Mountains, on western shore of Ross Sea.

Cape Campbell. Cape at northeast extremity of South Island, New Zealand.

Cape Crozier. Extreme eastern point of Ross Island.

Cape Evans. Base for Scott's Last Expedition. On west coast of Ross Island, at 77°38'S, 166°24'W.

Cape Hallett. Site of joint United States–New Zealand station, 1957–73, 72°20'S, 170°25'E.

Cape MacKay. The southeastern extremity of Ross Island, 77°42'S, 168°31'E.

Cape Royds. Shackleton's base for 1907–09 expedition. On west coast of Ross Island at 77°33'S, 166°09'E.

Castle Rock. Steep-sided, flat-topped rock, 415 metres high, 5 kilometres from Hut Point along Hut Point Peninsula.

Coulman Island. Island, about 25 kilometres long, 13 kilometres wide, off coast of northern Victoria Land, at 73°28' S, 169°45'E.

Debenham Glacier. Glacier inland from northern part of Wilson Piedmont Glacier, at 77°12'S, 162°38'E.

Deception Island. Volcanic, horseshoe-shaped caldera, in the South Shetlands, at 62°57'S, 60°38'W.

Dominion Range. Mountain range at 85°22'S, south of inland end of Beardmore Glacier.

Drake Passage. Thousand-kilometre stretch of ocean, separating South America and Antarctic Peninsula.

Ferrar Glacier. Glacier, about 55 kilometres long, flowing from near Royal Society Range into New Harbour, in south Victoria Land, at 77°45'S, 163°30'E.

Finger Mountain. Mountain on south side of Taylor Glacier, north of Turnabout Valley, at 77°45'S.

Fisher Massif. Massif, about 25 kilometres long, on west side of Lambert Glacier, at 71°27'S, 67°40'E.

Franklin Island. Small volcanic island, in Ross Sea, 130 kilometres east of Victoria Land, at 76°05'S, 168°18'E.

Gneiss Point. See Map 4.

Granite Harbour. At foot of Mackay Glacier, on east coast of south Victoria Land at 76°53'S, 162°44'E.

Harold Byrd Mountains. Mountains between head of Ross Ice Shelf and lower part of Leverett Glacier, at 85°26'S, 146°30'W.

Hogback Hill. See Map 4.

Horlick Mountains. Part of Transantarctic Mountains, east of Reedy Glacier, at 85°23'S, 121°W. Includes Ohio and Wisconsin Ranges and Long Hills.

Hut Point. Site of Scott's *Discovery* Expedition hut, at south end of Hut Point Peninsula on Ross Island, at 77°51'S, 166°38'E.

Kaskawulsh Glacier. Large valley glacier in Yukon Territory, Canada.

Kennar Valley. Partially ice-free valley on south side of Taylor Glacier, at 77°46'S, 160°20'E.

King Pin Nunatak. Also known as Speary's Knob. See Map 4.

Knobhead Mountain. Mountain, 2400 metres' elevation, west end of Kukri hills, between Taylor Valley and Ferrar Glacier, at 77°55'S, 161°32'E.

Koettlitz Glacier. Glacier flowing between Brown Peninsula and mainland of south Victoria Land, emptying into Ross Ice Shelf and McMurdo Sound. 78°20'S, 164°30'E.

Kukri Hills. Elevated area between Taylor Valley and Ferrar Glacier.

Lake Vanda. See Map 4.

Lake Vashka. See Map 4.

Lambert Glacier. Longest glacier in the world, draining part of East Antarctic Ice Sheet east and south of Prince Charles Mountains, at 71°S, 70°E.

Little America. Name for five United States bases between 1928 and 1959, on northern edge of Ross Ice Shelf.

Mackay Glacier. Glacier flowing from East Antarctic Ice Sheet, through Transantarctic Mountains of Victoria Land to Ross Sea at 76°38'S, forming Mackay Glacier Tongue.

McKelvey Valley. See Map 4.

McMurdo Ice Shelf. Part of Ross Ice Shelf flowing into McMurdo Sound.

MacRobertson Land. Part of coastal East Antarctic, centred on 70°S, 65°E.

Marble Point. See Map 4.

Marie Byrd Land. Large tract of West Antarctica, between Ross Sea and Ross Ice Shelf and Amundsen Sea.

Mawson Glacier. Flows from polar plateau of East Antarctica to coast of Victoria Land, where it forms the Nordenkjold Ice Tongue, 76°13'S, 162°05'E.

Menzies Range. On south side of Fisher Glacier in Prince Charles Mountains, at 73°30'S, 61°50'E.

Meserve Glacier. See Map 4.

Meyer Desert. Ice-free area at north end of Dominion Range, near confluence of Mill and Beardmore Glaciers, about 85°08'S, 166°45'E.

Mount Aoleus. Also known as A, a. See Map 4.

Mount Boreas. Also known as B, b. See Map 4.

Mount Brooke. Peak in Victoria Land, 2675 metres' elevation, 76°50'S, 159°56'E.

Mount Circe. Also known as C, c. See Map 4.

Mount Dido. Also known as D, d. See Map 4.

Mount Electra. Also known as E, e. See Map 4.

Mount Feather. Mountain on north side of Skelton Névé, 77°58'S, 160°20'E.

Mount Handsley. Peak two kilometres from Knobhead Mountain that overlooks Ferrar Glacier, 77°56'S, 161°33'E.

Mount Huggins. Conical peak, 3735 metres high, in Royal Society Range, at 78°17'S, 162°29'E.

Mount Insel. See Map 4.

Mount Jason. Also known as Peak 16. See Map 4.

Mount Loke. See Map 4.

Mount Newall. See Map 4

Mount Odin. Also known as Peak 105. See Map 4.

Mount Orestes. See Map 4.

Mount Theseus. Also known as Philosopher's Peak. See Map 4.

Mulock Glacier. Flows through Transantarctic Mountains into north-west corner of Ross Ice Shelf, at 79°S, 160°E.

North Fork. See Map 4.

Observation Hill. Hill, elevation 230 metres, one kilometre east of and overlooking McMurdo Station, 77°51'S, 166°41'E.

Odell Glacier. Flows into upper part of Mawson Glacier in south Victoria Land, 76°46'S, 159°47'E.

Olympus Range. See Map 4.

Ongul Island. Site of Japanese IGY station, at 69°01'S, 39°32'E.

Onyx River. See Map 4.

Pagodroma Gorge. Five-kilometre-long, steep-sided river, joining Radok and Beaver lakes in the Prince Charles Mountains, at 70°50'S, 68°08'E.

Pole Station. US station at South Geographic Pole.

Prince Charles Mountains. Main south range in MacRobertson Land, about 400 kilometres long.

Quelccaya Ice Cap. Large, high (5500 metres) ice cap in Andes of southern Peru.

Radian Glacier. Flows from east side of Royal Society Range towards Koettlitz Glacier, 78°13'S, 163°E.

Rawson Mountains. Range of tabular ice-covered mountains, extending to the west side of Robert Scott Glacier, at 86°43'S, 154°40'W.

Reedy Glacier. Two-hundred-kilometre-long glacier, flowing through Transantarctic Mountains from inland ice sheet to Ross Ice Shelf, between Michigan Plateau and Wisconsin Range, at about 85°30'S, 134°W.

Rennick Glacier. Three-hundred-kilometre-long glacier in northern Victoria Land, feeding into Rennick Bay on Oates Coast, 70°30'S, 160°45'E.

Ross Island. Volcanic island in the south-west corner of the Ross Sea. Approximately triangular in shape, being 70 kilometres from east to west and 70 kilometres from north to south.

Ross Sea. A southern extension of the Pacific Ocean, it forms a large embayment between Victoria Land and the shores of west Antarctica. The southern part is covered by the Ross Ice Shelf.

Royal Society Range. Along the western shores of McMurdo Sound between the Koettlitz and Ferrar Glaciers, at 78°10'S, 162°40'E and ranging above 4000 metres elevation.

Spitsbergen. Largest of the islands constituting Svalbard, an archipelago between 76° and 81°N, halfway from northern Norway to the North Pole.

Sponsors' Peak. Also known as Peak 13. See Map 4.

Tararuas. Mountain range in southern part of North Island, New Zealand.

Taylor Glacier. Flows from the inland plateau about 50 kilometres eastwards into the western end of Taylor Valley at 77°37'S, 162°E.

Tent Island. Largest (1.6 kilometres long) of four Dellbridge Islands in McMurdo Sound, at 77°41'S, 166°22'E.

Transantarctic Mountains. Range extending more than 3000 kilometres, from Cape Adare on Ross Sea, to Coats Land on Weddell Sea.

Victoria Valley. See Map 4.

West Groin. Rock spur on south side of Asgard Range, 77°39'S, 160°48'E.

Wilson Piedmont Glacier. Sometimes called 'The Piedmont'. Large low-lying glacier on western shore of McMurdo Sound. See Map 4.

Wood Bay. Indentation in west Coast of Ross Sea at 72°13'S, 165°30'E.

Wright Lower Glacier. See Map 4.

Wright Upper Glacier. See Map 4.

Wright Valley. See Map 4.

Conversion Table

When we went to Antarctica in 1958 New Zealand's weights and measures system, apart from its science, was still buried in the 19th century. However, they could see the way ahead and in 1969 began to introduce the metric system, completing it in 1976. The intervening years produced some amusing incidents. Once when I was visiting New Zealand on my way to Antarctica I saw in a Wellington newspaper something like 'In view of the impending move to the metric system, henceforth our four-inch timber will be sold in 10-feet, rather than 12-feet lengths.'

For those still in the Middle Ages, the following is offered to help find the imperial equivalent of the 'proper' units.

Temperatures

100 degrees on the Celsius scale = 180 degrees Fahrenheit.
Freezing (water) points are 32°F and 0°C.
Boiling (water) points are 212°F and 100°C.
Hence:
−10° Celsius = 14° Fahrenheit
0° Celsius = 32° Fahrenheit
10° Celsius = 50° Fahrenheit

Lengths

1 centimetre = 0.39 inches
2.54 centimetres = 1 inch
1 metre = 3.28 feet
1 kilometre = 0.62 statute miles

Weights

1 kilogram = 2.21 pounds

Capacity

1 litre = 2.11 pints (USA)

Index

Page references in italics refer to photographs

Adie, Ray 235
Allen, Tony 201
Amery Oasis 213, 251
Amundsen, Roald 12
ANARE 213, 214, 245
ANDRILL 203, 224, 226, 233, 245
Anson boots 46, 47, 104, *180*, 198, 199
Antarctic Research Centre 14, 202, 226, 234, *242*, 245
Asgard Range 66, *76*, 83, *86*, *87*, 126, 127, 128, *129*, 141, *173*, 226–227, 255
Askin, Rosemary 202
Bagshawe, Thomas 205
Balham, Ron 13, 26, 201, 223
Balleny, John 11
BANZARE 37, 230, 245
Barlow, Commander 66
Barrett, Peter 14, 16, 201, 203, 210
Bartley Glacier *87*, 88
Barwick (née MacEachern), Diane 229, 230
Barwick, Dick: 15, 21, 22, 28, 48–49, 50, 51, 52, 54, 55, 56–58, 60, 63, 64, 69, 70, 71, 73, 77–78, 79, 80, 82, 83, 88, 95, 107, 112, 116, 117, 141, 143, 163, 169, 171, 186, 194, 196; life after VUWAE-2 14, 16, 17–18, 42, 198, 200, 201, 219, 226, 228–232, 241; life before VUWAE-2 13, 21, 22–24, 26, 29, 35, 42, 47, 102,

228; photos of *23*, *65*, *81*, *89*, *94*, *100*, *106*, *111*, *116*, *156*, *157*, *174*, *175*, *192*, *194*, *242*; VUWAE-2 research 16, 35, 61, 73–74, 90, 92–93, 96, 97, 98, 99, 102, 104–105, 108, 109, 110, 112, 113, 115, 119, 120, 121, 124, 134, 135, 140, 144, 145, 146, 148, 150, 151, 152, 155, 158, 159, 160, 161, 162, 164, 166–167, 171, 172, 175, 176, 177, 178, 180, 182, 183, 185, 187, 188, 189, 191, 193, 197–198, 199, 243–244
Barwick, Laura 229, 230
basalt 137, 245
Beacon Heights 24, 251
Beacon Supergroup 108, 207, 223, 224, 245
Beardmore Glacier 35, 200, 212, 224, 251, 252, 253
Beaver Lake 213, 251, 254
Beehive Mountain 25, 214, 251
Behling, Bob 237
Bellingshausen, Thaddeus von 11
Bemmelen, Reinout Willem van 220
Bentley, Charlie 33
Biscoe, John 11
Blank, Dick 234
Borchgrevink, Carsten 11, 24
Brace, Gordon 41
Bradley, John 195, 216
Brady, Father Howard 209

Brecher, Henry 18, 236
Brooke, Dickie 13, 34, 55, 178, 189
Buckeye tillite 208
Bull, Andrew 202
Bull, Colin: 13, 14, 19, 21, 63, 69,
    70; life after VUWAE-2 14,
    15–16, 137, 188, 198–204, 211,
    219, 223, 226, 231, 233–241; life
    before VUWAE-2 9, 21, 27–30,
    31–39, 40–41, 46, 49–51, 53,
    117, 120–121, 144, 185, 197;
    photos of *29, 38, 50, 68, 81,
    84, 89, 111, 114, 116, 118,
    147, 156, 179, 190, 192, 194,
    242*; preparations for VUWAE-2
    21, 34–35, 37–39, 41–51,
    52–57, 71–72, 73–75, 77–78,
    197, 198; VUWAE-2 research
    88, 90, 92, 93, 95, 96–98, 104,
    105, 107, 108, 110, 112–113,
    115, 117, 121, 124–126, 133,
    134, 135, 136–140, 143, 150,
    151, 152–153, 155, 158–159,
    160–161, 164, 165–166,
    167–169, 171–172, 175,
    177–180, 182, 183, 185, 187,
    188, 189, 191, 193–194, 197,
    243–244
Bull, Gillian: marriage to Colin 28,
    29; painting 15, 32, 116; letters/
    calls to 16, 78, 79, 102, 112,
    144, 186; children 40, 200, 202;
    support/advice to Colin 17,
    29, 32, 34, 42, 47, 52, 239, 240;
    visits to Antarctica 241
Bull, H.J. 11
Bull, Julia 203
Bull, Nicky 16, 17, 42, 51, 52, 102,
    112, 116, 195, 202
Bull, Rebecca 200, 202

Bullard, Sir Edward 30
Byrd, Admiral Richard 12, 205
Byrd Polar Research Centre (see
    Institute of Polar Studies)
Byrd Station 64, 66, 77, 235, 237, 251
Cadbury 46–47, 48, 63, 182
Cameron, Dick 235
Campbell, Ken 230
Canham Glacier 210, 251
Cape Adare 11, 56, 251, 255
Cape Campbell 194, 251
Cape Crozier 71, 251
Cape Evans 27, 117, 251
Cape Hallett 12, 58, 117, 200, 251
Cape MacKay 72, 251
Cape Royds 27, 117, 251
Carey, Warren 216
Castle Rock 71, 72, 251
Caughley, Graeme 71, 189
Chinn, Trevor 126
Christchurch 33, 48, 51, 52, 54–56,
    193, 218, 228, 237
Christofferson, Chris 187
Clark, Bob: geology lectures 216;
    reporting to 79, 109, 119, 150,
    188, 195, 196; support for
    Antarctic expeditions 9, 13,
    17, 21, 27, 34, 37, 49, 197, 200,
    202, 203, 233, 234; tributes to 7,
    158-159
Clark Glacier 158
Claydon, John 26
Collier and Beale radios 48–49, 80,
    151, 177
Cook, Captain James 11, 46
Corbato, Charlie 239
Coulman Island 79, 102, 251
Crary, Bert 187
Crary's Traverse 56
Creech, Chic 73, 75

Dais *76*, 83, 85, *86*, 90, *101*, 109, 124, 128, 165, 166, 167, 169, 171, *172*, *173*, 189, 200
Dawson, Major 72–73
Debenham, Frank 12, 53
Debenham Glacier 178, 252
Deception Island 238, 241, 252
Deep Sea Drilling Project 208, 209, 222, 224
Denton Glacier *87*, 88
Department of Scientific and Industrial Research (DSIR) 17, 24, 33, 36, 49, 50, 187, 220, 246
Dickinson, Warren 203
dolerite: 246; Asgard Range 83, 126, 127, 128; Barwick and Balham Valleys 231; Beacon Valley 25; Beehive Mountain 214; Dais 85, 90, 165, 167, 169; Ferrar 12, 206; lichen on 191; Mount Jason 105; Mount Odin *91*; Mount Orestes 113, 115; Olympus Range 128, 130; paleomagnetic work on 197, 200, 201, 234; Taylor Valley 36; Wright Valley 75, 97, 117, 128, 158, 193; Wright Valley Hill 128
Dominion Range 212, 252, 253
Don Juan Pond 167, 172
Doorly, Gerald 47
Doumani, George 235
Drake Passage 241, 252
Drooger, Cornelius 220
Dry Valley Drilling Project 208, 210, 222
Dufek, Admiral 58, 60, 61, 67, 69
D'Urville, Dumont 11
dykes 82, *91*, 93, 96, 103, 107, 110, 115, 117, 124, 134, 171, 175, 193, 200

Ellison, Lt Cmdr 66
Enderby brothers 11
erratics 27, 246
Evans, Taffy 12
Falconer, Tamsin 203
Farrell, Lawrence 150
Feinmann, Lt Cmdr 147
Ferrar, Hartley 12, 25
Ferrar Glacier 25, *26*, 252, 253, 255
Ferrar Dolerite 12, 206
Finger Mountain 209, 252
Fisher Massif 213, 252
Fisher Glacier 253
Fleming, Charles 220
Fowlie, Walter 209
Franklin Island 11, 24, 102, 252
Freed, Dorothy 47, 48
Friedman, Imre 105
frost polygons 80, 105, 124, 136, 164, 178, 246
Fuchs, Vivian ('Bunny') 13, 22, 28, 34, 60, 110, 218
Gardner, Harvey 150
Garlick, John 234
Gawn, Ted 77
Gibson, Graham 201
Glossopteris 35, 201, 235, 246
gneiss 193, 246
Gneiss Point 26, 73, 145, 147, 252
Goldthwait, Richard ('Dick') 188, 202, 203, 234, 237
Goodspeed Glacier *87*, 88
Gore, Al 236
Gorton, Michael 207
Gossage, David 41
Granite Harbour 24, 252
Gregory, John 56, 173
greywacke 191, 235, 246
Gunn, Bernie 13, 55, 219
Hallett Station 219

Hamilton, Warren 58–59, 67, 71, 95, 202
Harold Byrd Mountains 211, 252
Harrington, Larry 51, 55, 59, 79, 117, 121, 132, 145, 186
Harrowfield, David 204
Hart Glacier 88
Harwood, David 211, 224
Hatherton, Trevor 13, 196
Hayes, Phil 58, 67, 71, 95
Helm, Arthur 140
Henderson, Bob 187
Hillary, Sir Edmund 13, 22, 26, 215, 218
HMNZS *Endeavour* 22, *23*, 24, 27, 96, 181, 186, 187, 188, 189, *190*, *192*, 194, 195, 196, 218, 219
HMS *John Biscoe* 22
Hogback Hill 73, 145, 149, 150, 151, 185, 252
Holdsworth, Gerry 138, 237
Hollin, John 235
Holmes, Arthur 34, 216
Homard, Roy 34
Horlick Mountains 208, 211, 235, 236, 252
hornfels 193, 246
Hornibrook, Norcott 220
horsts 36, 165, 191, 247
Humphries, John 70, 71, 187
Hut Point 72, 251, 252
Institute of Polar Studies 188, 202, 203, 205, 224, 234, 235, 236, 237
International Geophysical Year (IGY) 13, 54, 61, 219, 226, 248; NZ IGY 55, 67, 218; US IGY 24, 61, 67, 69, 188, 196
Irving, Ted 35, 200, 234, 235, 243
Jaeger, John 234

Kaskawulsh Glacier 237, 252
Kennar Valley 209, 252
Kennett, Jim 237
King Pin 25, 79, *81*, *87*, 128, 144, 186, 205, 207
King Pin Nunatak 73, 144, 145, 155, *157*, 185, 252
Kirkwood, Harry 22, 24, 196
Knobhead Mountain 25, *26*, 252, 253
Koenigswald, Ralph von 220
Koettlitz Glacier 202, 233, 234, 253, 254
Kohn, Barry 207
Kojima, Kenji 235
Kukri Hills 108, 248, 252, 253
Labyrinth 83, *129*, 165
Lake Brownworth 143, *157*
Lake Vanda 253; as site of Main Base *81*, *84*, 130, 132, 169; as site of Vanda Station 15, 183, 204; Christmas celebrations at 109, *118*; naming of 15, 85; photos of 76, *84*, *103*, *123*; research on 90, 92, 117, 121, 124, 126, 164, 171, 182–183, 185, 188, 191, 193; swim club 183, 188; temperature of 194, 237
Lake Vashka 27, 84, 201, 253
Lake Vida 27, 84, *111*, 127, 178, 201, 204
Lambert Glacier 212, 213, 251, 252, 253
lamprophyre 82, 175, 193, 247
Lauder, Ross 216
Leide, Jim 211
Lester, Charles 205
lichen 27, 61, 82, 93, 135, 157, 161, 180, 182, 191, 232

Lister, Hal 28, 34
Little America 61, 64, 66, 70, 71, 72, 205, 253
Loewe, Fritz 236
Long, Bill 208, 235, 236
Lower Depot 79, 82, 130, 139, 140, 156, 157, 167, 169, 172, 187
McGinnis, Lyle 208
MacKay, Stuart 230
Mackay Glacier 178, 210, 252, 253
McKelvey, Barrie: 15, 19, 21, 48, 50–51, 52, 60, 61, 63, 69–70, 71, 82, 85–86, 105, 107, 108, 109, 112, 113, 115, 116, 119, 134, 153, 160, 169, 182, 183, 186, 194; appetite 43, 64, 69, 83, 92, 104, 107, 108, 113, 115, *118*, 173, 187, 196, 243; life before VUWAE-2 13, 17, 21–22, 24–25, 26, 27, 29, 34, 36, 196, 216, 219; life after VUWAE-2 14, 16, 18, 55, 205–214, 216, 219, 222, 223, 224, 226; photos of *23, 26, 38, 65, 81, 84, 116, 118, 122, 129, 168, 181, 184, 192, 194, 242*; VUWAE-2 research 34, 58–59, 77, 79, 80, 90, 92, 95–96, 102, 104, 107, 108, 110, 120, 126–132, 140–141, 144, 150, 152, 160, 162, 165, 166, 169, 172–173, 175, 176, 177, 178, 181, 188, 189, 191–193, 197, 198, 199, 200, 243–244
McKelvey, Jan 207, 214
McKelvey Valley 96, 98, 107, 110, 140, 253
McMurdo Dry Valleys 6, 18
McMurdo Ice Shelf 56, 70, 185, 253
McMurdo Sound: 245, 253, 255; accidents in 72; as site for ANDRILL and MSSTS projects 210–211, 223, 233, 245; early exploration of 11, 12, 53; flights over 73; geographical features of 24, 29, 97, 193; maps of 6, 20; swimming in 188; views/photos of 58, 71, *74*, 85, 189, *192*; VUWAE-1 in 22, 24, 219; VUWAE-2 in 49, 50, 51, 56
McMurdo Sound Sediment and Tectonic Studies Project (MSSTS) 210, 211, 223
McMurdo Station: 69, 72, 195, 218, 254; communication with 151; facilities at 67, 208, 213; flights to and from 75, 77, 80, 82, 119, 146, 150, 169; photos/descriptions of *57*, 60–61, *62*; staff at 24, 26, 56, 58, 61, 187, 196, 209; transfer of Little America equipment to 70, 72; visitors from 188
MacRobertson Land 212, 253, 254
Madigan, Charles 230
Main Base: Christmas celebrations at 109, *116*; communication with 166, 169; equipment at 51, 63, 99, 111, 112; evacuation from 167, 170, 171; photos of *84, 86, 103, 163*; provisioning of 78, 80, *81*, 105, 162; research at 164, 175; returning to 115, 152, 153, 171, 173, 180, 186, 187; views from *87, 91*; weather conditions at 104, 107, 124, 132, 164, 167, 193
marble 193, 247

Marble Point: 253; access from
 Wilson Piedmont Glacier 73,
 146, 148; airstrip 67, 73, 77, 88,
 133, 145–146, 193; Dick and
 Colin's trip to 132, 133, 142,
 145–146, 154, 191; evacuation
 via 169, 185
Marie Byrd Land 12, 253
Markham, Geoffrey 13, 38, 49, 51,
 52
Marr, John 205
Martin, Lynden 63, 67, 69, 70, 169,
 170, 171
Mauri, Carlo 207
Mawson, Sir Douglas 37, 228, 230
Mawson Glacier 219, 253, 254
Menzies Range 213, 214, 253
Mercer, John 211, 212, 224, 236,
 238
Meserve Glacier *87*, 88, 136, 137,
 138, *139*, 193, 237, 253
Meyer Desert 212, 253
Miller, Harold 43, 46
Mogensen, Palle 66
moraines: 207, 231, 248;
 Beardmore Glacier 35; Bull Pass
 181; Meserve Glacier 136-137,
 139; North Fork 124, 164, 165,
 166; Pecten Moraine 110, 162;
 Philosopher's Peak 158, 159,
 160, 161; South Fork 92, 169;
 Wilson Piedmont Glacier 73;
 Wright Lower Glacier 140, 141,
 142, 143; Wright Valley 75, 80,
 97, 105, 107, 108, 134
Moulton, Ken 58, 64, 77
Mount Aoleus 85, *101*, 253
Mount Boreas 85, *122*, *129*, 227,
 253
Mount Brooke 210, 253

Mount Circe 85, 227, 253
Mount Dido 85, *129*, 227, 253
Mount Electra 85, *129*, 253
Mount Feather 209, 253
Mount Fleming *84*, 128
Mount Handsley 25, 253
Mount Huggins 104, 254
Mount Insel 85, 128, 177, 178, 254
Mount Jason *101*, *103*, 104, 110,
 113, 254
Mount Loke 115, 254
Mount Newall 55, 145, 155, 254
Mount Odin *86*, *87*, 90, *91*, 95, 96,
 102, 107, 108, 141, 171, 172,
 177, 189, 254
Mount Orestes *87*, 109, 110, 112,
 113, 254
Mount Theseus *74*, 158, 159, 161,
 162, 254
Mount Weller 25
Mulock Glacier 219, 254
Munro, Bobby 32, 46, 51
Munro, Elsie 51, 52
National Science Foundation
 (NSF) 17, 202, 204, 224, 225,
 234, 238, 248
New Zealand Geographic Board
 17, 25, 47, 141, 158
New Zealand Geological Survey
 51, 55, 59, 79, 186, 206, 207
Nichols, Bob 88, 150
North Fork 121, *123*, 124, *125*,
 164, 166, 167, *168*, 169, 171,
 191, 254
Observation Hill 60, *62*, 71, 254
Odell Glacier 210, 254
Ohio State University 14, 188, 202,
 203, 211, 223, 224, 234–235,
 236, 241
Ollier, Allessio 207

Olympus Range 76, 84, 86, 101, 126, 128, 129, 132, 153, 159, 207, 254
Ongul Island 200, 254
Onyx River 24, 74, 87, 254
Operation Deep Freeze 24, 55, 58, 201, 202, 218, 248, 250
Orheim, Olaf 238
Ostenso, Ned 33
Packard, Andrew 26
Pagodroma Gorge 213, 254
Parsons, Roy 48, 64
Peak 13 (see Sponsors' Peak)
Peak 16 (see Mount Jason)
Peak 105 (see Mount Odin)
Peak A (see Mount Aoleus)
Peak Alpha 113, 114, 198
Peak B (see Mount Boreas)
Peak C (see Mount Circe)
Peak D (see Mount Dido)
Peak E (see Mount Electra)
pectens 97, 98, 194
Pecten Moraine 110, 162
Peddie, George 51,
pegmatite 193, 248
penguins 12, 24, 71, 72, 160, 188, 191, 209, 250
phenocrysts 24, 248
Phillips, Peter 167, 183, 189
Philosopher's Peak (see Mount Theseus)
Pole Station 66, 69, 254
porphyry 193, 248, 249
Potter, Lieutenant 79
Priestley, Sir Raymond 117
Prince Charles Mountains 212, 213, 214, 234, 251, 253, 254
Prospect Mesa (see Pecten Moraine)
Purnell, C.W. 11

Pyne, Alex 209, 210
Quartermain, Les 13
Quarternmain Range 26, 207, 209, 210
Quelccaya Ice Cap 238–239, 254
Radian Glacier 202, 254
Rawson Mountains 56, 254
Reedy Glacier 211–212, 224, 252, 254
Reiss, Zeev 221
Rennick Glacier 210, 251, 255
Rich, Charlie 237
Robb, Murray 71, 77, 80, 189
Robertson, Eddie 9–10, 13, 17, 33, 36, 38, 42, 69
Rodley, Dawn 201
Ronne, Finn 88
Ross, James Clark 11, 24, 58
Ross Dependency Research Committee (RDRC) 9, 10, 13, 17, 37, 46, 49, 196, 197, 249
Ross Ice Shelf 11, 205, 211, 223, 236, 247, 251, 252, 253, 254
Ross Island 6, 11, 12, 20, 70, 71, 74, 188, 251, 252, 255
Ross Sea 11, 14, 24, 70, 96, 189, 222, 223, 251, 252, 253, 255
Ross Sea Committee 21, 22, 37, 196
Royal Society Range 58, 71, 104, 252, 254, 255
Ryder, Noel 31, 198
Sales, Len 189
sandstone 25, 75, 83
schist 193, 249
Schopf, Jim 235
Schytt, Valter 238
Scott, Robert Falcon: Discovery Expedition 12, 24, 25, 27, 36, 47, 72, 127, 252; Terra Nova

Expedition (Last Expedition)
12, 24, 27, 29, 35, 53, 71, 117,
127, 215, 220, 251
Scott Base: as NZ IGY/TAE
base 13, 26, 219; as source of
expedition supplies 28, 41, 42,
63, 77, 107, 110, 171, 173, 182,
187, 211; communication with
83, 88, 95, 98, 109, 112, 115,
117, 141, 145, 150, 151, 167,
169–171, 183; construction of
12, 24, 218; life at 49, 52–78,
97, 145, 151, 186, 187, 188, 193,
194; photos of 65, 68; transport
to and from 9, 21, 41, 49, 52, 56,
58, 79, 177, 181, 185, 186, 200,
201; staff 196, 201; visitors to
188, 202, 234
Scott Polar Research Institute 53,
240
seals, live 11, 61, 69–70, 72, 187–188
seals, mummified: found on
previous expeditions 12, 27, 35;
found by Dick 90, 92–93, 107,
109, 115, 121, 136, 160; found
by Peter and Barrie 102; found
by Colin 98, 165–166, 167;
examination/dissection of 107,
108, 109, 125, 150, 151, 161,
167, 171, 176, 182, 187, 189,
191, 243; fun with 118, 119;
photos of 94, 118, 125, 135
Shackleton, Ernest 12, 27, 29, 36,
205, 215, 251
Shirtcliffe, Tim 183
Simmers, Richie 51, 174, 182
Siple, Paul 205
SIPRE 182, 251
Sirius Group 212–213, 224
Sirius 'tillite' 209, 211, 212

Skelton Glacier 187, 207, 208, 209,
210, 223, 253
Smith, Bill 66, 67, 72
Smith, Phil 24, 26, 58, 61, 64, 66,
72, 196
Speary, Maurice 60, 69, 71, 77, 79,
80, 82, 85, 92, 93, 110, 141, 155,
185–186
Speary's Knob (see King Pin
Nunatak)
Spitsbergen 15, 19, 21, 27, 28, 33, 34,
40, 41, 42, 48, 117, 197, 202, 255
Sponsors' Peak 17, 18, 47, 177, 178,
179, 182, 199, 238, 255
Stewart, William 11
Stott, Lowell 211
Stuart, Al 235
Surko, Lieutenant 148, 150
Tararuas 201, 255
Tasman, Abel 11
Taylor, Griffith 6, 12, 29, 53, 54,
220, 229
Taylor, Larry 235
Taylor Glacier: 251, 252, 255;
as possible landing site for
VUWAE-2 66; Discovery
expedition 127; geology of 59,
202, 244; Hayes and Hamilton
in 59, 72, 95; naming of 29;
VUWAE-1 24, 25, 26, 205, 214
Taylor Valley: 13, 34, 46, 146, 252,
253, 255; first exploration of
12, 53; geology of 36, 208;
Hayes and Hamilton in 58, 67;
seals in 27, 35; views of 28–29;
VUWAE-1 24; VUWAE-6 237;
VUWAE-7 182–183
Tent Island 27, 255
tillite 208, 209, 210, 211, 212, 235,
250

Te Punga, Martin 216, 220
Thomson, Bob 71
Thomson, Carl 211
Thompson, Don 71
Thompson, Lonnie 236, 238–239
Trans-Antarctic Expedition
   (TAE): 34, 209, 215, 219, 250;
   equipment/supplies from 42,
   45, 63, 77, 80, 88, 107, 109, *111*;
   planning 9, 13, 28, 218–219;
   summer support team 9, 13, 22,
   218, 219; survey data from 55,
   59, 178, 189, 200
Transantarctic Mountains: 251,
   252, 253, 254, 255; exploration
   of 219, 235; geology of 12, 36,
   191, 202, 212, 224; views of 56,
   127, 214
Turnbull, Gordon 25, 36, 200
Turner, Mort 202, 225
Upper Depot 79, 80, 82, 83, *84*,
   86, 126, 128, 129, 130, 144, 152,
   172, 173
Vandals 15, 203, 204
Vanda Station 183, 185, 203, 204,
   226, 237, 241
ventifacts 97, 231, 250
Vickers, Bill 235
Victoria Land: coast of 51, 59, 73;
   discovery of 11; first view of 56;
   geology of 165, 193, 210, 214,
   245; ice-free areas in 9, 28, 35,
   46; maps of 52, 53; research in
   243–244; research stations in
   12–13; return to 207, 209, 210,
   211
Victoria University of Wellington:
   Antarctic Research Committee
   200; description of 31, 32,
   250; faculty 43, 46; Geology

Department 195, 205, 215–216;
   Physics Department 30, 33,
   37, 70, 195; staff working in
   Antarctica 9, 13, 14, 19, 21, 22,
   26, 27, 35, 182, 196–197, 210,
   226, 233, 234
Victoria Upper Glacier 178
Victoria Valley: 34, 36, 42, 96,
   110, 159, 201, 204, 255;
   descriptions/maps/photos of
   6, 53–54, *103*, 127, 178; first
   exploration of 13, 26–27, 29, 85,
   178; geology of 59, 181, 200,
   201, 234, 244; meteorite in 228,
   241; survey stations in 177, 189;
   VUWAE-2 work in 34, 35, 59,
   75, 191; weather stations in 204
Vince, George 72
VUWAE-1 13, 19, 197, 203, 214
VUWAE-2 13, 111, 198, 202, 203,
   204, 206, 207
VUWAE-4 202, 234
VUWAE-5 182, 237
VUWAE-6 237
VUWAE-7 182
VUWAE-13 207, 223
VUWAE-15 202
VUWAE-22 209
VUWAE-24 209
VUWAE-26 210
VUWAE-51 203
VUWAE-52 202, 233
VUWAE 50th Anniversary 203,
   226
VX-6 Squadron 24, 41, 49, 51, 59,
   66, 70, 77, 175, 197, 200, 250
Walker, Barry 210
Walker, Darcy 17, 31, 37
Warren, Guyon 6, 13, 18, 55, 73,
   104, 189, 219

Webb, Joan 224, 225, 241

Webb, Peter: 19, 43, 69, 82, 85, 102, 107, 109, 112, 134, 144, 150, 183, 186, 189, 191, 196, 205, 208; appetite 21, 64, 83, 92, 104, 113, 115, *118*, 173, 187, 243; life after VUWAE-2 14, 195, 206, 207, 208, 211, 212, 215–227, 239, 241, 243–244; life before VUWAE-2 13, 21, 22, 24–25, 26–27, 34–35, 53, 196, 201, 214; photos of *23, 26, 38, 65, 68, 116, 118, 122, 131, 192, 194, 242*; VUWAE-2 research 21, 34, 58–59, 67, 78, 80, 90, 95–96, 97, 102, 107–108, 110, 119, 120, 126–132, 140–141, 153, 162, 165, 166, 169, 172, 175, 176, 177, 181, 188, 189, 191, 197, 200, 243–244

Wegener, Alfred 35, 223, 236

Weiss, Lionel 34

Weller, W. Isaac 25

Wellington: descriptions of 31, 32; travel between Antarctica and 23, 31, 41, 52, 96, 188, 194; visits by Antarctic explorers 11, 218

Wellman, Harold 182

West Groin 25, 255

Wetter, Leslie H. 228

Wheeler, Ralph 201, 202

Whillans, Ian 239

Whitehurst, Jerry 148, 152

Wilkes, Charles 11

Wilkes Station 56, 117

Williams, Richard 72, 83

Williams, Vice-Chancellor J. 37, *38*, 50, 197, 198, 201, 236

Williams Air Facility 218 (see also McMurdo Station)

Willis, Ian 201, 234, 237

Wilson, Alec 182

Wilson, Edward 53

Wilson, Jim 187

Wilson Piedmont Glacier: 255; depot near 140; naming of 29, 53; outgrowths of 178; photos of *74, 147, 149, 156, 157, 160*; profile of 150, *190*, 191; travelling across 59, 64, 72, 73, 79, 80, 88, 133, 141, 143, 144, 146, 148, 152, 167, 185, 229

Wohlschlag, Donald ('Curly') 187–188

Wood Bay 59, 79, 255

Woodford, Keith 210

Woollard, George 36

Wright, Charles 12, 53, 237, 240

Wright Fjord 97

Wright Glacier 53, 74

Wright Lower Glacier 64, *74*, 85, *87*, 88, 90, 132, 140, *142*, *144*, 178, 191, 255

Wright Upper Glacier *76*, 83, 85, 128, 164, 255

Wright Lake (see Lake Brownworth)

Wright Valley: exploration of 13, 83, 96, 105, 107, 115, 127, 128, 132, 133, 141, 158–159, 161, 172, 237; geology of 158, *190*, 191, 200, 243, 244; mapping of survey stations in 55, 219; naming of 15, 53, 88; photos/descriptions of 17, *74, 76*, 81, 116, *138, 142, 168*; planning trip to 9, 197; research station in 15, 204; reserving for VUWAE-2 research 58–59, 79–80; sampling in 175, 177, 200; seals in 107, 125, 167,

191; tents in 96, 112; transport
   to and from 66, 74, 77, 234;
   weather in 185, 193, 204
Wright Valley Hill (see Mount
   Fleming)
Yeates, Peter 66, 73, 88, 94, 109,
   117, 141, 167,